Public Children Law: Contemporary Issues

Public Children Law: Contemporary Issues

Alexander Laing
Barrister, Coram Chambers
Dr Bianca Jackson
Barrister, Coram Chambers

Bloomsbury Professional
LONDON • DUBLIN • EDINBURGH • NEW YORK • NEW DELHI • SYDNEY

BLOOMSBURY PROFESSIONAL
Bloomsbury Publishing Plc
41–43 Boltro Road, Haywards Heath, RH16 1BJ, UK

BLOOMSBURY and the Diana logo are trademarks of Bloomsbury Publishing Plc

First published in Great Britain 2018

British Library Cataloguing-in-Publication Data

A catalogue record for this book is available from the British Library.

ISBN: PB: 978 1 52650 327 5
ePDF: 978 1 52650 329 9
ePub: 978 1 52650 328 2

Typeset by Compuscript Ltd, Shannon
Printed and bound by CPI Group (UK) Ltd, Croydon, CR0 4YY

To find out more about our authors and books visit www.bloomsburyprofessional.com. Here you will find extracts, author information, details of forthcoming events and the option to sign up for our newsletters

Foreword

The law relating to children does not seem to stand still long enough to have its photograph taken. For example, section 20 of the Children Act 1989 has been in force for over 25 years and the debate about children's evidence in proceedings has been going on for longer, yet these, and the other topics covered in this book, remain dynamic and, to a degree, controversial matters in professional circles. At the same time, the law must adapt to take on board cases of radicalisation, FGM and other developing topics, together with the impact of an international element in more and more cases.

The publication of this focused and most useful book introduces a novel hybrid into the family law library. Each of the dozen chapters focuses upon a different topic of current interest and importance. The topics have been well chosen and the treatment that each receives is partly that of an authoritative, in-depth journal article, partly a back-to-basics tutorial in the essential legal context, and partly sound pragmatic advice written by practitioners for practitioners. Even to the seasoned eye there will something to be gained from each chapter in addition to the value of having the learning on each issue drawn together in one easy article.

The authors are to be congratulated on the fruit of their endeavour, which reads well and is clearly pitched at a readership that is already familiar with the basic law but may value, or be reassured by, seeing the current law and practice teased out and examined with insight and skill.

It can confidently be predicted that the range of 'contemporary issues in public children law' will change and develop in the coming years. For the present, this most welcome publication succeeds in delivering a high-resolution and up to date image of the current law and practice. It is, however, to be hoped that the authors are already braced for the need to deploy their expertise once again before too long in order to attempt to take another photographic record of our law for the second and subsequent editions.

The Rt Hon Lord Justice McFarlane
16 April 2018

Preface

Public children law is at the sharp end of our legal system. It is the vehicle through which the State seeks to safeguard the most vulnerable of children, and in doing so, interferes profoundly with the lives of individuals and families up and down England and Wales. Its scope must take in the most needy – those with physical, mental and learning disabilities, and psychiatric and psychological conditions; those who have been exposed to significant trauma and abuse; and those suffering from addiction. It must protect the rights of all individuals involved in the process, including those rights afforded under the European Convention on Human Rights, and it must weather changing political moods, be alive to society's needs, and develop with cultural norms.

For the busy legal practitioner, social worker, children's guardian, and member of the judiciary, pressed by circumstances to deal with these most difficult and unpredictable cases as a matter of urgency, maintaining good practice can be a constant challenge. The proliferation of reported judgments, near infinite possibility of factual matrices, and sharp rise in applications for public law orders place considerable pressures on all of those involved in public children law. That is made harder still by the rise in the number of cases with an international dimension and the different jurisdictional schemes that apply. Recognition of that pressure, however, is not enough. All involved must strive to stay on top of case law, procedural rules, and evolving statutes and regulations.

The aim of this book is to help in that task. It is to synthesise, in one place, the myriad sources of our law. It is to set out, simply and clearly, the key cases and procedure in relation to 12 themes central to contemporary public children law. It is to assist with good practice, and to help us avoid the pitfalls.

Each chapter functions as a stand-alone guide to an important, current, and commonly misunderstood theme in public children law, providing an introduction to the relevant law, a discussion of the key principles, and a guide to the common, 'tricky' issues that may arise.

Commencing with pre-proceedings, Chapter 1 explores the widely used and often misused Children Act 1989, s 20, addressing the different types of accommodation under s 20, its uses, and claims in damages. Chapters 2 and 3 analyse particular issues that arise at the commencement of care proceedings. Whilst Chapter 2 examines the issue of threshold, in Chapter 3 we look at public law proceedings where the parties are foreign nationals and the difficulties that may arise out of this.

Chapters 4–9 consider pressing contemporary issues that are increasingly common in public law cases. Recognising the increasingly prominent role that children may play in public law proceedings, Chapter 4 examines the challenges that may arise from children's evidence, including the practical considerations and Achieving Best Evidence interviews. Chapter 5 analyses how the family court treats the risk or actuality of female genital mutilation, forced marriage, and/or honour-based violence. In Chapter 6, we explore the approach of the court in public law proceedings where the subject child and/or the parents have been trafficked, or there is the risk of child trafficking. In Chapter 7, we explore how the problem of radicalisation has been dealt with in care proceedings. Acknowledging the shift towards transparency, Chapter 8 tackles reporting restrictions and the variance between the right to privacy and freedom of expression. In Chapter 9, we consider secure accommodation and the particular care that these applications require from practitioners.

Chapters 10–12 explore the current changes in emphasis in public children law. Chapter 10 examines special guardianship orders, which have become more prevalent in recent years as the court seeks to balance a child's right to remain within her birth family and the need for a stable and caring placement. In Chapter 11, we investigate post-adoption contact, including the academic research on the benefits and detriments thereof and how the current legislation may be seen to discourage such contact. Finally, Chapter 12 investigates a number of interventions that function either inside of or as an adjunct to public children law proceedings and which have been developed to tackle the increasing number of care applications.

Contemporary Issues in Public Law offers a detailed and accessible guide to some of the challenges that arise in current public law proceedings, acting as a handbook for both seasoned professionals and those who are new to public children law.

Alexander Laing
Bianca Jackson
June 2018

Acknowledgments

I would like to thank the following people for their advice and assistance – my co-author, Alexander Laing; everyone at Bloomsbury Publishing, with a special thanks to Kiran Goss, Jenny Lank, and Maria Skrzypiec; the clerks and members of Coram Chambers, especially Dermot Casey, Katy Rensten, Lucinda Wicks and Helen Harper; Sir Andrew McFarlane; Dr Jenny Doubt; Professor Sara Binzer Holbolt; Carol and Michael Jackson; Lily, Joshua and Sadie Jackson; Sylwia Zielinska; Jonathan Morton; and Oscar Jackson-Morton.

Dr Bianca Jackson

And I would like to thank Bianca, as well as Kiran, Jenny and Maria. Also, Sir Andrew McFarlane for the encouraging nudge and writing the Foreword. Neil and Hannah too for their careful feedback. Mum and Dad for reading page after page of law. Jen for your gentle admonishments. And, last but not least, Liz-Ann, for the unstinting sustenance, support and patience through the winter and spring months.

Enjoy the read!

Alexander Laing

Acknowledgements

Contents

Table of Statutes

Table of Statutory Instruments

Table of European Legislation

Table of Cases

J

K

L

R

S

Chapter 1

SECTION 20 OF THE CHILDREN ACT 1989

INTRODUCTION

1.1 Section 20 of the Children Act 1989 (CA 1989) is of fundamental importance to the family justice system: to families, children, local authorities and practitioners. The latest Department for Education statistics show that the number of children looked after under s 20 in 2017 was 16,470. Indeed, the majority of children that enter the care system continue to do so under s 20: in 2014, this was 61 per cent of children, in 2015 it was 62 per cent, in 2016 it was again 61 per cent and in 2017 it fell to 53 per cent[1].

1.2 Section 20 is extremely broad in its application, both in terms of the types of family by whom it is used and the wealth of placements to which it applies. Its range covers: orphans; abandoned or relinquished babies; unaccompanied refugee children; children with disabilities; adolescents with behavioural problems; and homeless 16- and 17-year old young people. Placements under s 20 include: short-term respite care; therapeutic placements; residential and assessment units; secure units; homes of family members; mother-and-baby foster placements; foster care; and fostering-for-adoption placements.

1.3 A period of accommodation under s 20 has a significant impact not only on a child's immediate life, but also on her future, not least because it has the potential to weigh in the court's welfare balance and therefore influence the outcome of any court proceedings. As noted above, many children who become the subject of care proceedings have already been separated from their families and placed in alternative care under s 20. That period of accommodation is of particular importance in (the comparatively unusual) circumstances in which the

1 Department for Education, *Children looked after in England (including adoption) year ending 31 March 2017*, SFR 50/2017 (28 September 2017) pp 8 and 10, available online at www.gov.uk/government/uploads/system/uploads/attachment_data/file/647852/SFR50_2017-Children_looked_after_in_England.pdf.

placement is a fostering-for-adoption one. That point was fortified by the coming into force of the Children and Social Work Act 2017, s 9 on 31 October 2017, which amended the Adoption and Children Act 2002 (ACA 2002), s 1(4)(f) so that it reads (new addition in italics):

> '**1 Considerations applying to the exercise of powers**
>
> (4) The court ... must have regard to the following matters (among others):
>
> (f) the relationship which the child has with relatives, *with any person who is a prospective adopter with whom the child is placed,* and with any person in relation to whom the court ... considers the relationship to be relevant ...'.

1.4 Over the past decade, a wealth of case law guidance has come to rest on the bare words of the statute, although the 2017 Court of Appeal decision in *London Borough of Hackney v Williams*[2] has re-cast earlier judgments in a fresh light. This chapter examines:

(a) the history of s 20;

(b) different types of accommodation under s 20;

(c) the law post-*London Borough of Hackney v Williams;*

(d) proper (and improper) use of s 20;

(e) a draft s 20 agreement;

(f) claims for declaration and damages.

HISTORY OF THE CHILDREN ACT 1989, S 20 AND CURRENT PRESSURES

History

1.5 Section 20 is located within Part III of the CA 1989. Part III is entitled 'Support for Children and Families Provided by Local Authorities in England', and plays an important and distinct role within the CA 1989. It is the result of a careful calibration between competing historical trends. As explained by Bullock and Parker, for a long period, the paternal family was sacrosanct:

> 'For many years the father's family was perceived as sacrosanct and it was not until 1889 that a voluntary agency (the NSPCC) could enter a home to rescue a child from abuse. But thereafter, the state increased its power over families demanding education and responsible parenting, imposing penalties and instituting powers to remove children at risk of harm.

2 [2017] EWCA Civ 26, [2017] 3 WLR 59.

In the 1970s there was concern that the State's powers were too draconian and the voices of children and families were not being heard'[3].

1.6 The CA 1989 achieved a more equal balance of power between State and family. It marked the abolition of a 100-year-old policy of local authorities assuming parental rights over vulnerable children without recourse to a court[4]. This was a significant change in childcare law. In terms of legal principle and social policy, it signalled and continues to mark an alternative to the risk-focused child protection system that predominates in England, in favour of a family-oriented system.

Current pressures

1.7 There is currently an intense financial pressure on local authorities. That has an impact on a range of local authority services, including children's services. Resource pressures may function to make preventive (as opposed to reactive) children's services' work, including the principle of working together with struggling families, a less immediate priority for local authorities than 'fire-fighting' cases where there is an immediate risk of serious harm to a child. This pattern is not assisted by what is, in many local authorities, a high turnover rate of social workers – and, as fewer social workers work long-term in partnership with families, the skills of working together may not be passed on to successor social workers.

1.8 At the same time, there are particular financial pressures on families. Currently, almost one third of children under 15 are at risk of poverty or social exclusion, and the UK has higher rates of early parenthood (among 15–19 year olds) than other European countries[5]. At a time when more families may need greater help and support from local authorities, local authorities appear increasingly unable to offer it.

1.9 The current climate is characterised by an increase in the frequency of child protection investigations and the number of children subject to children protection plans. More specifically, there was a 79.4 per cent increase in child protection investigations from 2009–10 to 2014–15, and a doubling of the number of children subject to child protection plans from 2001–02 to the present day[6]. There is a risk – if not also a likelihood – that the number and range of children who may be subject at least to consideration by a local authority for accommodation under s 20 is going to increase.

---

3 R Bullock and R Parker, *A Review of Services for Children in Care in the UK since 1945 and a Comparison with the Situation in Jersey* (July 2014), available online at centreforsocialpolicy.org/inc/uploads/A_review_of_services_for_children_in_care_in_the_UK-since_1945_and_a_comparison_with_the_situation_in_Jersey_-_Roy_Parker_and_Roger_Bullock.pdf.

4 Ibid, p 24.

5 J Boddy, *Voluntary Placement Arrangements, A Scoping Review* (2017), which is set out as an Appendix to the Family Rights Group publication, *Cooperation or coercion* (FRG 2017).

6 Cited in the Family Rights Group publication, *Cooperation or coercion* (FRG 2017) at 4.4.4, p 31. First statistic: A Bilson and K Martin, 'Referrals and Child Protection in England: One in Five Children Referred to Children's Services and One in Nineteen Investigated before the Age of Five' (2016) *British Journal of Social Work* 1; second statistic: A Raff and A Brown, *Trends in Child Protection* (NSPCC, 2017), on the basis of limited data.

ACCOMMODATION UNDER S 20

Routes into s 20

1.10 Whilst we tend to talk in broad terms of 's 20 accommodation' there are, in fact, four routes into accommodation under s 20: two of those impose a compulsory duty on a local authority, and two a discretionary power.

1.11 The first compulsory duty is under s 20(1). It applies to children in need who appear to a local authority to require accommodation because of:

(a) no-one having parental responsibility;

(b) the child being lost or abandoned; or

(c) the carer being prevented from providing suitable accommodation or care.

Section 20(1) reads:

> '(1) Every local authority shall provide accommodation for any child in need within their area who appears to them to require accommodation as a result of –
>
> (a) there being no person who has parental responsibility for him;
>
> (b) his being lost or having been abandoned; or
>
> (c) the person who has been caring for him being prevented (whether or not permanently, and for whatever reason) from providing him with suitable accommodation or care'.

1.12 The second route is under s 20(3). Again, it is compulsory for the relevant local authority. It applies to children in need who are aged 16 or 17 and whose welfare the local authority think would be seriously prejudiced without accommodation:

> '(3) Every local authority shall provide accommodation for any child in need within their area who has reached the age of sixteen and whose welfare the authority consider is likely to be seriously prejudiced if they do not provide him with accommodation'.

1.13 The third and fourth routes into s 20 accommodation are discretionary duties: one for any child for whom it would safeguard or promote her welfare; and the other in a community home for 16–20-year-olds for whom it would safeguard or promote their welfare. Looking at those in full:

> '(4) A local authority may provide accommodation for any child within their area (even though a person who has parental responsibility for him is able to provide him with accommodation) if they consider that to do so would safeguard or promote the child's welfare.

'(5) A local authority may provide accommodation for any person who has reached the age of sixteen if they consider that to do so would safeguard or promote his welfare'.

1.14 It will, we suggest, be rare that any s 20 agreement (by which we mean the document that those with parental responsibility are often invited to sign by a local authority) spells out the statutory basis on which a child is being accommodated. Nevertheless, the distinct routes into s 20 can be important. For example, and as set out in Chapter 9 (see para 9.8), a young person who is 'looked after' under the CA 1989, s 20(5) cannot be made subject to a secure accommodation order.

Other statutory provisions: wishes and feelings; objections; and older children

1.15 As is well known, before providing accommodation, a local authority must 'so far as is reasonable practicable and consistent with the child's welfare' ascertain the wishes and feelings of the child about the proposed accommodation and 'give due consideration' to them[7]. As we also know:

(a) a person with parental responsibility who is 'willing and able' to provide or arrange for accommodation may 'object' to a child being accommodated under s 20[8];

(b) a person with parental responsibility may 'at any time' remove the child from that accommodation[9], except in the case of children who are 16 and over, who can themselves agree to accommodation, in doing so removing the legal ability of the person with parental responsibility to 'object' or 'remove'[10].

1.16 The CA 1989, s 20(8), which states that a person with parental responsibility may 'at any time' remove the child from s 20 accommodation, merits close consideration:

(a) the statute is explicit in its words: 'at any time'. That was endorsed *obiter* by Munby P in *Re N (Children) (Adoption: Jurisdiction)*[11], where the President said 'This means what it says. A local authority which fails to permit a parent to remove a child in circumstances within section 20(8) acts unlawfully, exposes itself to proceedings at the suit of the parent and may even be guilty of a criminal offence ... I am exceedingly sceptical as to whether a parent can lawfully contract out of section 20(8) in advance, as by agreeing with the local authority to give a specified period of notice before exercising their section 20(8) right';

7 CA 1989, s 20(6).
8 CA 1989, s 20(7). This has presented problems. It is discussed in detail at paras 1.21–1.27.
9 CA 1989, s 20(8).
10 CA 1989, s 20(11).
11 [2015] EWCA Civ 1112, [2017] AC 167 at [169]. The case was reversed on appeal to the Supreme Court on other grounds.

(b) nevertheless, that criticism has in turn been criticised academically. It has been said that a notice period continues to have an important role: it reminds a parent of the potentially disruptive effect on a child of removal (even removal to home); it affords time to plan for a child's return; discouraging notice periods undermines local authority-parent partnerships; and, focusing on a child's rights (including those under the European Convention on Human Rights (ECHR), Art 8) it would be 'shocking if the law did not allow a child in foster care a good night's sleep at the whim of a parent ...'[12].

CURRENT LAW IN RELATION TO S 20

Statutory guidance

1.17 Unlike in some areas of family law, where we have considerable statutory guidance to draw on, the law in relation to s 20 has been especially judge-led. Indeed, it is notable that the current statutory guidance on the CA 1989 – *The Children Act 1989 guidance and regulations: Volume 2: care planning, placement and case review*[13] – provides, despite its length, very little guidance on the interpretation and application of s 20. Rather, it:

(a) explains that s 20 does not impart parental responsibility to the local authority (paras 1.22 and 3.196);

(b) states that the 'agreement of all those with parental responsibility must be obtained in advance' (para 2.20);

(c) reminds the local authority that, for a young person who is 16 or over, her agreement to the care plan must be obtained (para 2.37);

(d) states that a parent must be invited to be involved in the health assessment (para 2.59);

(e) notes that the nominated officer's approval of the placement must be in writing, and 'should remind the birth parents of their right to remove the child from the local authority's care and should provide advice on access to legal advice and appropriate advisory bodies' (para 3.160);

(f) alerts us to the vulnerability of children accommodated under s 20 (para 5.4);

(g) discusses decision-making for young persons aged 16 and over (para 5.12);

(h) examines short breaks under s 20 (paras 6.4–6.5, 6.8, 6.12–6.13, 6.15–6.16); and

12 J Masson, 'Questioning the Use of Section 20' (2016) *Family Law Week* 26 November, available online at www.familylawweek.co.uk/site.aspx?i=ed151621.

13 (Department for Education, June 2015), available online at www.gov.uk/government/uploads/system/uploads/attachment_data/file/441643/Children_Act_Guidance_2015.pdf.

(i) looks at the interaction between remanding in custody and s 20 (paras 8.19, 8.14 and Annex 8).

1.18 With the exception, therefore, of stating the need for consent 'to be obtained in advance', it is silent on a number of the difficult central issues, including, in particular, the meaning of 'willing and able' and 'objects' in s 20(7).

Non-statutory guidance

1.19 In terms of other guidance, following case law[14] in which courts were critical of local authorities for allowing s 20 placements to 'drift' without issuing court proceedings, the Association of Directors of Children's Services (ADCS), Cafcass and ADCS Cymru produced a guidance document[15]. The relevant points on which it advises are:

— trust is key ('Best practice in the use of s20 hinges on a relationship of trust between the family and local children's services') (at para 12);

— written consent must be obtained, and monitored (at para 16); and

— care must be taken to ensure that consent is informed (at para 16).

Case law

1.20 Before turning to the considerable good practice guidance in relation to the use (and misuse) of s 20, it is necessary to consider the January 2017 judgment of the Court of Appeal in *London Borough of Hackney v Williams*[16].

London Borough of Hackney v Williams

1.21 Mr and Mrs Williams had eight children. On 5 July 2007, one of the older children was arrested on suspicion of shoplifting chocolate bars. He told the security guard that he needed money for food; when seen by the police, he said that he had been beaten by his father with a belt. The police visited the Williams' home: there, they found poor, unhygienic conditions and sticks or twigs bound together which suggested the use (or threat) of corporal punishment. The police took all eight of the children into police protection. In turn, the Williams were interviewed by the police and granted bail, which included the condition that neither was allowed unsupervised contact with any of their children.

---

14 Not least the judgment of Sir James Munby, President of the Family Division in *Re N (Children) (Adoption: Jurisdiction)* [2015] EWCA Civ 1112, [2017] AC 167, which was handed down in November 2015 (subsequently appealed to the Supreme Court as *Re N (Children) (Jurisdiction: Care Proceedings)* [2016] UKSC 15, [2017] AC 167).

15 *Practice guidance for the use of s 20 provision in the Children Act 1989 in England and the equivalent s 76 of the Social Services and Wellbeing (Wales) Act 2014 in Wales* (1 April 2016), available online at adcs.org.uk/assets/documentation/S20_Practice_Guidance_final_Apr_16.pdf.

16 [2017] EWCA Civ 26, [2017] 3 WLR 59.

1.22 The local authority, Hackney, decided not to issue public law proceedings and instead to work with the family under inter alia s 20. On 6 July 2007, the parents signed a 'safeguarding agreement', including that the children would for the present remain in foster care. Over the subsequent weeks, the Williams' solicitors wrote to Hackney to set out Mr Williams' intention to withdraw his consent under s 20, and providing a notice period of 10 days. Equally, Hackney's Children's Resources Panel met and determined that the children should return home, with the police to be spoken to about the bail conditions and the housing association to assist in getting the house in order. In the event, it was not until some time later, on 6 September 2007, that the police varied the bail conditions and not until 11 September 2007 that the children returned home.

1.23 In the following years, the Williams pursued their complaints against Hackney through its complaint procedures, the Local Government Ombudsman (and an application for judicial review) and civil litigation. A claim was brought on the basis of misfeasance in public office, race discrimination, negligence and breach of duty owed under the Human Rights Act 1998 (HRA 1998), s 6 and ECHR, Art 8.

1.24 Following a six-day trial in front of Sir Robert Francis QC, sitting as a deputy judge of the High Court, the actions for misfeasance, discrimination and negligence were dismissed, but the claim for breach of statutory duty was upheld and Hackney was ordered to pay damages of £10,000 per parent for breach of the ECHR, Art 8. Hackney appealed to the Court of Appeal.

1.25 The appeal was heard by the President of the Queen's Bench Division, Sir Brian Leveson P, McFarlane and Burnett LJJ. The Court of Appeal unanimously granted the appeal. Giving the lead judgment, Sir Brian Leveson P reviewed, at length, the case law up to that point. The key question, however, was found to be 'what, as a matter of law, as opposed to subsequently identified good practice, was required before the local authority were permitted to accommodate the Williams children under s 20 …' (at [62]). In answering that question, his Lordship held the following important points:

(a) in order for the Williamses to 'object' to the s 20 accommodation, they would have had to be 'willing and able … to provide accommodation … or arrange for accommodation to be provided' (at [67]). For the period during which the bail conditions remained in place, they were, as a function of those bail conditions, not 'willing and able' (at [75]);

(b) the word 'consent' does not appear in s 20. There is no express statutory requirement that a local authority obtain a positive expression of consent from a parent before accommodating a child. Neither is there any requirement that such consent be in writing, nor that any of the other 'good practice' requirements be met (at [68]);

(c) a failure to follow 'good practice' 'does not, of itself, give rise to an actionable wrong, or found a claim for judicial review' (at [77]).

1.26 Nevertheless, both Sir Brian Leveson P and McFarlane LJ stressed that, in the words of McFarlane LJ, 'nothing we have said is intended to dilute or amend the good practice guidance, which sits above the bare statutory requirements as set out by Sir James Munby P and Hedley J …' (at [89]).

1.27 The Williamses subsequently sought and were granted leave to appeal to the UK Supreme Court. That appeal was heard on 14–15 February 2018. At the time of writing, judgment is awaited. For the moment, then, the position is that: the 'good practice' guidance remains important – indeed, Sir Brian Leveson P described it as identifying 'clear, cooperative and sensible ways in which a voluntary arrangement can be made … and a description of the process that the family court expects to be followed' (at [77]) – but a failure to comply with that guidance is not in itself an actionable wrong.[17] The case raises a number of fundamental questions. They include: who is the arbiter of 'willing and able'? And, to what extent are the rights of families and children under the ECHR, Arts 6 and 8 protected in circumstances in which non-judicial actors (say, the police or a social worker) can determine that a person with parental responsibility is not 'willing and able' to provide accommodation, and therefore the non-consensual removal of a child into foster care can take place without court scrutiny (or the meeting of threshold under the CA 1989, ss 31 or 38)?

'Good practice' guidance

1.28 It is clear that, whilst as the law stands a breach of 'good practice' guidance is not itself an actionable wrong, that guidance remains important and a model for what should be followed. The key principles of that guidance can be summarised as follows:

(a) consent to accommodation under s 20 should be recorded in writing and evidenced by a signature[18];

(b) it should be 'clear and precise as to its terms, drafted in simple and straightforward language that the particular parent can readily understand'[19];

(c) it should 'spell out, following the language of s 20(8), that the parent can "remove the child" from the local authority accommodation "at any time"'[20];

(d) extreme scepticism as to whether a parent can 'contract out' of s 20(8) in advance, ie can sign up to a notice period before the removal of a child from s 20 accommodation[21]. As such the 's 20 agreement' should 'not seek to impose any fetters on the exercise of the parent's right under s 20(8)'[22];

(e) where the parent is not fluent in written English, 'the written document should be translated into the parent's own language and the parent should

17 In the words of McFarlane LJ, 'This claim for damages for breach of statutory duty must be determined on the basis of the clear wording of the statute'.

18 *R (on the application of G) v Nottingham City Council* [2008] EWHC 400 (Admin), [2008] 1 FLR 1668 at [54], per Munby J.

19 *Re N (Children) (Adoption: Jurisdiction)* [2015] EWCA Civ 1112, [2017] AC 167 at [170].

20 Ibid.

21 Ibid at [169].

22 Ibid at [170].

sign the foreign language text, adding, in the parent's language, words to the effect that 'I have read this document and I agree to its terms'[23].

1.29 Section 20 may be used as a 'short-term measure pending the commencement of care proceedings' but the use of s 20 'as a prelude to care proceedings for a period as long as here [eight months] is wholly unacceptable'[24]. That is not to say, however, that in other circumstances the prolonged use of s 20 is not appropriate and desirable: an obvious example in which it may not be appropriate to bring care proceedings is an unaccompanied asylum-seeking child[25].

1.30 In *Coventry City Council v C*[26], per Hedley J and endorsed by Munby P, guidance was given for social workers seeking to obtain consent from a parent immediately or soon after birth:

'i) Every parent has the right, if capacitous, to exercise their parental responsibility to consent under S 20 to have their child accommodated by the local authority and every local authority has power under S 20(4) so to accommodate provided that it is consistent with the welfare of the child.

ii) Every social worker obtaining such a consent is under a personal duty (the outcome of which may not be dictated to them by others) to be satisfied that the person giving the consent does not lack the capacity to do so.

iii) In taking any such consent the social worker must actively address the issue of capacity and take into account all the circumstances prevailing at the time and consider the questions raised by Section 3 of the 2005 Act, and in particular the mother's capacity at that time to use and weigh all the relevant information.

iv) If the social worker has doubts about capacity no further attempt should be made to obtain consent on that occasion and advice should be sought from the social work team leader or management.

v) If the social worker is satisfied that the person whose consent is sought does not lack capacity, the social worker must be satisfied that the consent is fully informed:

    a) Does the parent fully understand the consequences of giving such a consent?

    b) Does the parent fully appreciate the range of choice available and the consequences of refusal as well as giving consent?

    c) Is the parent in possession of all the facts and issues material to the giving of consent?

---

23 Ibid.

24 Ibid at [157], per Munby P.

25 See, for example, the words of Peter Jackson J (as he then was) in *Re J (Child Refugees)* [2017] EWFC 44, [2017] 4 WLR 192 at [25].

26 [2012] EWHC 2190 (Fam), [2013] 2 FLR 987 at [46].

vi) If not satisfied that the answers to a) – c) above are all "yes", no further attempt should be made to obtain consent on that occasion and advice should be sought as above and the social work team should further consider taking legal advice if thought necessary.

vii) If the social worker is satisfied that the consent is fully informed then it is necessary to be further satisfied that the giving of such consent and the subsequent removal is both fair and proportionate.

viii) In considering that it may be necessary to ask:

a) what is the current physical and psychological state of the parent?

b) If they have a solicitor, have they been encouraged to seek legal advice and/or advice from family or friends?

c) Is it necessary for the safety of the child for her to be removed at this time?

d) Would it be fairer in this case for this matter to be the subject of a court order rather than an agreement?

ix) If having done all this and, if necessary, having taken further advice, the social worker then considers that a fully informed consent has been received from a capacitous mother in circumstances where removal is necessary and proportionate, consent may be acted upon.'

A DRAFT S 20 AGREEMENT

1.31 In line with the 'good practice' guidance, we suggest that a s 20 agreement should meet the following basic criteria:

— be in writing, signed and dated;

— be written in simple language;

— mirror the words of s 20(8);

— include no notice period for removal; and

— be translated if necessary.

A template s 20 agreement might look as follows.

Agreement between [local authority] and [persons with parental responsibility] for the accommodation under s 20 of the Children Act 1989 of [children]

- This is an agreement between [local authority] and [persons with parental responsibility].
- The agreement is that [children] will be placed in [say, foster care] by [local authority].

- In legal terms, that placement is happening under [sub-section of s 20 of the 1989 Act].
- It [has/has not] been possible to find out the [children's] wishes and feelings. [The children's] wishes and feelings are [wishes and feelings].
- [The persons with parental responsibility] do not at the moment object to [the children] being placed in [say, foster care].
- [The persons with parental responsibility] may at any time remove [the children] from the [say, foster care].
- Signed and dated:
  - [The persons with parental responsibility]
  - [Local authority]
- This document has been written in English and translated into [foreign language]. The [persons with parental responsibility] have read it in [foreign language]. Signed and dated in [foreign language]: ['*I have read this document and agree to its terms*'].

CLAIMS FOR DECLARATION AND DAMAGES

1.32 In the past 24 months or so, there has been a surge in applications for claims for declarations and damages against local authorities for the misuse of the CA 1989, s 20. The majority of those applications have been made under the HRA 1998 for breach of ECHR rights, most commonly rights under Arts 6 and 8. Equally, however, it is possible to (and there have been numerous instances of) make a claim under common law on the basis of negligence, breach of statutory duty and a range of torts.

1.33 This section focuses on the major growth area: claims under the HRA 1998. It examines:

(a) the basics, ie what a claim under the HRA 1998 actually is;

(b) the procedure for issuing a claim, including the limitation period and pre-action protocol;

(c) calculating damages;

(d) costs, including offers under the Civil Procedure Rules 1998 (CPR), Part 36 and the statutory charge.

1.34 Three points should immediately be emphasised. First, this is an area that requires forethought and careful consideration *prior to* the issuing of a claim. Unlike in much of family law, there can be significant cost consequences for procedural missteps. Second (and whilst this section focuses on the HRA 1998), given the low level of damages, if any, likely to be awarded, it may well be preferable to bring the claim instead under common law where awards could be significantly higher. Depending on the factual basis of the claim, specialist civil advice may be required. And third, this is *civil* litigation: it is governed by the CPR and not the Family Procedure Rules 2010 (FPR 2010).

The basics: what is a claim under the HRA 1998?

1.35 It is helpful to look at the broad picture and functioning of the HRA 1998:

(a) it is 'unlawful' for a public authority to act in a way which is 'incompatible' with a ECHR right[27];

(b) a public authority includes a court or tribunal or 'any person certain of whose functions are functions of a public nature'[28]. That includes a local authority;

(c) anyone who is or would be 'a victim' of that unlawful act can bring proceedings[29];

(d) if a court finds that an act is unlawful, it may grant 'such relief or remedy' as 'it considers just and appropriate'[30];

(e) damages will only be awarded where doing so is 'necessary to afford just satisfaction'[31].

1.36 So, to take the example of the type of claim commonly pleaded and issued: where a child is subject to a long period of accommodation under s 20, without court proceedings, who has suffered harm during that period, he can assert that the local authority's actions have been incompatible with one or more of the child's ECHR rights – say, Articles 6 and 8. The child (or the child's parent, on behalf of the child) can seek a declaration that the local authority has acted incompatibly with those rights, and can also argue that damages are required, in addition to a declaration.

Procedure for issuing a claim, including the limitation period and pre-action protocol

Limitation period

1.37 In many civil claims, the limitation period – ie the period within which any claim must be brought – is governed by the Limitation Act 1980. That provides for fixed time periods for claims. Importantly, however, time limits do not start running in relation to children until they obtain their majority[32].

---

27 HRA 1998, s 6(1).
28 HRA 1998, s 6(3).
29 HRA 1998, s 7(1).
30 HRA 1998, s 8(1).
31 HRA 1998, s 8(3).
32 Limitation Act 1980, s 28.

1.38 The HRA 1998, however, provides for its own statutory limitation period. That is not paused or affected by being a child. The limitation period is: (1) one year from when the act took place; or (2) such longer period as considered equitable[33]. The HRA 1998, s 7(5) provides:

> '(5) Proceedings brought under subsection (1)(a) must be brought before the end of –
>
> (a) the period of one year beginning with the date on which the act complained of took place; or
>
> (b) such longer period as the court or tribunal considers equitable having regard to all of the circumstances'.

1.39 It is worth noting that, in a case such as an extended unlawful period of s 20 accommodation, the date of the 'act complained of' may not be immediately obvious. It is, we suggest, dangerous to be drawn in to a situation in which one is obliged to make the date of the unlawful act ever later so as to fall within the limitation period when, in doing so, one is ever reducing the potential amount of damages. A more sensible argument, we suggest, is to say that the unlawful act was an on-going state of affairs, with the limitation period running from the end of that act (say, the issuing of proceedings following the prolonged use of the CA 1989, s 20). For a fuller discussion on the interpretation and functioning of the HRA 1998, s 7(5)(a), practitioners should read the judgment of the UK Supreme Court in *O'Connor v Bar Standards Board*[34], which concerned a claim by a practising barrister against the BSB alleging discrimination under the ECHR, Arts 14 and 6, on the grounds of her race in bringing disciplinary proceedings against her. In particular, Lord Lloyd-Jones held that:

> 'The expression "the date on which the act complained of took place" is apt to address a single event. However, the provision should not be read narrowly. There will be many situations in which the conduct which gives rise to the infringement of a Convention right will not be an instantaneous act but a course of conduct. The words of section 7(5)(a) should be given a meaning which enables them to apply to a continuing act of alleged incompatibility ... The primary provision in 7(5)(a) must be capable of providing an effective and workable rule for situations where the infringement arises from a course of conduct'[35];

He held that 'time runs from the date when the continuing act ceased, not when it began'[36], ie where we are concerned with an on-going act, limitation starts to run from the end (and not the beginning) of that on-going act.

33 In fact, the limitation period applies only to a 'person who bring proceedings against the authority under this Act in the appropriate court or tribunal' and not the ability to 'rely on the Convention right or rights concerned in any legal proceedings': HRA 1998, s 7(1) and (5).

34 [2017] UKSC 78, [2017] 1 WLR 4833.

35 At [23].

36 At [30].

1.40 Having established that any potential claim meets the limitation requirement, the next step *before* issuing proceedings is to apply the pre-action protocol. A pre-action protocol is, of course, the list of steps that must be taken prior to the issuing of a claim; the focus is on settlement.

Pre-action protocol

1.41 Unlike in certain civil claims, for claims under the HRA 1998, there is no specific pre-action protocol. Instead, we use the general Practice Direction on Pre-Action Conduct and Protocols in the CPR[37]. The provisions of that include the following:

(a) the parties must exchange information, including considering a form of alternative dispute resolution (at para 3);

(b) that will normally take the form of the claimant writing to the defendant with 'concise details of the claim' to include 'the basis on which the claim is made, a summary of the facts, what the claimant wants from the defendant and, if money, how the amount is calculated' (at para 6). This is known as a letter before action. It is an important document and requires care in its drafting: it should set out fully and clearly the basis of the claim and the remedy sought;

(c) in turn, the defendant should respond – within 14 days in a simple case and within three months in a complex one – to include 'confirmation as to whether the claim is accepted and, if it is not accepted, the reasons why, together with an explanation as to which facts and parts of the claim are disputed' and any counterclaim (at para 6);

(d) equally, parties should disclose key documents (at para 6). In a s 20 claim, that may well include a request for confirmation that the local authority holds the decision-making documents for the various looked-after children (LAC) and panel meetings that caused the child to continue to remain accommodated.

1.42 The effect of a failure to comply with the general Practice Direction on Pre-Action Conduct and Protocols can be stark. In the event of non-compliance, a court can order:

— that proceedings be stayed whilst the defect be remedied;

— that sanctions be applied;

— an order for costs, including on an indemnity basis; and

— a reduced or increased rate of interest on any damages (at para 16).

1.43 Importantly, pre-action protocols explicitly do not impact on limitation periods[38], so compliance with the general Practice Direction on Pre-Action Conduct and Protocols should not be left to the last minute.

---

37 Available at www.justice.gov.uk/courts/procedure-rules/civil/rules/pd_pre-action_conduct.

38 See, for example, general Practice Direction on Pre-Action Conduct and Protocols at para 17.

Issuing a claim

1.44 For a period, the process in relation to issuing a claim for declarations and damages under the HRA 1998 was uncertain. The position is now much clearer, following the two 2017 judgments of Cobb J in *Re CZ (Human Rights Claim: Costs)*[39] and *Re SW & TW (Human Rights Claim: Procedure) (No 1)*[40].

1.45 The key principles to extract from those authorities in terms of issuing a claim correctly are:

(a) if a HRA 1998 claim arises in and on the same facts as proceedings under, say, the CA 1989, Part IV, that claim can be considered within those proceedings;

(b) any application – even if within CA 1989 proceedings – should be issued formally: that means under the CPR 1998 on an application form and not simply on a Form C2 as one might under the FPR 2010, or flagged up in writing;

(c) the claim is formally issued under the CPR 1998, Part 8;

(d) a child requires a litigation friend to proceed with the claim. That litigation friend cannot be the child's Cafcass guardian.

1.46 Focusing on the need for a litigation friend, practitioners should be aware that, in broad terms:

(a) the starting point is that a child must have a litigation friend to conduct proceedings on her behalf[41]. Without that litigation friend, no step can be taken in the proceedings except issuing and serving the claim form and applying for the appointment of a litigation friend[42];

(b) a person can become a litigation friend without a court order. To do so, that person must complete, serve and file a certificate of suitability[43]. That certificate must state that the proposed litigation friend: can fairly and competently conduct proceedings on behalf of the child; has no interest adverse to the child; if the child is a claimant, undertakes to pay any costs which the child may be ordered to pay, subject to any right to be re-paid from the child's assets[44];

(c) to have a litigation friend appointed by court order, an application must be made under CPR, Part 23 and it must be supported by evidence[45];

39 [2017] EWFC 11, [2017] 1 WLR 2467.
40 [2017] EWHC 450 (Fam), [2017] 2 FLR 1609.
41 CPR 21.2(2).
42 CPR 21.3(2)(b).
43 CPR 21.5(4).
44 CPR 21.4(3).
45 CPR PD 21, 3.2 and CPR 21.6(4).

(d) equally, it is possible to invite the court to permit a child to proceed without a litigation friend[46]. It is perhaps notable that, at the time of writing, there is no reported case in the family context in which this has occurred, nor does the 2017 *White Book* contain any reference to such a case.

1.47 So, going back to the standard 'misuse of s 20' type claim, a litigation friend could be, say, a parent or grandparent who satisfies the terms of the certificate of suitability and is willing to fill the role. Or, if there is no appropriate person available, a request can be made to the Official Solicitor.

1.48 That leaves two commonly encountered questions unanswered:

(a) despite Cobb J's words, is the CPR, Part 8 process appropriate for all HRA 1998 claims? The CPR distinction between Parts 7 and 8 is that Part 7 (which includes, for example, formal case pleadings) is used instead of Part 8 where there is significant factual dispute. This, of course, might be the case in a freestanding HRA 1998 claim, especially where there have not ever been any proceedings under the CA 1989 and any facts found in those proceedings;

(b) is the Family Division of the High Court the appropriate division in which the claim should be issued? It may well be the case that many defendants to claims would rather the proceedings run in, say, the Queen's Bench Division, where the emphasis is on procedural rules (and, therefore, reductions in damages and orders for costs where, say, the pre-action protocol is not properly complied with) might be felt more firmly. Equally, claimants would no doubt prefer the Family Division and the expertise in relation to 'family' issues. This has not been addressed fully in any reported case.

Calculating damages

1.49 An intrinsic part of claiming, defending and determining an HRA 1998 claim for declarations and damages is calculating the appropriate amount of damages for any unlawful act. The calculation of damages in this context is an art and not a science. Nevertheless, there are a number of fundamental principles that are, we suggest, important:

(a) no award of damages will be made unless 'necessary to afford just satisfaction'[47];

(b) in determining whether to award, and the amount of any damages, the court must 'take into account' the principles applied by the European Court of Human Rights (ECtHR) in relation to the award of compensation under the ECHR, Art 41,[48]. In looking at Art 41, it is clear that: a clear causal link

46 CPR 21.2(3).

47 CA 1989, s 8(3).

48 ECHR, Art 41 provides, 'If the Court finds there has been a violation of the Convention or the protocols thereto, and if the internal law of the High Contracting Party concerned allows only partial repatriation to be made, the Court shall, if necessary, afford just satisfaction to the injured party'.

must be established between damage claim and violation alleged; damages are compensatory and not punitive; non-pecuniary damage is, by nature, not amenable to precise calculation;

(c) nevertheless, there is very little guidance from the ECtHR (in the form of applicable principles) as to the quantification of non-pecuniary loss in HRA 1998 claims;

(d) the court's focus will be on bringing an infringement of ECHR rights to an end, with any damages very much secondary to that. For example, in the leading case of *Anufrijeva v Southwark London Borough Council*[49], Lord Woolf noted that, 'Where an infringement of an individual's human rights has occurred, the concern will usually be to bring the infringement to an end and any question of compensation will be of secondary, if any, importance'.

1.50 It is widely suggested that the non-pecuniary damages awards made by the ECtHR are unpredictable or inconsistent. As noted above, there is little guidance by way of applicable principles on which to calculate future awards. That is a function, however, of the ECtHR: it does not provide that guidance because it does not seek to do so. In contrast, courts in England and Wales have endeavoured to draw up comparative tables[50].

1.51 Despite the attempts of the courts in England and Wales, the correct focus in any given case remains the ECtHR principles under the ECHR, Art 41. As such, we suggest that the best starting point for those who wish to think deeply and justify the quantification of damages on an empirical basis is an empirical study of ECtHR awards under the ECHR, Art 41 for non-pecuniary damage.

1.52 In a very thorough empirical analysis, dated November 2016,[51] it was suggested that, in looking for applicable principles to calculate non-pecuniary damages, we should focus on:

— the seriousness of the violation: its character (which ECHR right is breached), intensity, duration and consequences;

— applicant-related factors, such as age, status, moral conduct and 'contributory negligence; and

— the overall context, which is to say, the local economic circumstances (so, the same breach in Germany would result in a higher award than in Bulgaria).

49 [2003] EWCA Civ 1406, [2004] QB 1124 at [53].

50 Most notably, the table drawn up and relied upon in *Medway Council v M* [2015] EWFC B 164, at [90], per HHJ Lazarus.

51 Professor Dr Anne Peters, Dr Szilvia Altwicker-Hamon and Dr Tilman Altwicker, 'Measuring Violations of Human Rights: An Empirical Analysis of Awards in Respect of Non-Pecuniary Damage Under the European Convention on Human Rights', available at www.mpil.de/files/pdf4/Quant_Human.Rights.pdf.

CONCLUSION

1.53 The statute is simple: the CA 1989, s 20. In terms of case law, if you are arguing about the quality (or otherwise) of a s 20 agreement, it is important still to go back to the guidance in *R (on the application of G) v Nottingham City Council*[52], *Coventry City Council v C*[53], and *Re N (Children) (Adoption: Jurisdiction)*[54].

1.54 If, on the other hand, you are looking at a claim under the HRA 1998, you will need to have with you the two 2017 judgments of Cobb J in *Re CZ (Human Rights Claim: Costs)*[55] and *Re SW & TW (Human Rights Claim: Procedure) (No 1)*[56], plus *London Borough of Hackney v Williams*[57].

1.55 In terms of key arguments to consider:

(a) looking at the s 20 agreement: is it in writing, signed and dated; is it written in simple language; does it mirror the words of s 20(8); does it include no notice period for removal; and, has it been translated if necessary?

(b) in any claim for declarations and damages under the HRA 1998, have all of the (many) procedural requirements been complied with (see paras 1.37–1.48), including limitation, pre-action protocol and proper issuing?

(c) if bringing, defending or advising on a claim under the HRA 1998 for damages, have you considered the merits of using a thorough, empirical analysis of ECtHR case law to justify quantum?

52 [2008] EWHC 400 (Admin), [2008] 1 FLR 1668.
53 [2012] EWHC 2190 (Fam), [2013] 2 FLR 987.
54 [2015] EWCA Civ 1112, [2017] AC 167.
55 [2017] EWFC 11, [2017] 1 WLR 2467.
56 [2017] EWHC 450 (Fam), [2017] 2 FLR 1609.
57 [2017] EWCA Civ 26, [2017] 3 WLR 59.

Chapter 2

THRESHOLD: CHILDREN ACT 1989, SECTIONS 31 AND 38

INTRODUCTION

2.1 The threshold test ('threshold') is the gateway to public children law: the test that must be passed before Parliament permits interference in this context with the lives of families. It is, or should be, at the centre of proceedings, but is often overlooked or mistreated.

2.2 Indeed, the purpose of threshold is absolutely central to the family justice system. It is to prevent the State interfering in the upbringing of children simply on the basis that it could do better than the parents. In *Review of Child Care Law*[1] it was put in the following terms:

> '… "the child is not the child of the state" and it is important in a free society to maintain the rich diversity of lifestyles, which is secured by permitting families a large measure of autonomy in the way in which they bring up their children. This is so even, or perhaps, particularly, in those families who through force of circumstances are in need of help from social services or other agencies. Only where their children are put at an unacceptable risk should it be possible compulsorily to intervene. Once such a risk of harm to the child has been shown, however, his interests must clearly predominate'[2].

2.3 Another way of putting that, of course, is in the (very) well-known words of Hedley J, in *Re L (Care: Threshold Criteria)*[3]:

> '… society must be willing to tolerate very diverse standards of parenting, including the eccentric, the barely adequate and the inconsistent. It follows too that children will inevitably have both very different experiences of parenting and very unequal consequences flowing from it. It means that some children will experience disadvantage and harm, while others flourish

1 DHSS, *Review of Child Care Law* (HMSO, 1985).
2 Quoted by Hale LJ in *Re G (Care Proceedings: Threshold Conditions)* [2001] EWCA Civ 968, [2001] 2 FLR 1111 at [8].
3 [2007] 1 FLR 2050, [2007] Fam Law 297 at [70].

> in atmospheres of loving security and emotional stability. These are the consequences of our fallible humanity and it is not the provenance of the state to spare children all the consequences of defective parenting. In any event, it simply could not be done'.

2.4 Recently, the senior courts have been keen to remind family practitioners of the fundamental points in relation to threshold and to emphasise the need for compliance with these basic principles. For example, in an excoriating judgment, Sir James Munby P described the case of *Re A (A Child)* as 'an object lesson in, almost a textbook example of, how not to embark upon and pursue a care case'[4].

2.5 This chapter addresses:

(a) the basic principles of the Children Act 1989 (CA 1989), ss 31 and 38, including interpreting the statute, burden and standard of proof, and credibility and memory;

(b) tricky issues: female genital mutilation (FGM) and circumcision, relinquished babies and pools of (possible) perpetrators;

(c) the use of split hearings;

(d) pleading threshold: a guide.

BASIC PRINCIPLES OF THE CA 1989, SS 31 AND 38

Section 31

2.6 Section 31(2) of the CA 1989 reads:

> '(2) A court may only make a care order or a supervision order if it is satisfied –
>
> (a) that the child concerned is suffering or likely to suffer significant harm; and,
>
> (b) that the harm or likelihood of harm is attributable to –
>
> (i) the care given to the child, or likely to be given to him if the order were not made, not being what it would be reasonable to expect a parent to give him; or
>
> (ii) the child's being beyond parental control'.

From that, however, a number of points merit emphasis.

2.7 First, 'is suffering' demands an existing state of affairs. One might initially think – and the Court of Appeal has previously held – that that state of affairs must exist at the time of disposal. However, the House of Lords in *Re M (A Minor)*

4 *Re A (A Child)* [2015] EWFC 11, [2016] 1 FLR 1 at [7].

(Care Order: Threshold Conditions) firmly refuted that suggestion, Lord Templeman describing it as 'an illustration of the tyranny of language' and 'a preoccupation with the present tense'[5].

2.8 In that case, the House of Lords made clear that there is nothing in the wording of the CA 1989, s 31(2) that requires the satisfaction of the threshold conditions to be disassociated from the time of the making of the application by the local authority. So, where at the time the application is to be disposed of there are in place 'arrangements for the protection of the child by the local authority on an interim basis which protection has been continuously in place for some time, the relevant date with respect to which the court must be satisfied is the date at which the local authority initiated the procedure for protection under the Act from which these arrangements flowed'[6]. Equally, if interim protective arrangements are in place, and then terminated, in subsequent proceedings 'it would not be possible to found jurisdiction on the situation at the time of initiation of these arrangements'[7].

2.9 We might well question what the situation is where there are *not* interim protective measures in place: does threshold require satisfaction at the point of disposal, or at the point of issuing the proceedings? As family practitioners, we all work on the basis of the latter. Authority for that proposition comes from the speech of Lord Mackay, in which it is noted that:

> 'Indeed, I think there is much to be said for the view that the hearing that Parliament contemplated was one which extended from the time the jurisdiction of the court is first invoked until the case is disposed of and that was required to be done in the light of the general principle that any delay in determining the question is likely to prejudice the welfare of the child'[8].

If the hearing extends from issuing to disposal, it is the point of issuing which – absent any interim and pre-dating protective measures – is relevant.

2.10 As is well known, the process of evidence-gathering to support threshold can and often does continue post-threshold date. Many of us will have seen local authority threshold documents marked up with a standard paragraph to that effect. In *Re G (Care Proceedings: Threshold Conditions)*[9], Hale LJ delineated three types of post-commencement-of-proceedings matters:

(a) *information* discovered after the relevant date: such information – for example, medical evidence about the injuries that prompted removal; new complaints by a child about abuse in the home; and admissions by the parents – evidences the facts as they were at the relevant date. This can clearly evidence threshold;

5 [1994] 2 FLR 577 at 588 and 589.
6 At 583.
7 At 583.
8 At 583.
9 [2001] EWCA Civ 968, [2001] 2 FLR 1111.

(b) *new events* – for example, substance abuse, neglect or acts of violence that occur during the course of proceedings – which may, or may not, be capable of demonstrating a risk of substance abuse, neglect or acts of violence at the time proceedings were brought. The difficulty here, as flagged up by Hale LJ, is the 'obvious dangers of retrospectively validating a concern which was not in fact justified at the time: there may, after all, be other reasons for things to go badly wrong after proceedings are started'[10]. These, then, may be capable of evidencing threshold;

(c) *entirely new events* that introduce a new and different risk that was not there at the relevant date – say, for example, injuries suffered by a baby, leading to her removal, are found to be accidental, but the stress of proceedings has led to the violent breakdown of the parents' relationship. These are therefore not evidence of threshold.

2.11 Second, 'or is likely to suffer' looks to the future, as does much of children law. The relevant time for that evaluation is, however, the same as with 'is suffering', ie the date of the public law application or, if temporary protective measures have been continuously in place from an earlier date, the date when those arrangements were initiated[11].

2.12 In terms of defining 'likely', what is required is a 'real possibility that it will occur'[12] or 'a real possibility, a possibility that cannot sensibly be ignored having regard to the nature and gravity of the feared harm in the particular case'[13] with that conclusion 'based upon a fact or facts established on a balance of probabilities'[14]. In addition, the following points made by Lady Hale in her (dissenting) judgment in the 2013 case of *Re B (Care Proceedings: Appeal)*[15] bear remembering: a comparatively low threshold of likelihood is adopted because some harm is so catastrophic that even a relatively small degree of likelihood should be sufficient to justify the State intervening before it happens. In other words, the 'more serious the harm, the less likely it has to be' and 'the less serious the harm, the more likely it has to be'. Also, that it is extremely difficult to predict the future and to predict future harm, especially in relation to emotional or psychological harm. In addition, the degree of likelihood of future harm must be sufficient to justify compulsory intervention now, for there is always the possibility of compulsory intervention later should the 'real possibility' solidify[16].

2.13 Third, 'what it would be reasonable to expect a parent to give him' is an objective test. We are not concerned with the parent of the subject child, nor is the comparator a parent with the same or similar characteristics to that parent. If it were so, then the subject child would only be protected – threshold could only be met – in circumstances in which her parent was capable, but unwilling,

---

10 At [15].
11 *Southwark London Borough Council v B* [1998] 2 FLR 1095, [1999] 1 FCR 550.
12 *Re B (Care Proceedings: Appeal)* [2013] UKSC 33, [2013] 2 FLR 1075 at [24], per Lord Wilson.
13 *Re B (Care Proceedings: Appeal)* [2013] UKSC 33, [2013] 2 FLR 1075 at [187], per Baroness Hale.
14 *Re B (Care Proceedings: Appeal)* [2013] UKSC 33, [2013] 2 FLR 1075 at [24], per Lord Wilson.
15 [2013] UKSC 33, [2013] 2 FLR 1075.
16 *Re B (Care Proceedings: Appeal)* [2013] UKSC 33, [2013] 2 FLR 1075 at [188]–[190].

of providing reasonable care. The test is an objective one: 'It is abundantly clear that a parent may unhappily fail to provide reasonable care even though he is doing his incompetent best'[17].

2.14 Fourth, 'harm' is defined by statute, by the CA 1989, s 31(9) (as subsequently amended by the Adoption and Children Act 2002):

> '"harm" means ill-treatment or the impairment of health or development including, for example, impairment suffered from seeing or hearing the ill-treatment of another'.

And reference should be had also to the CA 1989, s 31(10), which sets out that, where harm is focused on 'health or development', it should be compared 'with that which could reasonably be expected by a similar child' – so, whilst the test in relation to a parent is objective, the test here in relation to the child is subjective.

Section 38

2.15 The interim threshold test – set out in the CA 1989, s 38 – is equally familiar terrain. Here, a court must be satisfied that there are, 'reasonable grounds for believing that circumstances with respect to the child are as mentioned in s 31(2) [of the CA 1989]'.

2.16 The key points here, we suggest, are:

(a) the object of an interim order is to hold the balance: 'an interim order or decision will usually be required to establish a holding position, after weighing all relevant risks, pending the final hearing'[18];

(b) it is rarely appropriate to make findings of disputed facts[19];

(c) satisfaction of interim threshold is not in itself sufficient to permit interim removal of a child from her parent: instead, the court must find that the child's safety demands immediate separation[20].

Burden of proof

2.17 It is well known that the burden of proof rests on the applicant local authority. There is, however, a subtler point that bears remembering – one which requires practitioners to tread a fine line between two Court of Appeal authorities. The first authority is *Re M (Fact-Finding Hearing: Burden of Proof)*[21], a successful appeal by parents against a first-instance finding that both parents were possible

17 *Re D (Care Order: Evidence)* [2010] EWCA Civ 1000 at [35], per Hughes LJ.

18 *Hampshire County Council v S* [1993] 1 FLR 559 at 567.

19 For example, *Hampshire County Council v S* [1993] 1 FLR 559 at 567.

20 The well-known test is set out in eight Court of Appeal authorities, most notably, in *Re H (A Child) (Interim Care Order)* [2002] EWCA Civ 1932 at [39].

21 [2012] EWCA Civ 1580.

perpetrators of a number of bruises to the arms and legs of an 8-week-old baby. In his judgment, Wall LJ held that, in the context of an injury to the child, the absence both of a parental explanation and a satisfactory benign explanation does not without more lead to the conclusion that there must be a malevolent explanation. To hold otherwise is to reverse the burden of proof and is to place a burden on the parents to show that an injury is not 'non-accidental'[22].

2.18 In the second, *Re M-B (Children)*[23], the Court of Appeal was concerned with the death of a 10-month-old child from an unascertained cause. During the post-mortem, at least seven fractures were discovered that occurred prior to the date of his death. In granting the appeal, Macur LJ revisited Wall LJ's conclusion and described the first-instance judge's reliance on it as having been 'wrongly to elevate to a point of legal principle Ward LJ's clearly fact-specific determination in *Re M* that the judge was wrong in that case to equate lack of parental explanation with a malevolent explanation'[24]. *Re M-B* was, like *Re M*, characterised by injuries in relation to which there was an absence both of a (credible) parental explanation and a satisfactory benign explanation. Nevertheless, the Court of Appeal held that, on the basis of the unanimous medical evidence – including that 'The appearance of the individual fractures were not diagnostic of culpable injury but the number, multiple sites and absence of a history of significant memorable accidental injury which would be expected to have led to hospital attendance were highly suggestive of that fact'[25] – the first-instance judge's fact-finding exercise was fatally flawed and a re-hearing required.

Standard of proof

2.19 The essential principles of the standard of proof are simply stated: it is the ordinary civil standard of balance of probabilities. A binary system is employed, under which, if a judge finds it more likely than not that something has taken place, then it is treated as having occurred, and if a judge does not find it more likely than not, then it is treated as having not occurred. In other words, the court deals in black and white: there is no room for shades of grey.

2.20 Other key points to be remembered are:

(a) the standard of proof is affected by neither the seriousness of the allegation nor the seriousness of the consequences. To borrow Peter Jackson J's example on the latter: 'Whether a man was in a London street at a particular time might be of no great consequence if the issue was whether he was rightly issued with a parking ticket, but it might be of huge consequence if he has been charged with a murder that day that occurred in Paris. The evidential

22 *Re M (Fact-Finding Hearing: Burden of Proof)* [2012] EWCA Civ 1580, [2013] 2 FLR 874 at [15]. It is noted that the term 'non-accidental' has been noted by Ryder LJ to be a tautology: *Re S (A Child)* [2014] EWCA Civ 25 at [19]. For ease, we use it in this book.

23 [2015] EWCA Civ 1027.

24 At [15].

25 At [8].

standard to which his presence in the street must be provided is nonetheless the same'[26];

(b) inherent improbability is no more than something to be taken account of, where relevant, in deciding where the truth lies. Again, to return to Peter Jackson J, this time citing counsel before him, 'Improbable events occur all the time. Probability itself is a weak prognosticator of occurrence in any given case. Unlikely, even highly unlikely, things do happen. Somebody wins the lottery most weeks; children are struck by lightning. The individual probability of any given person enjoying or suffering either fate is extremely low'[27];

(c) and, once an event has been found to have happened – say, an inherently improbable injury to a baby – it has happened, and the inherent improbability of it having done so has no impact on the determination of the culprit.

2.21 The limits – and our pushing of the boundaries – of medical and scientific evidence need also to be remembered in all such cases. Senior courts across all areas of law – criminal, general, civil and family – have sought to describe the difficulties inherent in this when looking at perpetrators of injuries. In 2004, the President, Butler-Sloss P, considering a criminal judgment in the Court of Appeal, noted that, 'The judge in care proceedings must never forget that today's medical certainty may be discarded by the next generation of experts or that scientific research will throw light into corners that are at present dark'[28]. In 2011, Hedley J described it in the following terms:

> '... a conclusion of unknown aetiology in respect of an infant represents neither professional nor forensic failure. It simply recognises that we still have much to learn and it also recognises that it is dangerous and wrong to infer non-accidental injury, merely from the absence of any other understood mechanism. Maybe it simply represents a general acknowledgement that we are fearfully and wonderfully made'[29].

Credibility and memory

2.22 Relevant too to the standard of proof are the linked questions of credibility and memory. Credibility, of course, is central to many a first-instance judgment; in addition, the appeal books are thick with assertions that one of the significant advantages of the first-instance judge is her ability to live the case and assess a witness's credibility.

2.23 Scratch beneath the surface, however, and the concepts of credibility and memory become difficult for a judge safely to handle. The most compelling

26 *Re BR (Proof of Facts)* [2015] EWFC 41 at [7](2).
27 *Re BR (Proof of Facts)* [2015] EWFC 41 at [7](3).
28 *Re U, Re B (Serious Injury: Standard of Proof)* [2004] EWCA Civ 567 at [23].
29 *Re R (Care Proceedings: Causation)* [2011] EWHC 1715 (Fam) at [19].

criticisms of the court's failures properly to manage these concepts are set out in a multi-million-pound commercial claim tried by Leggatt J – a discussion later adopted by Mostyn J in *Lachaux v Lachaux*[30] – and by Lord Bingham, in an extra-judicial essay.

2.24 Turning first to Leggatt J, in a lengthy passage – which merits reading in full – his Lordship held that,

> '15. An obvious difficulty which affects allegations and oral evidence based on recollection of events which occurred several years ago is the unreliability of human memory.
>
> 16. While everyone knows that memory is fallible, I do not believe that the legal system has sufficiently absorbed the lessons of a century of psychological research into the nature of memory and the unreliability of eyewitness testimony. One of the most important lessons of such research is that in everyday life we are not aware of the extent to which our own and other people's memories are unreliable and believe our memories to be more faithful than they are. Two common (and related) errors are to suppose: (1) that the stronger and more vivid is our feeling or experience of recollection, the more likely the recollection is to be accurate; and (2) that the more confident another person is in their recollection, the more likely their recollection is to be accurate.
>
> 17. Underlying both these errors is a faulty model of memory as a mental record which is fixed at the time of experience of an event and then fades (more or less slowly) over time. In fact, psychological research has demonstrated that memories are fluid and malleable, being constantly rewritten whenever they are retrieved. This is true even of so-called "flashbulb" memories, that is memories of experiencing or learning of a particularly shocking or traumatic event. (The very description "flashbulb" memory is in fact misleading, reflecting as it does the misconception that memory operates like a camera or other device that makes a fixed record of an experience.) External information can intrude into a witness's memory, as can his or her own thoughts and beliefs, and both can cause dramatic changes in recollection. Events can come to be recalled as memories which did not happen at all or which happened to someone else (referred to in the literature as a failure of source memory).
>
> 18. Memory is especially unreliable when it comes to recalling past beliefs. Our memories of past beliefs are revised to make them more consistent with our present beliefs. Studies have also shown that memory is particularly vulnerable to interference and alteration when a person is presented with new information or suggestions about an event in circumstances where his or her memory of it is already weak due to the passage of time.

---

30 [2017] EWHC 385 (Fam).

19. The process of civil litigation itself subjects the memories of witnesses to powerful biases. The nature of litigation is such that witnesses often have a stake in a particular version of events. This is obvious where the witness is a party or has a tie of loyalty (such as an employment relationship) to a party to the proceedings. Other, more subtle influences include allegiances created by the process of preparing a witness statement and of coming to court to give evidence for one side in the dispute. A desire to assist, or at least not to prejudice, the party who has called the witness or that party's lawyers, as well as a natural desire to give a good impression in a public forum, can be significant motivating forces.

20. Considerable interference with memory is also introduced in civil litigation by the procedure of preparing for trial. A witness is asked to make a statement, often (as in the present case) when a long time has already elapsed since the relevant events. The statement is usually drafted for the witness by a lawyer who is inevitably conscious of the significance for the issues in the case of what the witness does nor does not say. The statement is made after the witness's memory has been "refreshed" by reading documents. The documents considered often include statements of case and other argumentative material as well as documents which the witness did not see at the time or which came into existence after the events which he or she is being asked to recall. The statement may go through several iterations before it is finalised. Then, usually months later, the witness will be asked to re-read his or her statement and review documents again before giving evidence in court. The effect of this process is to establish in the mind of the witness the matters recorded in his or her own statement and other written material, whether they be true or false, and to cause the witness's memory of events to be based increasingly on this material and later interpretations of it rather than on the original experience of the events.

21. It is not uncommon (and the present case was no exception) for witnesses to be asked in cross-examination if they understand the difference between recollection and reconstruction or whether their evidence is a genuine recollection or a reconstruction of events. Such questions are misguided in at least two ways. First, they erroneously presuppose that there is a clear distinction between recollection and reconstruction, when all remembering of distant events involves reconstructive processes. Second, such questions disregard the fact that such processes are largely unconscious and that the strength, vividness and apparent authenticity of memories is not a reliable measure of their truth.

22. In the light of these considerations, the best approach for a judge to adopt in the trial of a commercial case is, in my view, to place little if any reliance at all on witnesses' recollections of what was said in meetings and conversations, and to base factual findings on inferences drawn from the documentary evidence and known or probable facts. This does not mean that oral testimony serves no useful purpose – though its utility is often disproportionate to its length. But its value lies largely, as I see it, in the opportunity which cross-examination affords to subject the documentary

record to critical scrutiny and to gauge the personality, motivations and working practices of a witness, rather than in testimony of what the witness recalls of particular conversations and events. Above all, it is important to avoid the fallacy of supposing that, because a witness has confidence in his or her recollection and is honest, evidence based on that recollection provides any reliable guide to the truth'[31].

2.25 The short words of Lord Bingham, to much the same effect, are 'The human capacity for honestly believing something which bears no relation to what actually happened is unlimited'[32].

TRICKY ISSUES

Female genital mutilation and circumcision

2.26 A particular difficulty in the application of threshold has arisen in the context of female genital mutilation (FGM) and male circumcision. It has been held that a distinction is drawn between FGM and male circumcision (not least given the severity of male circumcision when compared with FGM WHO Type IV, and the need for FGM in all forms to satisfy threshold) in that, whilst both constitute significant harm, FGM is not a procedure which it would be 'reasonable to expect a parent' to impose on a child, whereas male circumcision does not, without more, satisfy that part of threshold[33].

2.27 Explaining the justification for that distinction in *Re B and G (Children) (No 2)*[34], the President first turned to Oliver Wendell Holmes – and his famous observation that:

> 'The life of the law has not been logic; it has been experience. The felt necessities of the time, the prevalent moral and political theories, intuitions of public policy, avowed or unconscious, even the prejudices which judges share with their fellow-men, have had a good deal more to do than the syllogism in determining the rules by which men should be governed'[35].

Munby P then noted that:

> 'The explanation, it must be, is simply that in 2015 the law generally, and family law in particular, is still prepared to tolerate non-therapeutic male circumcision performed for religious or even for purely cultural or

31 *Gestmin SGPS SA v Credit Suisse (UK) Ltd & Credit Suisse (Europe) Ltd* [2013] EWHC 3560 (Comm).

32 Cited by Mostyn J in his extra-judicial speech, 'The Craft of Judging and Legal Reasoning', 8 December 2014.

33 *Re B and G (Children) (No 2)* [2015] EWFC 3, [2015] 1 FLR 905 at [58]–[73], per Munby P. FGM is discussed in more detail at paras 5.63–5.111.

34 [2015] EWFC 3.

35 OW Holmes, *The Common Law* (American Bar Association, 1881) at p 1.

> conventional reasons, whilst no longer being willing to tolerate FGM in any of its forms'[36].

In particular, the President suggested, the distinction between FGM and male circumcision is predicated on two aspects: first, FGM has no basis in any religion; male circumcision is often performed for religious reasons; and second, FGM has no medical justification and confers no health benefits; male circumcision is seen by some (although opinions are divided) as providing hygienic or prophylactic benefits[37].

Relinquished babies

2.28 Babies relinquished by their biological families have also presented difficulties in terms of formulating and satisfying threshold. In a thorough and humane judgment, Baker J, in *A Local Authority v A Mother*[38], examined the topic in detail. The key point to remember is that a mother's relinquishment of her baby for adoption will not, in itself, satisfy threshold, especially in circumstances where that process has been conducted in a planned manner.

2.29 In reaching that conclusion, Baker J discussed the historical and on-going importance of adoption and the need for a civilised society to respect difficult decisions that parents may reach. His Lordship quoted an earlier judgment of Holman J:

> 'Adoption exists to serve many social needs. But high among them has been, historically, the desire or need of some mothers to be able to conceal from their own family and friends the fact of the pregnancy and birth ... There is, in my judgment, a strong social need, if it is lawful, to continue to enable some mothers, such as this mother, to make discreet, dignified and humane arrangements for the birth and subsequent adoption of their babies, without their families knowing anything about it, if the mother, for good reason, so wishes'[39].

Holman J then went on to emphasise that we must differentiate in 'relinquished baby cases' between a scenario in which, say, a mother simply abandons a baby on a doorstep – there, it is likely threshold will be met – and, one in which a mother has made responsible plans for the relinquishment of the baby in a way which minimises the risk of harm, in which case, even if the baby suffers harm from no longer being in her mother's care, it does not follow is either attributable to the mother's care or as a result of unreasonable care[40].

---

36 *Re B and G (Children) (No 2)* [2015] at [64].
37 *Re B and G (Children) (No 2)* [2015] at [72].
38 [2016] EWFC 36.
39 *Z County Council v R* [2001] 1 FLR 365 at 367.
40 CA 1989, s 31(2)(b); *A Local Authority v A Mother* [2016] EWFC 36 at [19].

Pools of (possible) perpetrators

2.30 In a significant number of public children law cases, the local authority presents – and the court is confronted with – a range of possible culprits for a particular event (say, a series of fractures suffered by a baby). In those cases, there is a pool of (possible) perpetrators.

2.31 Where there is a pool of (possible) perpetrators, a number of additional considerations apply in relation to the standard of proof. We can extract the following from the relevant case law:

(a) the public interest here is that those who cause serious non-accidental injuries to children be identified, wherever such identification is possible. By definition in such cases, the perpetrator denies responsibility and those close to or emotionally engaged with the perpetrator likewise deny any knowledge of how the injuries occurred. Any process 'which encourages or facilitates frankness' is welcome[41];

(b) the public interest here is also that children 'have the right, as they grow into adulthood' to know the truth about who injured them when they were children, and why. The burden for any child removed from her parents as a result of 'non-accidental' injury is a heavy one. If the truth can be ascertained, children need to know it[42];

(c) equally, if, for example, it is clear that a child was assaulted by one or other of two people, the fact is that one of them did and the question for the tribunal is simply whether it is more probable that one rather than the other was the perpetrator[43];

(d) nevertheless, if that identification is not possible – because, for example, at the end of a fact-finding hearing, a judge remains genuinely uncertain, and cannot find on the balance of probabilities that A rather than B caused the injuries to the child, and that neither A nor B can be excluded as a perpetrator – the judge's duty is to state that as her conclusion. In other words, the judge should not 'strain to identify the perpetrator', nor start from the premise that it will only be in exceptional circumstances that it will not be possible to identify the perpetrator[44];

(e) in identifying a pool of (possible) perpetrators – ie where there is insufficient evidence positively to identify a perpetrator – the judge should ask herself, 'is there a likelihood or real possibility that A or B or C was the perpetrator or a perpetrator of the inflicted injuries?'[45];

(f) where a pool of (possible) perpetrators is found at a fact-finding hearing (threshold having, by definition, been met on the basis of physical harm,

41 *Re K (Children)* [2004] EWCA Civ 1181 at [57].

42 *Re K (Children)* [2004] EWCA Civ 1181 at [57].

43 *Re B* [2003] UKHL 18 at [15], per Lord Hoffmann.

44 *Re D (Care Proceedings: Preliminary Hearing)* [2009] EWCA Civ 472, [2009] 2 FLR 668 at [12].

45 *North Yorkshire County Council v SA* [2003] EWCA Civ 839 at [26].

even though the perpetrator cannot be identified), the court at the welfare stage will 'have regard, to whatever extent is appropriate' to that finding. To do otherwise – to proceed at welfare stage on the footing that, because neither A nor B, considered individually, has been proved to be the perpetrator, the child is at risk from neither – would be 'grotesque'[46];

(g) however, a finding that a person, A, is in a pool of (possible) perpetrators – which, by definition, is not a finding on the balance of probabilities that A is a perpetrator – cannot be used to found a prediction of future harm (ie 'likely to suffer significant harm': CA 1989, s 31(2)(a))[47];

(h) disquiet has been expressed by Lords Wilson and Sumption about what they understood to be the suggestion of other members of the Supreme Court that, whilst A being in the pool of (possible) perpetrators could not itself found a prediction of future harm, it might, in conjunction with other facts found, be capable of so doing. The point is a simple – and, in our view compelling – one. To quote from the headnote of *Re J (Care Proceedings: Possible Perpetrators)*, 'The suggestion was illogical that although [A's] consignment to a pool could not alone constitute a factual foundation for a prediction of likely significant harm, it could, if weighed together with other facts which were on any view relevant, figure as part of the requisite factual foundation. If, for the purpose of the requisite foundation, [A's] consignment to a pool had a value of zero on its own, it could, for this purpose, have no greater value in company'[48].

USE OF SPLIT HEARINGS

2.32 The tendency in the past few years has been to seek to avoid, wherever possible, separate fact-finding hearings and instead hold (both in public and private children law) combined fact-finding and welfare hearings.

2.33 The rationale for split hearings in public law proceedings was set out by Bracewell J back in 1996, drawing on the Annual Report of the Children Act Advisory Committee 1994–95. Her Ladyship adopted the view of the CAA Committee that the early resolution of issues such as physical or sexual abuse would enable the welfare hearing to proceed more speedily and to focus on the child's welfare with greater clarity[49].

2.34 The starting point in the change of approach can be traced back to the President's judgment, whilst sitting in the Court of Appeal, in the case of *W (Children)*[50]. There, Wall P emphasised the time-consuming nature of and delays

46 *Re O and N; Re B* [2003] UKHL 18, [2003] 1 FLR 1169 at [27]–[28].

47 *Re J (Care Proceedings: Possible Perpetrators)* [2013] 1 FLR 1373 at [43] and [49].

48 *Re J (Care Proceedings: Possible Perpetrators)* [2013] 1 FLR 1373 at [80] and [92].

49 *Re S (Care Proceedings: Split Hearing)* [1996] 2 FLR 773 at 773–774.

50 [2009] EWCA Civ 644.

caused by fact-finding hearings and the need to ensure that such a hearing is 'strictly necessary':

> 'The judge who directs [a fact-finding hearing], and the advocates who seek it, both owe a duty to the children in the case and to the system itself to ensure that such a hearing is strictly necessary, and that in the terms of the overriding objective such a hearing, where required, addresses appropriate issues and is given an appropriate share of the court's resources'[51].

2.35 Shortly after, the President issued his *Guidance on split hearings*[52]. In that guidance, Wall P set out his view that, even where a fact-finding element of a hearing is required, 'it will be a rare case'[53] that demands a separate fact-finding hearing.

2.36 More recently, Ryder LJ, in *Re S (A Child)*[54], set out the Court of Appeal's (firm) view as to the use – and in that case, inappropriate use – of split hearings in public children law. There, his Lordship set out a number of important points, which now in practice tend to govern courts' decisions on whether to sanction a split hearing:

> 'Unless the basis for such a decision [listing a split hearing] is reasoned so that the inevitable delay is justified it will be wrong in principle in public law children proceedings. Even where it is asserted that delay will not be occasioned, the use of split hearings must be confined to those cases where there is a stark or discrete issue to be determined and an early conclusion on that issue will enable the substantive determination (ie whether a statutory order is necessary) to be made more expeditiously'[55].

2.37 The type of cases for which a split hearing is appropriate is limited to:

(a) the most simple cases where there is really only one factual issue to be decided and where, if the local authority does not make out its case on that issue, threshold is not met and the proceedings will come to an end; and

(b) the most complex medical causation cases where death or very serious medical issues have arisen and where an accurate medical diagnosis is integral to the future care of the child concerned[56].

Ryder LJ held that, 'For almost all other cases, the procedure is inappropriate' and the 'erroneous justification for them that a split hearing enables a social care assessment to be undertaken is simply poor social work and forensic practice'[57].

---

51 At [33].
52 (May 2010).
53 *Guidance (May 2010)* at [7].
54 [2014] EWCA Civ 25.
55 At [27].
56 At [29].
57 At [29].

PLEADING THRESHOLD: A GUIDE

2.38 The senior courts have been keen to remind family practitioners of a number of fundamental points about threshold and to emphasise the need for compliance with these basic principles. Those points, adapted from the President's judgment in *Re A (A Child)*[58], are as follows[59]:

(a) threshold is a pleading. A pleading asserts facts; it does not set out evidence. So, a threshold document does not assert '*A saw B doing X*' – that is evidence; it is A's evidence – but rather it asserts the plain fact that the applicant will seek to prove, namely '*B did X*'. To give a tangible example: we should not write, '*The school has reported that Sally was, most days, very hungry mid-morning, as if she had not been fed her breakfast*' but rather '*Sally was often not fed breakfast and was often very hungry mid-morning at school.*' You plead, simply, the fact that you will prove;

(b) threshold is a particular sort of pleading: it is the assertion of facts that satisfy threshold. So, a fact must be *linked to* significant harm, either current or future: if the linkage is obvious, then so be it; but, in very many cases, it will require stating, ie state the way in which the fact pleaded causes or is likely to cause significant harm to the subject child;

(c) part of that means that the type of significant harm should itself be asserted: is it physical, emotional, sexual?

(d) a pleaded assertion that '*Mr Jones does not admit that Sally is hungry and does not understand the local authority's concerns*' is, by itself, of a no value. For an applicant to rely on a lack of understanding of its concerns, the applicant has *first* to prove the veracity of that asserted concern: so, it must *first* be proved that Sally is hungry, then that a parental failure to appreciate Sally's hunger has or would cause Sally significant harm, and only then does the pleading that '*Mr Jones does not understand the local authority's concerns*' have any force or relevance.

2.39 What, then, should a properly pleaded threshold look like? In his *Second, View from the President's Chambers*[60], Munby P provides a model core threshold (ie excluding the introductory section) for a simple case of alleged neglect:

'The parents have neglected the children. They have:

- Not fed them properly
- Dressed them in torn and dirty clothes
- Not supervised them properly

---

58 [2015] EWFC 11, [2016] 1 FLR 1.

59 One should note also Munby P's discussion of the importance of primary evidence in *Re A (A Child)* [2015] EWFC 11, [2016] 1 FLR 1 at [9]. This needs to be read alongside, and contrasted with, the considered and detailed views of Hayden J in *Re H (A Child) (Interim Care Order: Fact-Finding)* [2017] EWHC 518 (Fam) at [15]–[26].

60 [2013] Fam Law 458.

- Not got them to school or to the doctor or hospital when needed
- Not played with them or talked to them enough
- Not listened to the advice of social workers, health visitors and others about how to make things better: and now will not let the social worker visit the children at home [the evidence to support the case being identified by reference to the relevant page numbers in the bundle]'.

2.40 A fuller example, for a different and more complex factual scenario, is set out below. Notably, we include here a suggestion of how to address a common difficulty: how properly to plead threshold in circumstances in which some allegations (here, allegations against members of the maternal family of child sexual abuse) are historic, not live and not going to be adjudicated upon in proceedings: see, in particular, 9–11.

Example threshold: complex, factual scenario

Key:

M – the mother

C1, C2, C3 – the children

MU – maternal uncle

MGF – maternal grandfather

Mr A, Mr F – other adults (ex-partners of the mother)

1 The local authority asserts that, at the time protective measures were taken (14 December 2016, ie the date that the children were made subject to police protection) there were reasonable grounds to believe that the children were suffering or likely to suffer significant harm, the care being given to the children or being likely to be given to them not being what it would be reasonable to expect a parent to give.

2 In particular, the local authority asserts that the children suffered and/or were at risk of suffering significant emotional and physical harm and neglect for the following reasons:

Presentation of M

3 On 9 January 2016 and 13 April 2016, M threatened to kill the children and herself if the children were removed from her care.

4 M has failed to seek or engage with mental health support:

   a On 9 August 2016, M self-medicated with alcohol;

   b On 18 October 2016, M stopped taking anti-depressants;

c Having been referred to Talking Therapies by her GP, M declined to engage, and she has declined to undergo a mental health assessment;

all of which caused the children to suffer significant emotional harm and neglect.

Emotional and physical harm

5 C1 suffers from soiling and blocked intestines.

6 M is unable to meet C1's physical needs, in that:

a On 23 September 2016, M informed the allocated social worker that C1's soiling was 'C1's problem';

b On 21 October 2016, M failed to take C1 to a hospital appointment;

c M has, repeatedly, referred to C1 as 'dirty and disgusting'.

7 On 14 December 2016, M encouraged the children to block the police entering their home.

Association with undesirable individuals

8 M has failed to protect the children from suffering and witnessing domestic violence:

a On 16 April 2012, C2 witnessed Mr A grab C1 by the neck and push her back into a wardrobe;

b In or around May 2013, C1, C2 and C3 witnessed Mr F physically assault M;

c In or around April 2014, Mr F told C3 that he would kill M.

9 There are historic allegations of sexual abuse against MU and MGF. It was M's view that C1, C2 and C3 required safeguarding from them. It was M's view that this included the children not having unsupervised contact with them.

10 On:

a 14 July 2016 and 2 September 2016, M refused to sign a safeguarding agreement to stop contact between C1, C2, C3 and MU;

b 5 October 2016, M refused to sign a safeguarding agreement to stop contact between C1, C2, C3 and MU and MGF;

11 The children have continued to have unsupervised, staying contact with MGF.

CONCLUSION

2.41 The statute is simple: we are looking no further here than the CA 1989, ss 31 and 38. In terms of case law, however, this chapter has covered a lot. To help, we have referred to a number of cases in the text and the accompanying footnotes. We suggest that practitioners, if necessary, read more deeply into the case law on whichever sub-topic within this chapter is of particular relevance.

2.42 The significant practical point that this chapter covers is drafting threshold documents. We would suggest that, if instructed to plead a tricky threshold – or seeking to discredit one drafted on behalf of a local authority when representing, in particular, a parent – you remind yourself of the President's guidance in *Re A (A Child)*[61] and the two examples provided above, including that drawn from the *View from the President's Chambers.*

61 *Re A (A Child)* [2015] EWFC 11, [2016] 1 FLR 1.

Chapter 3

INTERNATIONAL PUBLIC LAW ORDERS

INTRODUCTION

3.1 As any public law practitioner knows, the impact of international issues – both practical and legal – on public children law proceedings is significant. Whilst it is yet to be seen how Brexit will impact on these issues, it is safe to say that the increasing internationalism of modern life makes it unlikely that there will be any drastic reduction in the need for English and Welsh courts to deal with foreign national parents and children. Indeed, the move to a post-Brexit legal landscape will, no doubt, throw up novel and difficult legal questions to answer.

3.2 The need for child protection and family justice systems to grapple with international considerations is global. Nevertheless, England and Wales receive a particular focus from European neighbours, given both the number of non-British Europeans living on these shores and what is perceived to be the unusual approach of our courts, particularly in relation to adoption. It is frequently – and wrongly – said that English courts are unique or near-unique in permitting non-consensual adoption; in fact, confining ourselves to the EU Member States, it has been demonstrated that a number of our neighbours have mechanisms for permitting adoption without parental consent in certain circumstances. What appears to be distinct about our system is not the mechanism itself for non-consensual adoption, but rather the frequency with which it is deployed by our courts[1]. This theme was picked up by the President, Sir James Munby, in the 2014 case of *Re E*[2], in which his Lordship noted,

> '... there is a wider context that cannot be ignored. It is one of frequently voiced complaints that the courts of England and Wales are exorbitant in their exercise of the care jurisdiction over children from other European

1 The Directorate General for Internal Policies of the EU Parliament, Policy Department C: Citizens' Rights and Constitutional Affairs has published a study for the Peti committee, *Adoption without consent* (2015) PE 519.236, by Dr Claire Fenton-Glynn of King's College London (see Annex III to the report).

2 *Re E (A Child)* [2014] EWHC 6 (Fam), [2014] 1 WLR 2670.

countries. There are specific complaints that the courts of England and Wales do not pay adequate heed to BIIR and that public authorities do not pay adequate heed to the Vienna Convention'[3].

His Lordship said, highlighting the corollary of the exercise of English jurisdiction over foreign children, that,

> '... the outcome of care proceedings in England and Wales may be that a child who is a national of another European country is adopted by an English family notwithstanding the vigorous protests of the child's non-English parents. No doubt, from our perspective that is in the best interests of the child – indeed, unless a judge is satisfied that it really is in the child's best interests no such order can be made. But we need to recognise that the judicial and other State authorities in some countries that are members of the European Union and parties to the BIIR regime may take a very different view and may indeed look askance at our whole approach to such cases'[4].

3.3 Linked to this is a second difficulty: a recognition on our own part that, just as we impose English law in relation to foreign children, so do our neighbours apply their laws to child protection concerns in relation to British children. This too was noted by the President in his address to the International Hague Network of Judges Conference at Windsor in 2013. It can, as his Lordship set out, lead to conclusions that are not (for us) immediately palatable,

> 'It is so deeply engrained in us that the child's welfare is paramount, and that we have a personal responsibility for the child, that we sometimes find it hard to accept that we must demit that responsibility to another judge, sitting perhaps in a faraway country with a very different legal system. But we must, and we do. International comity, international judicial comity, is not some empty phrase; it is the daily reality of our courts. And be in no doubt: it is immensely to the benefit of children generally that it should be'[5].

3.4 The role of this chapter is to function as a guide to those public children law cases that contain an international element.[6] We take you through:

(a) introductory procedural tips;

(b) care orders: jurisdiction;

(c) care orders: welfare;

(d) placement and adoption orders: jurisdiction and welfare;

---

3 [2014] EWHC 6 (Fam) at [13].

4 Ibid at [15].

5 Cited in *Re E (A Child)* [2014] EWHC 6 (Fam), [2014] 1 WLR 2670 at [20].

6 What this chapter does not do, however, is address each and every detail and nuance in this complex area; for that, further reading will be required.

(e) placing children abroad: adoption, special guardianship orders, Brussels II Revised (BIIa)[7], Art 56 and the Hague Convention 1996[8];

(f) relinquished babies.

INTRODUCTORY PROCEDURAL TIPS

3.5 The key to the successful navigation of a public children law case marked by international complexity is early identification and good case management. That is for two reasons: there may well be steps (communication with foreign authorities, etc) that require taking at the start of proceedings, and there will be certain additional demands (securing specialist legal advice, conducting assessments out of the jurisdiction) that can prove time-consuming and are likely, unless quickly identified, to cause delay.

3.6 Indeed, early identification has been exhorted by the President in various cases and is now an in-built part of the template orders, in which the question of jurisdiction must explicitly be tackled.

3.7 What, then, should one do? We suggest that, on first becoming involved in any public children law case, a practitioner should immediately be alert to the international issue lurking buried in the papers: be it a foreign national parent and/or child, a latent dispute about jurisdiction or the possibility of a placement with family members abroad.

3.8 The first two issues to think about are:

(a) jurisdiction: does the English and Welsh court have jurisdiction over the subject child and, if so, on what basis? This is explored further, below;

(b) communication: what is the impact on the proceedings of the obligations under the Vienna Convention on Consular Relations of 24 April 1963?

3.9 The 1963 Vienna Convention is unlikely to be especially familiar to readers. Two provisions, however, bear noting: Art 36, which deals with communication and contact with nationals of the sending State; and Art 37, which addresses information in cases of death, guardianship or trusteeship, wrecks and air accidents. There are a handful of simple points to be drawn from the Convention.

3.10 Article 36 states, inter alia, that,

> '1 (a) consular officers shall be free to communicate with nationals of the sending State and to have access to them. Nationals of the sending State

7 Council Regulation (EC) No 2201/2003 of 27 November 2003 concerning jurisdiction and the recognition and enforcement of judgments in matrimonial matters and the matters of parental responsibility, repealing Regulation (EC) No 1347/2000.

8 Convention of 19 October 1996 on applicable law, recognition, enforcement and co-operation in respect of parental responsibility and measures for the protection of children.

shall have the same freedom with respect to communication with and access to consular officers of the sending State'.

As a matter of good practice, therefore, its effect is to discourage a family court from sheltering behind the Administration of Justice Act 1960, s 12, and the fact of its sitting in private, and from curtailing in any way free communication and access between a foreign national party and her consular authority.

3.11 The President has suggested that practical steps should be taken, including:

> 'Whenever the court is sitting in private it should normally accede to any request, whether from the foreign national or from the consular authorities of the relevant foreign state, for
>
> (a) permission for an accredited consular official to be present at the hearing as an observer in a non-participatory capacity; and/or
>
> (b) permission for an accredited consular official to obtain a transcript of the hearing, a copy of the order and copies of other relevant documents'[9].

3.12 Further, Art 36 1(b) provides that,

> '(b) if he [the person arrested, imprisoned or detained] so requests, the competent authorities of the receiving State shall, without delay, inform the consular post of the sending State if, within its consular district, a national of that State is arrested or committed to prison or to custody pending trial or is detained in any other manner ...'.

3.13 Article 37 requires inter alia that,

> 'If the relevant information is available to the competent authorities of the receiving State, such authorities shall have the duty:
>
> (b) to inform the competent consular post without delay of any case where the appointment of a guardian or trustee appears to be in the interests of a minor or other person lacking full capacity who is a national of the sending State. The giving of this information shall, however, be without prejudice to the operation of the laws and regulations of the receiving State concerning such appointments; ...'

Where a guardian ad litem is appointed to represent a foreign national child – ie in all public children law cases – the court should immediately ascertain whether that appointment has been brought to the attention of the relevant consular officials. If it has not, that should be done without delay. This duty has been held to apply in particular to the applicant local authority[10].

---

9 *Re E (A Child)* [2014] EWHC 6 (Fam), [2014] 1 WLR 2670 at [47].

10 *Re CB (A Child)* [2015] EWCA Civ 888 at [79].

CARE ORDERS: JURISDICTION

Principles of jurisdiction

Introduction

3.14 Jurisdiction in respect of private law proceedings (including special guardianship orders[11]) is set out in statute. The Family Law Act 1986 (FLA 1986), ss 2–3, which explicitly refers to the jurisdictional provisions of BIIa and the Hague Convention 1996, makes clear that those international instruments sit alongside the statutory jurisdictional scheme of presence and/or habitual residence. Equally, jurisdiction for the adoption of a child is set out in statute, in the Adoption and Children Act 2002 (ACA 2002), as discussed at para 3.43.

3.15 Curiously, however, statute is totally silent in relation to the jurisdiction of the English and Welsh courts in *public* children law proceedings – ie the question of the class of children in relation to whom the State can exercise these fundamental powers is not contained in any statute. Instead, in the context of national law, it had been left to judges to formulate the jurisdictional scheme. Starting with Singer J in *Re R (Care Orders: Jurisdiction)*[12], then Hale J in *Re M (Care Orders: Jurisdiction)*[13] and subsequently Bodey J in *Lewisham London Borough Council v D (Criteria for Territorial Jurisdiction in Public Law Proceedings)*[14], it has been held that – in part by reason of analogy with private law jurisdiction under the FLA 1986 – jurisdiction requires presence and/or habitual residence.

BIIa and the Hague Convention 1996: founding of jurisdiction

3.16 All member states of the European Union (except Denmark) are bound by the provisions of BIIa. This includes England and Wales. As such, since its introduction over a decade ago, it is BIIa to which we must first turn when determining jurisdiction in children law. BIIa, Art 1, addressing 'scope', makes it clear that BIIa applies to 'the attribution, exercise, delegation, restriction or termination of parental responsibility'. In 2007, the Grand Chamber confirmed that BIIa applies to care proceedings[15].

3.17 Whilst BIIa is a European instrument, its central jurisdictional scheme, set out in BIIa, Arts 8–14 and on which more below, has been held by the UK Supreme Court to apply in England and Wales to *all* children law cases that fall within its 'scope', and not only those in which the competing jurisdiction is another BIIa Member State[16].

11 FLA 1986, s 1(1)(aa).
12 [1995] 1 FLR 711.
13 [1991] 1 FLR 456.
14 [2008] 2 FLR 1449.
15 Case C-435/06, *Re C* [2008] 1 FLR 490.
16 *Re I (A Child) (Contact Application: Jurisdiction)* [2009] UKSC 10 at [17]–[20] and *A v A (Children: Habitual Residence) (Reunite International Child Abduction Centre Intervening)* [2013] UKSC 60 at [30] and [59].

3.18 It should be recognised from the outset that BIIa operates as one part of the international child protection jigsaw and needs to be read alongside its sister instruments, most notably the Hague Convention 1996, Hague Convention 1980 and even the Luxembourg Convention[17].

3.19 The Hague Convention 1996, which came into force in the UK on 1 November 2012, is best understood as supplementing and building on existing powers and duties as opposed to introducing new concepts. Provisions introduced or supplemented by the Hague Convention 1996 include: the taking of urgent, protective measures (such as interim care orders); transfers of jurisdiction; requests to another Contracting State to take urgent measures; help in tracing a child; and information gathering[18]. Unlike BIIa, which is a purely European instrument, the Contracting States to the 1996 Hague Convention are truly international[19].

3.20 BIIa explicitly provides for its own predominance over both the Hague Convention 1980 (BIIa, Art 60(e))[20] and, where the child is habitually resident in a BIIa Member State, the Hague Convention 1996 (BIIa, Art 61)[21]. That presents a number of legal uncertainties and potential problems, not least in relation to the transfer of cases, as examined at paras 3.28–3.40.

Children law generally

3.21 BIIa itself sets out a complete jurisdictional scheme for children law which, at its culmination, points us back to jurisdiction under national statute and common law. It is a scheme of no little complexity and its application is predicated on the type of order sought. One way[22] to conceptualise it is in the following hierarchy:

(a) jurisdiction rests with the Member State in which a child is habitually resident[23] at the time the court is seised[24];

---

17 The limited relevance of the Luxembourg Convention (properly, the European Convention on Recognition and Enforcement of Decisions concerning Custody of Children and on Restoration of Custody of Children 20/05/1980) (limited given the operation of the 1980 Hague Convention) is not examined in this book.

18 Respectively, Arts 11, 8–9, 32(b), 31(c) and 32(a).

19 The (evolving) list of Hague Convention 1996 Contracting States can be found on the Hague Conference on Private International Law website at www.hcch.net/en/instruments/conventions/status-table/?cid=70.

20 Albeit often BIIa and the Hague Convention 1980 will be used together: see, for example, BIIa, Arts 11 and 62.2.

21 It should be noted that the precise scope of this predominance – ie the extent to which a child who has her habitual residence in a BIIa Member State is precluded from the protection available under the Hague Convention 1996 – is complex and yet to be authoritatively determined.

22 Whether it is strictly hierarchical in any given case depends in part on the proper interrelationship between BIIa and the Hague Convention 1996 as defined by BIIa, Art 61.

23 The definition of habitual residence is now well known: it is a question of fact, and not a legal concept, and is 'the place which reflects some degree of integration by the child in a social and family environment in the country concerned', for example, in *A v A (Children: Habitual Residence) (Reunite International Child Abduction Centre Intervening)* [2013] UKSC 60 at [54(iii)].

24 BIIa, Art 8.

(b) where a child's habitual residence cannot be established, including but not limited to in relation to refugee children and those internationally displaced[25] (and there has been no prorogation of jurisdiction under BIIa, Art 12), jurisdiction is held by the Member State in which the child is present[26];

(c) where no Member State has jurisdiction under BIIa, Arts 8–13, jurisdiction shall be determined, in each Member State, by the national law of that Member State[27];

In the event, therefore, that it is BIIa, Art 14 that applies – ie jurisdiction cannot be founded on Arts 8–13 in *any* Member State – BIIa tells us to depart from BIIa itself and look elsewhere for jurisdiction:

(d) the next instrument to consider in children law generally is the Hague Convention 1996 (because, depending on the type of order sought, *either* the combined operation of FLA 1986 and BIIa, Art 61(a) points us toward the Hague Convention 1996, *and/or* the direct effect[28] of the Hague Convention 1996 kicks in, as circumscribed by BIIa, Art 61(a));

(e) where there is no jurisdiction under the Hague Convention 1996, we turn next to national statute and the FLA 1986, which provides jurisdiction primarily in relation to orders under the CA 1989, s 8 (ie classic private law orders) and orders made under the inherent jurisdiction 'so far as it gives care of a child to any person or provides for contact with, or the education of, a child'[29] and founds jurisdiction on habitual residence and/or presence;

(f) finally, failing that, we have recourse to the inherent jurisdiction – or, more properly, to those parts of it not affected by the operation of FLA 1986 – and the making of orders based on presence and, to be used sparingly, nationality.

3.22 So, in children law generally, we look for habitual residence under BIIa, **or**, if that cannot be established we fall back on presence under BIIa, **or** if a child is not habitually resident or present in *any* Member State, we consider the Hague Convention 1996, **then** we turn, depending on the nature of the order sought, to habitual residence and/or presence under FLA 1986, **then** to orders under the inherent jurisdiction on the basis of presence or, exceptionally, nationality, to be exercised sparingly.

Care orders and interim care orders

3.23 In the context of public law orders under the CA 1989, ss 31 and 38, the provisions of the FLA 1986 and the inherent jurisdiction have little or no application: see para 3.21(e) and (f). In public law cases in which substantive

25 BIIa, Art 13.2.

26 BIIa, Art 13.

27 BIIa, Art 14.

28 The Hague Convention 1996 has direct effect pursuant to the European Communities Act 1972, s 2, and the European Communities (Definition of Treaties) (1996 Hague Convention on Protection of Children etc) Order 2010, SI 2010/232.

29 FLA 1986, s 1(1)(d).

jurisdiction cannot be established under BIIa or the Hague Convention 1996, those instruments provide instead for the taking of emergency measures. That includes, in the public law context, the making of an interim care order.

3.24 Under BIIa, an interim care order can be made under Art 20:

> '1. In urgent cases, the provisions of this Regulation shall not prevent the courts of a Member State from taking such provisional, including protective, measures in respect of persons ... as may be available under the law of that Member State, even if, under this Regulation, the court of another Member State has jurisdiction as to the substance of the matter.
>
> 2. The measures referred to in paragraph 1 shall cease to apply when the court of the Member State having jurisdiction under this Regulation as to the substance of the matter has taken the measures it considers appropriate'

Under the Hague Convention 1996, on the other hand, the relevant provisions are Arts 11–12:

> '**Article 11**
>
> (1) In all cases of urgency, the authorities of any Contracting State in whose territory the child or property belonging to the child is present have jurisdiction to take any necessary measures of protection.
>
> (2) The measures taken under the preceding paragraph with regard to a child habitually resident in a Contracting State shall lapse as soon as the authorities which have jurisdiction under Articles 5 to 10 have taken the measures required by the situation.
>
> (3) The measures taken under paragraph 1 with regard to a child who is habitually resident in a non-Contracting State shall lapse in each Contracting State as soon as measures required by the situation and taken by the authorities of another State are recognised in the Contracting State in question.
>
> **Article 12**
>
> (1) Subject to Article 7, the authorities of a Contracting State in whose territory the child or property belonging to the child is present have jurisdiction to take measures of a provisional character for the protection of the person or property of the child which have a territorial effect limited to the State in question, in so far as such measures are not incompatible with measures already taken by authorities which have jurisdiction under Articles 5 to 10.
>
> (2) The measures taken under the preceding paragraph with regard to a child habitually resident in a Contracting State shall lapse as soon as the authorities which have jurisdiction under Articles 5 to 10 have taken a decision in respect of the measures of protection which may be required by the situation.

(3) The measures taken under paragraph 1 with regard to a child who is habitually resident in a non-Contracting State shall lapse in the Contracting State where the measures were taken as soon as measures required by the situation and taken by the authorities of another State are recognised in the Contracting State in question.'

3.25 Clearly, therefore, neither BIIa, Art 20 nor the Hague Convention 1996, Arts 11–12 can be used as a mechanism to subvert the fundamentally important idea of judicial comity and equal respect for distinct legal systems and practices.

3.26 As such, the jurisdictional interrelationship here between BIIa and the Hague Convention 1996 is as follows:

(a) for European cases, if a child is habitually resident in Member State B, but present in Member State A, Member State A can make an interim care order under BIIa, Art 20, ie a child must be habitually resident in *a* Member State;

(b) for non-European cases, both where the competing jurisdiction is a Hague Convention 1996 Contracting State and where it is a third (ie non-Contracting) State:

   (i) if a child is habitually resident in Contracting State B, but present in Contracting State A, Contracting State A can make an interim care order under the Hague Convention 1996, Arts 11–12;

   (ii) if a child is habitually resident in a third state – ie a country that is neither a Member State nor a Contracting State – but present in Contracting State A, Contracting State A can make an interim care order under the Hague Convention 1996, Arts 11–12.

3.27 A practical example may help to illustrate the issues that may arise:

Piotr and his wife, Aleksandra, are due to have a baby, with Aleksandra heavily pregnant. They already have a 3-year-old daughter, Verginia. Aleksandra travels to England to stay with friends and Verginia accompanies her, with Piotr remaining at home in another BIIa Member State. Whilst here, Aleksandra gives birth. Due to ill health, Aleksandra and the children remain in England for a couple of months. Following a suspicious injury suffered by Verginia, a local authority issues care proceedings in relation both to Verginia and the baby. Who, then, has jurisdiction for each of the subject children?

The points to consider are:

(a) at the time of the trip to England, Verginia was habitually resident in another BIIa Member State. Has the time that Verginia has spent in England – and her level of integration, including that of Aleksandra, on whom she relies – been sufficient so as to mean that she has ceased to be habitually resident in the other Member State and is now habitually resident here? Or, does she remain habitually resident in her country of origin? Or, is it impossible to establish her habitual residence, in which case jurisdiction can be founded on her presence in England?

(b) as for the baby, has the baby acquired a habitual residence in England? Or, given her firm reliance on the habitual residence of her mother, Aleksandra (who perhaps remains integrated in her country of origin and is detained in England only by reason of ill-health) is the baby without a habitual residence at all?

These questions are highly fact-specific and may not permit of easy answers. Such questions need explicitly to be flagged up at the commencement of proceedings and a hearing listed to determine them. In the absence of these steps being taken, the English court may be operating in a jurisdictional void, save for any urgent orders founded on BIIa, Art 20.

Transfer of jurisdiction

BIIa

3.28 In every case that has a BIIa element the court should consider whether, despite the founding of jurisdiction in England and Wales under BIIa, Arts 8–14, the case should be transferred to another Member State.

3.29 That transfer is effected by way of the mechanism set out in BIIa, Art 15, which acts as an exception to the jurisdictional scheme of BIIa, Arts 8–14. It is (or should be) predicated on 'the principle of mutual trust and on the assumption that the courts of all member states are in principle competent to deal with a case'[30].

3.30 From around 2013 onwards, a significant body of case law built up in relation to BIIa, Art 15. That now needs to be reconsidered in light of the two leading cases. The first, in the Supreme Court, *Re N (Children)*[31]; and the second, in the Court of Justice of the European Union, *Child and Family Agency v JD*[32]. Practitioners must also be alive to the tensions between the two decisions, with the UK Supreme Court having handed down its judgment only a few months before the CJEU ruling.

3.31 For an Art 15 transfer to take place, three criteria must be satisfied in addition to the founding of jurisdiction in Member State A:

(a) the child must have a '*particular connection*' with Member State B. 'Particular connection' is defined, exhaustively[33], within Art 15 itself and means: has become or is a former habitual residence of the child; is the place of

30 *Re N (Children) (Adoption: Jurisdiction)* [2015] EWCA Civ 1112, [2017] AC 167 at [4], citing the BIIa *Practice Guide.*

31 *Re N (Children) (Jurisdiction: Care Proceedings)* [2016] UKSC 15, [2017] AC 167.

32 *Child and Family Agency v JD* Case C-428/15, CJEU.

33 *Child and Family Agency v JD* Case C-428/15 CJEU at [51].

the child's nationality; is the habitual residence of a holder of parental responsibility; or, in certain circumstances which are unlikely to apply to care proceedings, is where the child's property is located[34];

(b) Member State B must be 'better placed' to hear the case. The Court of Justice of the European Union has explained, in *Child and Family Agency v JD*[35], that 'better placed' requires that the court in Member State B be able 'to provide genuine and specific added value, with respect to the decision to be taken in relation to the child, as compared with the possibility of the case remaining before that court'. Also, it can include consideration of 'the rules of procedure in the other Member State, such as those applicable to the taking of evidence required for dealing with the case'. But, it must not take into account 'the substantive law of that other Member State'[36];

(c) the transfer to Member State B must be in the 'best interests' of the child. Authoritative guidance on the meaning of 'best interests' under Art 15 has been provided by the Supreme Court in *Re N (Children) (Jurisdiction: Care Proceedings)*, in which Lady Hale in the lead judgment held that, 'The question is whether the *transfer* is in the child's best interests. That is a different question from what eventual *outcome* is in the child's best interests … The factors relevant to deciding the question will vary according to circumstances. It is impossible to be definitive. But there is no reason at all to exclude the impact upon the child's welfare, in the short or the longer term, of the transfer itself … It is deciding whether it is in the child's best interests for the court currently seised of the case to retain it or whether it is in the child's best interests for the case to be transferred to the requested court'[37];

3.32 The Court of Justice of the European Union in *Child and Family Agency v JD* explained that the 'best interests' requirement

> 'implies that the court … must be satisfied, having regard to the specific circumstances of the case, that the envisaged transfer of the case to the court of another Member State is not liable to be detrimental to the situation of the child concerned' and that the court must assess 'any negative effects that such a transfer might have on the familial, social and emotional attachments of the child concerned in the case or on the child's material situation', at [58]–[59].

The Court of Justice's interpretation, therefore, which post-dates by a few months the Supreme Court's decision, is importantly different in emphasis: the Court of Justice speaks not of the need to demonstrate that a transfer is *positively* in a child's best interests, but rather that it would not cause a child to

34 BIIa, Art 15(3).

35 *Child and Family Agency v JD* Case C-428/15 CJEU.

36 At [57].

37 *Re N (Children) (Jurisdiction: Care Proceedings)* [2016] UKSC 15, [2017] AC 167 at [44] (emphasis in original).

suffer *detriment*. It remains to be seen how this principle will now be developed in our national courts.

3.33 The Court of Justice also made clear that, when evaluating the BIIa, Art 15 criteria, whilst any detriment to the right of freedom of movement of the subject child could be relevant, the effect on the right of freedom of movement on other persons concerned or the reason(s) why the parent(s) of that child exercised the right to move to Member State A prior to Member State A being seised are *not* to be taken account of, save to the extent that such considerations are liable to have adverse repercussions on the situation of the child[38].

3.34 Article 15 of BIIa is not, however, the full story. That is for two reasons: one, the proliferation of non-European (properly, non-BIIa cases); and two, the uncertainty as to the lifespan of BIIa in domestic terms post-Brexit.

Non-European cases[39]

3.35 As set out above, the jurisdictional scheme in BIIa, Arts 8–14, has been held in England and Wales to apply to all public children law cases, and not only those in which the competing jurisdiction is another BIIa Member State. But it remains uncertain whether the transfer scheme under BIIa, Art 15 has as broad an application. It has been held at first instance not to apply so broadly.[40]

3.36 Article 15 of BIIa reads:

> '1. By way of exception, the courts of *a Member State* having jurisdiction as to the substance of the matter may, if they consider that a court of *another Member State* ... (a) stay a case or the part thereof and invited the parties to introduce a request before the court of that other Member State ... or (b) request a court of another Member State to assume jurisdiction ...' (authors' emphasis),

It is, therefore, explicit in stating that we are concerned with a transfer from Member State A to Member State B. So, Lady Hale's reasoning in relation to the broad scope of BIIa, Arts 8–14, does not easily apply[41].

3.37 As such, when considering transfer in a non-European case (ie transfer from England and Wales to a non-BIIa Member State) careful consideration is required about other mechanisms for transfer.

---

38 *Child and Family Agency* (Case C-428/15) at [64]–[67].

39 Properly, non-BIIa, ie EU save for Denmark.

40 *Re M (Children) (Suspected Trafficking: Competent Authority)* [2017] EWFC 56, per Parker J at [15]. Her Ladyship's decision appears to have been *obiter* and without detailed submissions on the point. It explicitly relies on pre-BIIa reasoning. The case does not appear since to have been considered by an appellate court.

41 *Re I (A Child) (Contact Application: Jurisdiction)* [2009] UKSC 10 at [17]–[20] and *A v A (Children: Habitual Residence) (Reunite International Child Abduction Centre Intervening)* [2013] UKSC 60 at [30] and *Re I (A Child) (Contact Application: Jurisdiction)* [2009] UKSC 10 at [17]–[20].

3.38 One option is consideration of a transfer under the Hague Convention 1996, Art 8. Article 8 is, of course, a well-trodden route: with both the legal test ('would be better placed in the particular case to assess the best interests of the child') and procedure familiar. The potential block is the operation of BIIa, Art 61[42]. In the event that:

(i) BIIa, Art 61 precludes the use of the 1996 Hague Convention where a child is habitually resident in a BIIa Member State; and

(ii) BIIa, Art 15 cannot be deployed where the country of intended transfer is not a BIIa Member State,

we are in the unfortunate position in which (a) a BIIa Member State can transfer to another BIIa Member State, (b) a 1996 Hague Convention Contracting State can transfer to another Contracting State but (c) a Member State cannot transfer to a Contracting State that is not itself a Member State because the available mechanisms are made inapplicable by the interoperation of the very instruments intended to promote international child protection.

3.39 Another possibility, of course, is for the English court simply to stay its proceedings under traditional *forum non conveniens* principles, permit the subject family to return home to their country and allow the foreign equivalent of children's services to take the necessary child protection measures. The legal capability of the court here to decline to exercise jurisdiction where a non-Member State might be thought 'better placed' to determine the issues is complex and uncertain[43]: see Lady Hale sitting in the Supreme Court in *Re A (Jurisdiction: Return of Child)*[44] and a recent line of domestic authority which has held, without detailed argument, that the power exists[45].

3.40 Beyond that, there is a practical problem with a stay. As it stands, there is no scheme for a transfer of child protection measures to take effect. Judges will not, of course, want to send care proceedings into an abyss. Firm and detailed information will be required from the receiving country as to what, if any,

42 For a more detailed consideration of this potential block – and the competing arguments for a narrow (relying on the *Practice Guide for the application of the Brussels IIa Regulation* and the operation of Article 7, 1996 Hague Convention) and broad (on a plain reading of Article 61, BIIa) interpretation – readers should consult a dedicated international family children law text. Regard should also be had to the view of Theis J in *Re H (A Child) (Care Proceedings: Jurisdiction)* [2014] EWHC 2550 (Fam), at [30].

43 See, for example, the view of *Dicey, Morris & Collins on the Conflict of Laws* (15th edn, Sweet and Maxwell) at 19-062, which says that the power of the English and Welsh court to stay proceedings (under its inherent power or the FLA 1986, s 5) in which jurisdiction is founded on BIIa is 'a matter of some uncertainty' and 'The drafting of s 5(2) [of the FLA 1986] is not determinative'.

44 [2013] UKSC 60, in which her Ladyship comments on, 'whether the courts of a Member State which has jurisdiction in respect of parental responsibility under BIIR is obliged to exercise that jurisdiction even though there is a third country which would be better placed to hear the case', and suggests that 'it might, therefore, be thought anomalous for this [a transfer] to be precluded in a case where the courts of a non-Member State were better placed to hear the case', both at [32].

45 See *Re K (A Child)* [2015] EWCA Civ 352; *MB v GK* [2015] EWHC 2192 (Fam); *SF v HL* [2015] EWHC 2891 (Fam); *AB v AB* [2015] EWHC 2422 (Fam) and *Re G (Children) (Habitual Residence)* [2017] EWHC 2111 (Fam).

child protection measures would be taken. The likelihood of receiving that from a (perhaps) disinterested foreign authority is low. Indeed, that takes on particular importance when it is considered that the 'stay' argued for would, it seems, be illusory: once the foreign national subject family is on the plane, with a settled intention to leave, jurisdiction under BIIa will quickly disappear and, without the children having British nationality, no residual inherent jurisdiction will remain: once they are off, they are off.

CARE ORDERS: WELFARE

3.41 In any case with an international dimension, particular focus will be placed on the child's social, cultural and religious background when evaluating the welfare checklist under the CA 1989, s 1(3). Beyond that, there is, we suggest, no impact on welfare considerations, save for the legal and practical issues relating to placing children abroad, as set out at paras 3.47–3.63.

PLACEMENT AND ADOPTION ORDERS: JURISDICTION AND WELFARE

3.42 Unlike with orders made under the CA 1989, ss 31 and 38, in relation to which BIIa is the governing jurisdictional instrument, placement and adoption orders are governed solely by domestic statute. That is for the simple reason that BIIa, Art 1.3, addressing scope, makes clear that BIIa does not apply to 'decisions on adoption, measures preparatory to adoption …'. The position, then, is simpler. We look solely at the ACA 2002.

3.43 The ACA 2002 sets out the jurisdictional scheme. The key points to bear in mind are that:

(a) jurisdiction to make a placement order is set out in the ACA 2002, ss 21–22;

(b) jurisdiction to make an adoption order is based on the domicile or habitual residence for one year of the applicant(s)[46], so there may be jurisdiction to adopt a child irrespective of the child's nationality, domicile or habitual residence and irrespective of the natural parent(s)' nationality, domicile or habitual residence. Indeed, this jurisdiction to adopt a non-British subject has existed since the enactment of the Adoption of Children Act 1949, which removed the nationality requirement introduced by the Adoption of Children Act 1926;

(c) wherever an English court has jurisdiction to place a child for adoption, it is English law that shall be applied, including when dispensing with the consent of the natural parent(s). That is the case despite the academic arguments to the contrary[47].

46 ACA 2002, s 49(2)–(3).

47 *Re N (Children) (Adoption: Jurisdiction)* [2015] EWCA Civ 1112, [2017] AC 167 at [91]–[103].

3.44 The making of a placement or adoption order with an international dimension demands a particular welfare focus. Section 1(4) of the ACA 2002 provides that:

> 'The court … must have regard to the following matters (among others) … (c) the likely effect on the child (throughout his life) of having ceased to be a member of the original family and having become an adopted person, (d) the child's age, sex, background and any of the child's characteristics which the court … considers relevant …'

3.45 A defining characteristic of a child's adoption is the impact on her (legal) status: she is, in law, no longer the child of her natural parents, but instead now the child of her adoptive parents. She becomes, in law, part of a new family. Both her status and that of her natural parents is radically altered. But, that status is altered only as a matter of our national law; in a relevant foreign law, the adoption order may not be recognised. That would create what has been coined academically as a 'limping infant', a term referred to in case law as far back as 1968, by Goff J:

> 'The court cannot shut its eyes to the possibility of creating the "limping infant" referred to in *Cheshire's International Private Law*, 7th ed (1965), p 382, and if the child is domiciled in a country where the English order would not be recognised, he may "limp" not only there but in other places, and may find himself faced with a dispute in other countries whether the English order should be recognised or not'[48].

The result of this is that:

> '… in all cases where there is such a foreign element … evidence should be furnished to show that the order, if made, will be recognised by the foreign court and, if so, then the English court is free to proceed regardless of any question of foreign law or procedure, but if not, then the court will have to weigh the disadvantages of the child having one status here and another in other countries, or even a doubtful one, against the other considerations that they may be in favour of adoption. The disadvantages may of course be serious in such matters as liability for military service, taxation (including death duties) and succession to property'[49].

3.46 That analysis has more recently been picked up by the President, in terms that, 'Unless the foreign country is one which, under the International Convention, is bound to recognise an English adoption order, the English court will need to address the issues identified by Goff J, having ensured that it has the necessary evidence to enable it to do so'[50].

48 *Re B (S) (An Infant)* [1968] Ch 204 at 212.
49 *Re B (S) (An Infant)* [1968] Ch 204 at 212–213.
50 *Re N (Children) (Adoption: Jurisdiction)* [2015] EWCA Civ 1112, [2017] AC 167 at [111].

PLACING CHILDREN ABROAD: ADOPTION AND SPECIAL GUARDIANSHIP ORDERS, BIIA, ART 56 AND PLACEMENTS UNDER THE HAGUE CONVENTION 1996

3.47 It is not, of course, only through a transfer of the proceedings that a child in relation to whom public law proceedings are commenced in England may find herself transferred abroad. It is equally open to the English court, through a range of mechanisms, to make a welfare order that authorises the (final) placement of the child abroad. Indeed, in the words of Lady Hale in 2016, quoting the written intervention of the Family Rights Group, 'the courts have been arranging foreign placements for years'[51].

Adoption

3.48 Section 85 of the ACA 2002 establishes a blanket ban on the removal from the UK of any child who is a Commonwealth citizen or habitually resident in the UK for the purpose of adoption, save in cases in which the proposed adopters have parental responsibility by virtue of the ACA 2002, s 84[52].

3.49 A court may grant parental responsibility only to a proposed adopter who does not meet the jurisdictional requirements – domicile or habitual residence of one year – imposed by the ACA 2002, s 49, ie the normal jurisdictional requirements for the making of an adoption order.

3.50 However, the CA 1989, Sch 2, para 19 acts to modify the ACA 2002, ss 84–85. This means that the ACA 2002, s 85 is disapplied in cases where a child is to live outside of England and Wales with the approval of the court given under the CA 1989, Sch 2, para 19. Except in cases in which a local authority is placing a child for adoption with prospective adopters, in which case the CA 1989, Sch 2, para 19 is itself disapplied[53].

3.51 Where, then, does that leave us? The view of Baker J in *Re JL v AO (Babies Relinquished for Adoption)*[54] (there in the context of a consensual adoption coupled with a dispute over the country in which the child would be adopted) was that, absent a successful ACA 2002, s 84 application, the court was prohibited from the blanket ban in the ACA 2002, s 85 from making an order authorising the removal of the subject baby to Hungary for adoption. That was because the subject baby was not in the care of the local authority and therefore not within the provisions of the CA 1989, Sch 2, para 19(6)[55]. The solution suggested to the local authority by his Lordship was for it to consider whether it wished to issue care proceedings and then apply under the CA 1989, Sch 2, para 19 to place the baby abroad.

---

51 *Re N (Children) (Jurisdiction: Care Proceedings)* [2016] UKSC 15, [2017] AC 167 at [48].

52 ACA 2002, s 85(1) and (2)(a).

53 See CA 1989, Sch 2, para 19(6) and (9).

54 [2016] EWHC 440 (Fam).

55 At [82]–[89].

3.52 We suggest, therefore, that the position is as follows:

(a) for a child to be placed abroad with specific adopters, those specific adopters must obtain an order under the ACA 2002, s 84. That is because: (i) the blanket ban in s 85 is subject to the ACA 2002, s 84; and (ii) the disapplication of the blanket ban where the child is in local authority care is itself disapplied where there are specific adopters[56];

(b) a child cannot be placed abroad for the purpose of adoption (ie without, we suggest this must mean, specific adopters being identified) if the child is not in the care of a local authority. Equally, this cannot be effected under the inherent jurisdiction as to do so would cut across the statutory scheme[57];

(c) a child can be placed abroad for the purpose of adoption, without the identification of specific adopters, if the child is in the care of a local authority and an order is made under the CA 1989, Sch 2, para 19.

A child in local authority care: interim care orders and care orders

3.53 As set out above, tucked away in the CA 1989, Sch 2, para 19 is the important provision that:

> '(1) A local authority may only arrange for, or assist in arranging for, any child in their care to live outside England and Wales with the approval of the court',

which requires that, for the placement abroad of any child subject to an interim or (final) care order, a court order must first be obtained.

3.54 In determining such an application, the court applies the factors set out at the CA 1989, Sch 2, para 19(3)–(5), which require that: (i) it be in the child's best interests; (ii) suitable arrangements be in place; (iii) the child either consents or has insufficient understanding to consent; and (iv) every person with parental responsibility consents, cannot be found, is incapable of consent or is judged to be withholding consent unreasonably.

Special guardianship orders; child arrangements orders

3.55 Special guardianship and child arrangements orders are private law orders. Nevertheless, because of their utility in and relevance to public law proceedings, it is convenient at this stage to consider the provisions in relation to them. Either may be the appropriate welfare order to secure the placement of a child with a family member.

3.56 A child arrangements order presents no particular legal complications. As in any private law dispute, the order will be made under the CA 1989, s 8 and

---

56 CA 1989, Sch 2, para 19(6) and (9).

57 *Re JL v AO (Babies Relinquished for Adoption)* [2016] EWHC 440 (Fam) at [86]–[88].

then recognised and enforced abroad (with very little scope for non-recognition and/or non-enforcement) under Chapter III of BIIa and Chapter IV of the Hague Convention 1996.

3.57 The position in relation to special guardianship orders can prove more problematic. First, because a special guardianship order – ie a private law order providing for enhanced parental responsibility for the holder – may not be an order that exists in or is known to the foreign state. Specialist advice will often be required on the terms in which any order should be expressed. Second, because, whilst an English reading of BIIa, Art 56, would place a special guardianship order outside of its provisions, other BIIa Member States (for example, Cyprus) may view a special guardianship order as falling within the definition of '*in institutional care or with a foster family*' triggering the BIIa, Art 56 provisions. Again, expert advice and/or communication with the relevant Central Authority will be required to establish that.

3.58 Also important is the CA 1989, s 14C(3)(b), which allows the court to make an order permitting a special guardian to remove a child from the UK indefinitely.

Inherent jurisdiction

3.59 Equally, in the event that the child is not subject to a public law order, the High Court's inherent jurisdiction might be used in a flexible way so as to secure the placement of a child abroad[58].

BIIa, Art 56; Hague Convention 1996, Art 33

3.60 BIIa, Art 56 and the Hague Convention 1996, Art 33 provide mandatory consultative and consent provisions when the plan is for the 'placement of a child in institutional care or with a foster family and where such placement is to take place in another Member State'[59], or, 'placement of a child in a foster family or institutional care, or the provision of care by kafala or an analogous institution'[60].

3.61 The consultation and consent demanded by BIIa is:

(i) the court shall first consult the foreign Central Authority or other authority having jurisdiction in the latter state where public authority intervention in that Member State is required for domestic cases of child placement;

(ii) a judgment on foreign placement shall only be made if the foreign state consents to that placement;

---

58 See Lady Hale's *obiter* comments in *Re N (Children) (Jurisdiction: Care Proceedings)* [2016] UKSC 15, [2017] AC 167 at [48], and the operation of the CA 1989, s 100(2).

59 BIIa, Art 56.

60 Hague Convention 1996, Art 33.

(iii) the procedures for consultation and consent are to be governed by national law of the foreign state, except in cases where a decision is made to place a child in a foster family in a foreign state in which no public authority intervention is required in domestic cases of child placement, in which case the foreign Central Authority shall simply be informed of the decision to place the child[61].

3.62 The consultation and consent required under the Hague Convention 1996 is that:

(i) the English authority shall first consult with the foreign Central Authority;

(ii) the English authority shall transmit a report on the child together with the reasons for the proposed placement or provision of care; and

(iii) the decision to place the child in the foreign state may only be made if that country has consented to the placement or provision of care, taking into account the child's best interests[62].

3.63 In either case, in the event that the required consultation does not take place, the order made may be refused recognition under BIIa, Art 23(g) and the Hague Convention 1996, Art 23(2)(f).

RELINQUISHED BABIES

3.64 The 'typical' adoption in England has changed drastically over the past 50 years. It was described in 2015 by Sir James Munby P in the following terms:

> 'Until the late 1960s, the typical adoption was of an illegitimate child born to a single mother who, however reluctantly, consented to the adoption of her child. Non-consensual adoption was comparatively rare. A combination of dramatic changes in the 1960s – the readily availability of the contraceptive pill, the legalisation of abortion, the relaxation of divorce laws and a sea-change in society's attitude to illegitimacy – led to a drastic reduction in the number of adoptions of the traditional type .... The typical adoption today is of a child who has been the subject of a care order under the 1989 Act and where parental consent has been dispensed with in accordance with s 52(1)(b) of the 2002 Act'[63].

3.65 Nevertheless – and despite the sea-change in society's attitude and the new 'typical' adoption – cases of relinquished babies still remain. A number of these have an international element. Following a dearth of authority on relinquished, foreign babies, the now-leading case is *Re JL v AO (Babies Relinquished for Adoption)*[64], which contains a detailed and considered judgment by Baker J.

61 BIIa, Art 56.2–4.

62 Hague Convention 1996, Art 33(2).

63 *Re N (Children) (Adoption: Jurisdiction)* [2015] EWCA Civ 1112, [2017] AC 167 at [16].

64 [2016] EWHC 440 (Fam).

3.66 From his Lordship's judgment, the following points are relevant:

(a) such applications, certainly within the domestic context, almost always proceed by consent, with no contested hearing or judgment, thus accounting for the limited case law[65];

(b) the wishes and feeling of the parents – or, often, simply the mother – will carry significant weight in evaluating the child's best interests[66];

(c) where parents have – or a mother has – relinquished their baby and expressed a wish that she be adopted outside the natural family, the degree of interference with family life rights is less than where the parent-child relationship is severed against the parents' wishes. When determining, therefore, whether the State's interference with the ECHR, Art 8 rights of the child and parents is necessary and proportionate, the actively consensual nature of the proposed adoption will carry weight. There is no requirement that, following *Re B (A Child) (Care Proceedings: Threshold Criteria)*[67] and *Re B-S (Children)*[68], 'nothing else will do', given the impact of the parents' wishes on the level of interference with their ECHR, Art 8 rights[69];

(d) where that parental consent is given in the prescribed way, the local authority need not apply for – indeed, the court may have no jurisdiction to make – a placement order, with that placement for adoption instead taking place under the ACA 2002, s 19[70];

(e) by reason of the voluntary nature of the taking into care and/or adoption, Art 36 1(b) of the Vienna Convention – as referred to at para 3.12 – is not triggered. But, a local authority may still conclude that it is necessary to contact foreign authorities so as to further its enquiries[71].

CONCLUSION

3.67 In summary, then, the proliferation of international issues means that, on a daily basis, courts and those involved in the family justice system must confront international complexities and show familiarity with the different jurisdictional and legal schemes involved. Importantly, whilst the future of international family law post-Brexit is uncertain, the internationalism of modern life means that the need for practitioners and judges to be on top of these sometimes-tricky matters will continue.

65 [2016] EWHC 440 (Fam) at [46].
66 [2016] EWHC 440 (Fam) at [49]–[50].
67 [2013] UKSC 33.
68 [2013] EWCA Civ 1146.
69 [2016] EWHC 440 (Fam) at [52]–[55]. In reaching this conclusion, Baker J explicitly drew on the step-parent adoption analogy as examined by the Court of Appeal in *Re P (Adoption: Step-parent's Application)* [2014] EWCA Civ 1174.
70 [2016] EWHC 440 (Fam) at [57].
71 [2016] EWHC 440 (Fam) at [60]–[70].

Chapter 4

CHILDREN'S EVIDENCE: 'ACHIEVING BEST EVIDENCE' AND COURT EVIDENCE

INTRODUCTION

4.1 Historically, the suggestion that a child should attend a family court to give evidence was treated with incredulity and distrust. The pre-2010 law was simply stated:

> 'The correct starting point ... is that it is undesirable that a child should have to give evidence in care proceedings and that particular justification will be required before that course is taken. There will be some cases in which it will be right to make an order. In my view they will be rare'[1].

4.2 March 2010 – and the case of *Re W (Children) (Abuse: Oral Evidence)*[2] – marked a legal turning point. Gone was the presumption against children giving evidence in public children law proceedings: instead, what was required was a careful balancing act, taking account of ECHR, Arts 6 and 8. In practice, however, the shift has been small. Six years later, the Court of Appeal felt moved to comment, in strident terms, that:

> '... this court has been told that the previous culture and practice of the family courts remains largely unchanged with the previous presumption against children giving evidence remaining intact. That state of affairs is plainly contrary to the binding decision of the Supreme Court which was that such a presumption is contrary to Article 6 of the European Convention on Human Rights'[3].

4.3 Indeed, the contrast between the family and criminal justice systems is now sharp: in criminal proceedings, it is said that some 40,000 children give

---

1 *LM v Medway Council, RM and YM* [2007] EWCA Civ 9 at [44], per Smith LJ.

2 [2010] UKSC 12, [2010] 2 All ER 418.

3 *Re E (A Child) (Evidence)* [2016] EWCA Civ 473, [2017] 1 FLR 1675 at [56], per McFarlane LJ.

live evidence each year, including those of a very young age[4]. As practitioners are aware, it remains relatively unusual in the family justice system.

4.4 This chapter examines:

(a) the achieving best evidence (ABE) process, including tips for challenging ABE interviews;

(b) children giving evidence in family proceedings: guidance and tips;

(c) children giving evidence in family proceedings: advocacy;

(d) children meeting judges.

ACHIEVING BEST EVIDENCE: THE PROCESS

4.5 The starting point is the relevant guidance for criminal proceedings: *Achieving Best Evidence in Criminal Proceedings, Guidance on interviewing victims and witnesses, and guidance on using special measures* (the *Achieving Best Evidence Guidance*)[5]. It is of great utility not only in criminal proceedings but also in family proceedings and to family practitioners[6]. It was described in *TW v A City Council*[7] as being one of three pivotal documents, along with the Report of the Inquiry into Child Abuse in Cleveland 1987 (especially chapter 12) and the Report of the Advisory Group on Video Evidence 1989 (the Pigot Report).

4.6 The *Achieving Best Evidence Guidance* explains that the ABE process has a number of stages, even pre-interview: decisions about whether or not to conduct an interview; decisions about whether it should be video-recorded; careful planning; and, the interview itself[8]. These are taken in turn.

4.7 Before delving into the subject, it is worth making explicit a fundamental point: ABE interviews are *not* an evidence-gathering exercise in the sense of eliciting a specific narrative, nor an opportunity to encourage a child to repeat on camera what she may already have said[9], but rather, they are, as the name makes clear, about achieving the *best* evidence.

---

4 Ibid at [46], per McFarlane LJ.

5 *Achieving Best Evidence in Criminal Proceedings, Guidance on interviewing victims and witnesses, and guidance on using special measures* (Ministry of Justice, March 2011), available online at www.cps.gov.uk/publications/docs/best_evidence_in_criminal_proceedings.pdf.

6 See also the view of Baker J, sitting in the Court of Appeal, in *Re W and F (Children)* [2015] EWCA Civ 1300 at [33]: 'It is accepted that [the guidance's] relevance is not confined to criminal proceedings but extends to proceedings in the family courts'.

7 [2011] EWCA Civ 17. An appeal to the Court of Appeal in public children law proceedings.

8 *Achieving Best Evidence Guidance* at para 1.3.

9 See, for example, Wall LJ's ringing criticism in *TW* [2011] at [52]. That fundamental point has subsequently been cited and repeated in more recent cases, such as *Re W and F (Children)* [2015] EWCA Civ 1300 at [42] and *Re E (A Child) (Evidence)* [2016] EWCA Civ 473, [2017] 1 FLR 1675 at [26].

Initial contact

4.8 Clearly, initial questioning may take place prior to any formal, video-recorded ABE interview. In family cases, we are well used to that: by the time the formal ABE interview takes place, a child may well have spoken and been spoken to by an assortment of teachers, police, social workers and medical child protection professionals. That is often unavoidable, as the need to take immediate action requires or provokes initial discussions.

4.9 That initial questioning should seek to elicit only a brief account of what is said to have happened, with a more detailed account to await the formal ABE interview. It is suggested that such questioning should focus simply on *where* and *when* the alleged incident took place and *who* was involved or present, that information being required to take immediate investigative steps[10]. Subsequently, the Court of Appeal has suggested the following formulation:

> '... with the benefit of experience of many similar cases I would suggest that discussions about the facts in issue in respect of an allegation as distinct from whether and what allegation is being made against whom, should be rare and should not be a standard practice which avoids the purpose of a full ABE interview where the recording can pick up the nuances of suggestion and demeanour'[11].

Part of the reason for this, of course, is that the more times the child is asked about the same subject, the less weight can be put on the answers given[12].

4.10 Even at this stage, any conversation should bear in mind the following principles: listen to the witness; do not stop freely recalled narrative; try to ask open-ended questions; ask only those questions that are necessary to take immediate action; make a note of the conversation – including, importantly, the timing, setting and people present, as well as the questions asked (ie not just the answers); and, make a note of the witness's demeanour[13].

4.11 These principles apply as strongly to social workers as they do to police officers. It was emphasised by Butler-Sloss LJ as far back as in 1998 that:

> 'Social workers, in particular, must consider the purpose of the interview and whether it is being conducted with a view to taking proceedings to protect the child or for separate therapeutic purposes where the restrictions upon prompting would not apply but the interview would not be for the purposes

---

10 *Achieving Best Evidence Guidance* at para 2.5.

11 *Re S (A Child) (Fact-finding)* [2013] EWCA Civ 1254 at [16].

12 *Re D (Child Abuse: Interviews)* [1998] 2 FLR 10 at 18, 'It may be difficult to obtain the information which the young child has to impart within a single session which almost must not go on for too long. It may be necessary to interview the child again. But the more often the child is asked questions about the same subject the less one can trust the answers given'. It should be noted that Butler-Sloss LJ gives no explanation or justification for this assertion: instead her Ladyship goes on to note that 'To remind a child of earlier answers ... has its own dangers' (at 18).

13 *Achieving Best Evidence Guidance* at para 2.6.

of court proceedings. It is essential to distinguish between interviewing the child to ascertain the facts and interviewing to provide the child with help to unburden her worries. The therapeutic interview would seem to be generally unsuited to use as part of the court evidence, although there may be rare cases in which it is necessary to use it'.[14]

Planning for the ABE interview

4.12 The first point to bear in mind is that planning is *key*: 'The importance of planning cannot be overstated'[15]. Particular attention should be paid to the extent to which the child has already had contact with child protection professionals and services. Especially in cases in which a child has had limited contact with such professionals, any investigating team should include not only representatives from the police but also from children's services[16].

4.13 Equally, whilst the police retain responsibility for a criminal investigation (a recommendation of Lord Laming's report following the Independent Statutory Inquiry into the death of Victoria Climbié) – including the formal ABE interview that forms part of it – the interview itself need not be conducted by a police officer. Where a properly trained social worker is available, either the police or the social work team can lead the interview: that decision should depend on who is able to establish the best rapport with the child[17].

4.14 At the start of the investigation, members of the investigating team (including the police and social work teams) should give an explanation of their roles to the child and her carer. From then on, the child's understanding and knowledge should be monitored and maintained[18].

4.15 In determining how a child's evidence should be obtained (ie how the ABE process should achieve the child's best evidence), interviewers should consider: the child as an individual, her needs, and her age, gender, culture, religion, confidence and developmental level and any disability[19].

4.16 The child, and those with parental responsibility for her, should be given sufficient information so as to come to an informed decision about taking part in a video-recorded interview. Advice must be given that, should the case proceed (and that, of course, can mean either in a criminal or public children law context) they may be required to attend court and give evidence, irrespective of the decision as to whether to participate in a video-recorded interview[20]. Whilst written consent from the child is not required, it is, self-evidently, undesirable to

---

14 *Re D (Child Abuse: Interviews)* [1998] 2 FLR 10 at 18.
15 *Achieving Best Evidence Guidance* at para 2.1.
16 *Achieving Best Evidence Guidance* at para 2.20.
17 *Achieving Best Evidence Guidance* at para 2.22.
18 *Achieving Best Evidence Guidance* at para 2.25.
19 *Achieving Best Evidence Guidance* at para 2.29.
20 *Achieving Best Evidence Guidance* at paras 2.32–2.33.

video-record an interview with a reluctant or hostile child[21]: at the very least, that will affect the quality of the evidence and the success of the process.

4.17 Generally, those caring for the child will be informed of her interview before it takes place. The exception to that is where circumstances dictate that they should not be informed: say, where a child may be threatened, important evidence would be destroyed, or a competent child does not wish the carer to be involved[22].

4.18 The need for a pre-interview assessment of the child is a question for the interviewers. It depends on the needs of the child and the needs of justice. Where the child has had no, or limited, contact with children's services, an assessment may be required. Such an assessment may require multiple sessions. Importantly, an assessment provides an opportunity for the interviewers to ascertain basic, but vital, pre-interview information. That includes: the child's preferred form of address; her ability and willingness to talk within a formal setting; an explanation to the child of the reasons for the interview; the ground rules; an opportunity to practise answering open questions; an assessment of the child's cognitive, emotional and social development; any day-to-day requirements of the child; any apparent clinical or mental health problems; and an assessment of the child's competency to give consent to interview and medical examination[23].

4.19 It also – and this, we suggest, is of particular utility – permits the child's language and understanding of relative concepts (perhaps most obviously: time) to be assessed. In many instances, this assessment can, should and does mould the interviewer's questioning style and subsequent analysis of and weight placed on the video-recorded interviewer.

4.20 The distinction between a preliminary assessment and the interview itself must be maintained: each has distinct goals. The *Achieving Best Evidence Guidance* suggests the following explanation to the child of the purpose of the preliminary assessment:

> 'We will talk about the things you are concerned about tomorrow. Today, I want to get to know you a bit better and explain what will happen if we do a video interview tomorrow'[24].

Setting up the ABE interview

4.21 Thought needs to be given to who will perform each role within the ABE interview: the interviewer (a person with whom the child has developed a rapport); the interview monitor (with consideration given to whether he is present in the interview room – in effect becoming or appearing to become a

21 *Achieving Best Evidence Guidance* at para 2.37.

22 *Achieving Best Evidence Guidance* at para 2.40.

23 *Achieving Best Evidence Guidance* at Box 2.7 beneath para 2.54.

24 *Achieving Best Evidence Guidance* at para 2.56.

second interviewer – or remains in the adjoining room as an observer) and the equipment operator[25].

4.22 Witnesses should be interviewed in the language of their choice. As such, an interpreter may be required. If so, the interpreter should be involved in the planning process[26].

4.23 For children, an intermediary is often required. The intermediary plays an important role in the planning process: he can give advice on how questions should be asked. During the interview itself, intermediaries will often desist from communicating all questions and instead observe and intervene where miscommunication is likely, helping to re-phrase questions or repeat answers[27]. Clearly, before performing his role, the intermediary will need to meet with the child and conduct one or more assessments. In those, the allegations themselves should not be discussed and a responsible third party must at all times be present. The assessment(s) assist also in building rapport between child and intermediary[28].

4.24 Children may well also require an interview supporter. That is a person whose role is to provide emotional support to a child. It is *not* the same as an 'appropriate adult' (an 'appropriate adult' has, since 1 April 2003, not been required). Equally, from a forensic perspective, it is likely to be suitable to have a parent present at the interview[29].

4.25 The interview should take place in a place in which the child feels comfortable: that may be in an interview suite or a (sufficiently quiet) setting with which the child is comfortable. That may even be at the child's home – however, care should be taken to ensure that the home cannot subsequently be identified by visual or verbal clues[30].

4.26 Timing, too, is important, both in terms of finding a balance between interviewing any witness relatively quickly and not giving too much time for memory to fade, and looking at the child's routine to ensure that she is not overly fatigued[31].

4.27 As would be expected, the interview should go at the witness's pace, with breaks factored in accordingly[32]. In interviews of children, one will often see multiple and sometimes lengthy breaks when the child is permitted to leave the room. The danger, of course, is that a break (during which, say, a younger child is permitted to play with toys) is seen by the child as an inducement or a reward for saying or not saying certain things during the course of the interview, so this must be managed carefully.

---

25 *Achieving Best Evidence Guidance* at paras 2.178–2.185.
26 *Achieving Best Evidence Guidance* at paras 2.188–2.189.
27 *Achieving Best Evidence Guidance* at para 2.196.
28 *Achieving Best Evidence Guidance* at para 2.198.
29 *Re N (Child Abuse: Evidence)* [1996] 2 FLR 214 at 218. See also the Cleveland Report at 12.35.
30 *Achieving Best Evidence Guidance* at paras 2.206–2.208.
31 *Achieving Best Evidence Guidance* at paras 2.209–2.211.
32 *Achieving Best Evidence Guidance* at para 2.212.

4.28 A child is likely to require significant pre-interview preparation: that will include an explanation of the reason for and purpose of the interview, the role of anyone present, its location and time, the general structure and any ground rules. The evidence itself should not be discussed at this stage. Instead, focus should be on topics such as school, favourite teachers and friends, TV programmes, favourite games and the journey to, say, the police station at which the interview is being conducted. Even at this stage, the pattern of the interview should be established: open-ended questions should be used with the child given the chance to speak in free narrative. This also allows the interviewer a chance to increase rapport with the child and gain further knowledge of the child's understanding and communication levels. A full written record must be kept[33].

4.29 Indeed, a written record must be kept of all decisions made during the pre-interview planning and setting up process. That should include the information and justification for those decisions[34].

Conducting the ABE interview

4.30 Irrespective of the video-recording of any interview, detailed notes should be taken. Normally, the responsibility for doing so will fall to the interview monitor if in the adjoining room or, if not, to the recording equipment operator. Interviewers may choose to take brief notes to assist later in the interview, but they should not take a detailed note as this may well distract the witness, obstruct the flow of recall and slow down the interview process[35].

4.31 Generally[36], a child's ABE interview must have four phases, with the pre-ABE planning having assisted in determining the goals for each of those phases. The phases are:

(a) establishing rapport;

(b) free narrative;

(c) questioning;

(d) closure.

We deal also with the use of drawings, pictures, dolls, and other props.

Establishing rapport

4.32 The first phase has, in effect, four parts to it: preliminaries; discussion of neutral topics to continue rapport; explanation of ground rules; and 'truth and lies'.

---

33 *Achieving Best Evidence Guidance* at paras 2.223–2.237.

34 *Achieving Best Evidence Guidance* at para 2.222.

35 *Achieving Best Evidence Guidance* at para 2.177.

36 Indeed, a departure from the guidance requires the agreement of a senior manager or interview adviser. *Achieving Best Evidence Guidance* at para 3.2.

4.33 The preliminaries are simple: the interviewer should say out loud the day, date, time and (not detailed) address of the interview and say who is present. The reason for the interview should be stated, without referring to the allegations[37].

4.34 Rapport is built at various stages through the pre-interview process. It must be continued during the interview itself. To assist, the interviewer should talk to the child about neutral (ie non-allegation) topics. This should be brief and should, as with the pre-interview process, follow the interview pattern, that is to say focus on open-ended questions and allow the child to speak freely[38].

4.35 Next, simple ground rules need to be set out. These are: if the child does not understand a question, she should say so; if the interviewer misunderstands an answer, she should also say; a break can be had at any time; and, depending on the child's age and development, a reminder that the interviewer was not present at the time of the alleged events, does not know what happened and that detail is helpful[39].

4.36 At the end of the rapport phase, a 'truth and lies' exercise should be carried out. It is done at this phase – and not later – because otherwise a child may feel that she is being accused of not having told the truth to date. A readily understandable (and age appropriate) scenario is given to the child. That scenario must (but often does not) include an intent to deceive another person. The child is then able to demonstrate her understanding of the difference between the truth and a lie. If the child cannot demonstrate that, the interview may need to be stopped for an expert assessment of the child's abilities[40]. Example scenarios are,

> **Preamble**
>
> 'Now [name], it is very important that you tell me the truth about things that have happened to you. So before we begin, I want to make sure you understand the difference between the truth and a lie.'
>
> **Example for Younger Children**
>
> 'Let me tell you a story about John. John was playing with his ball in the kitchen and he hit the ball against the window. The window broke and John ran upstairs into his bedroom. John's mummy saw the broken window, and asked John if he had broken the window. John said, 'No mummy.'
>
> 'Did John tell a lie or the truth, or don't you know?'
>
> [*Child responds*]

37 *Achieving Best Evidence Guidance* at para 3.7.
38 *Achieving Best Evidence Guidance* at paras 3.8–3.10.
39 *Achieving Best Evidence Guidance* at paras 3.12–3.14.
40 *Achieving Best Evidence Guidance* at paras 3.18–3.20.

'What should he have said?'

[*Child responds*]

Example for Older Children

'So, for example, Tony was having a smoke in his bedroom, after his mum had told him not to. He heard his mum coming and hid the cigarette. His mum said 'Have you been smoking?' Tony said, 'No mum.'

'Did Tony tell a lie or the truth, or don't you know?'

[*Child responds*]

'What should he have said?'

[*Child responds*]

'Why do you think he said 'no mum'?'

[*Child responds*][41].

Free narrative

4.37 The second phase – free narrative – is self-explanatory. It is the heart of the ABE process. Here, the child should be encouraged and then left to give an uninterrupted and free narrative account of the allegation that provoked the interview. Questions should be kept for later. The interviewer will likely have to demonstrate active listening (for example, repeating back to the child what she has said; albeit this, in fact, is not as easy as it sounds, given the need to avoid consciously or subconsciously indicating approval or disapproval of a given statement) and prompting through simple, open questions and prompts such as, 'Tell me', 'Did anything else happen?', 'Can you explain what happened next?', etc[42].

4.38 For many particularly distressing allegations – an obvious one being child sexual abuse – a child may initially be unwilling to talk freely about what has happened. Gentle encouragement may be required.

4.39 Particular care must be taken to avoid acquiescence: that is to say, a vulnerable child answering affirmatively to every question, whatever its nature. Any questions or prompts should be simple and not suggestive; equally, the interview should not be conducted in an obviously authoritative way[43].

41 *Achieving Best Evidence Guidance*, Appendix G.
42 *Achieving Best Evidence Guidance* at paras 3.24–3.31.
43 *Achieving Best Evidence Guidance* at para 3.32.

Questioning

4.40 Whilst the free narrative stage is often the least well performed by ABE interviewers, it is the questioning phase that requires the most skill and thought. Before commencing questioning, it is helpful to signpost the change in phase in the interview: to explain that some questions will now be asked based on the narrative given. It is sensible also, especially with a younger child, to repeat the ground rules, in particular that, if she does not understand a question, she should say[44].

4.41 For each (relevant) given topic within the free narrative, the interviewer should: re-open that topic by an open-ended invitation to the child to return to it; and conduct a systematic questioning of that topic, using open-ended and specific-closed questions, to elicit the detail that is required for any criminal or public children law proceedings[45].

4.42 Key points to remember during the questioning phase are:

(a) open-ended questions elicit the best evidence: 'Tell me ...', 'Describe ...', 'What happened ...' etc, ie the sort of question that practitioners will be familiar with from examination-in-chief;

(b) next best are specific-closed questions, which provide for some control but aim not too heavily to shape the answers: these again can take the form of 'Who ...' and 'Why ...' questions, but in a narrower context that therefore allows for a narrower range of responses;

(c) although 'why ...' questions can be confusing and require care: if about someone else, they are speculative; and they can arouse feelings of guilt or shame;

(d) forced-choice questions are questions of last resort: an example being, 'Would you like tea of coffee?'. The danger is that a witness may guess or acquiesce;

(e) unsurprisingly, multiple questions are (as with cross-examination) to be avoided and leading questions have the power not only to influence the answer given but also to distort the child's memory of the event;

(f) interviewers should not summarise as a matter of routine, and, if required, should do so only at the end of a given topic;

(g) a child should not (or only most exceptionally) be challenged over an inconsistency: instead, any inconsistency should be repeated in a sense of puzzlement, with a suggestion that the interviewer has not quite understood[46];

(h) putting the same question multiple times is – unsurprisingly – unhelpful. If a question does have to be repeated (even in different terms), it should be

44 *Achieving Best Evidence Guidance* at para 3.36.

45 *Achieving Best Evidence Guidance* at para 3.38.

46 All, *Achieving Best Evidence Guidance* at paras 3.44–3.68.

made clear to the child that it is not that the first response was 'wrong' but rather that the interviewer wants to check that he understood[47].

4.43 The difficulty a child witness may have in understanding relative concepts should not be forgotten: in particular in relation to dates and times, the length and frequency of events, and weight, height and age estimates. As a rule of thumb, telling the time is learned on average at about seven, but an awareness of days of the week and the seasons takes another year[48].

Closure

4.44 The final phase has two elements: recapitulation and closure. In the first – if appropriate and including if the child is not too worn out – the child's evidence can be summarised, which might lead to further retrieval[49]. In the second, the interviewer should talk again to the child about neutral topics. The aim is that the child leaves happy as opposed to distressed – but, clearly, praise or congratulations for giving certain evidence must be avoided[50]. Finally, the child should be asked if she has any questions and, once answered, the time at the end of the interview noted[51].

Use of drawing, pictures, dolls and other props

4.45 Drawing, pictures, photographs, symbols, dolls, figures and props can be and are all used during recorded interviews to assist. Their use can help assess a child's language or understanding, keep a child calm and settled, support a child's recall of events and enable a child to give an account. They can prove especially important when eliciting evidence from children with communication difficulties[52].

4.46 The benefits of the use of such tools are obvious: children may be better at showing than speaking; two modes of communication can provide greater clarity than one; and, it can feel less stressful or imposing for the child. It is important to remember, however, that these tools carry with them a number of risks: props such as anatomical dolls can lead to distortions and inaccuracies, and normal 'toys' (such as teddies, animals and doll houses) might encourage a child to slip into play or fantasy mode[53]. Anyone who has watched the Netflix programme, *Making A Murderer*, will be only too aware of the combined power of drawings and leading questions to distort evidence[54].

---

47 *Achieving Best Evidence Guidance* at para 3.76.

48 *Achieving Best Evidence Guidance* at para 3.74.

49 *Achieving Best Evidence Guidance* at paras 3.80–3.83.

50 *Achieving Best Evidence Guidance* at paras 3.84–3.85.

51 *Achieving Best Evidence Guidance* at paras 3.86–3.87.

52 *Achieving Best Evidence Guidance* at paras 3.103–3.105.

53 *Achieving Best Evidence Guidance* at paras 3.106–3.108.

54 In the context of Brendan Dassey's interview by Michael O'Kelly, shown in episode 4, available online at www.netflix.com.

4.47 The *Achieving Best Evidence Guidance* makes the sensible points that, when using props, the interviewer should always ensure that the child's facial expressions, gestures and body language (as well as the props themselves) remain open to the camera and do not become closed and focused on the object and those props should be preserved for production, if required, in court[55].

Challenging ABE evidence

4.48 Regrettably, it is common that a busy police force will conduct its ABE interviews in ignorance and/or in breach of chunks of the guidance that has been set out so far in this chapter. We suggest that, when representing a client whose case requires the challenge of ABE evidence, careful consideration should be given to the ABE evidence at the hearings in advance of trial. It is likely to be important to obtain from the police the written records of the various pre-ABE planning stages. It is our experience that, on receipt, it is often easy to locate either aspects of the planning that do not tally with the guidance and/or parts of the interview that fall foul of the planning. That is fertile ground for cross-examination.

CHILDREN GIVING EVIDENCE IN FAMILY PROCEEDINGS: GUIDANCE AND TIPS

4.49 As McFarlane LJ's loud reminder[56] slowly echoes its way through the family justice system, we as practitioners will begin to feel its reverberation.

> '... this court has been told that the previous culture and practice of the family courts remains largely unchanged with the previous presumption against children giving evidence remaining intact. That state of affairs is plainly contrary to the binding decision of the Supreme Court which was that such a presumption is contrary to Article 6 of the European Convention on Human Rights'[57].

Principally, that is likely to mean an increase in the number of children giving evidence in family proceedings. In this section, therefore, we set out the key principles against which decisions about children giving evidence fall to be determined.

4.50 The starting point is *Re W (Children) (Abuse: Oral Evidence)*[58]. The appeal was in care proceedings, following a decision by the first-instance judge, subsequently upheld by the Court of Appeal, that a 14-year-old girl, given the name Charlotte in the Supreme Court, who had made allegations of sexual abuse against her father, should not be called to give evidence at a fact-finding hearing

55 *Achieving Best Evidence Guidance* at paras 3.09 and 3.12.

56 *Re E (A Child) (Evidence)* [2016] EWCA Civ 473, [2017] 1 FLR 1675 at [56].

57 *Re E (A Child) (Evidence)* [2016] EWCA Civ 473, [2017] 1 FLR 1675 at [56], per McFarlane LJ.

58 [2010] UKSC 12, [2010] 2 All ER 418.

into those allegations. The father appealed. The question for the Supreme Court, then, was whether the existing starting point or presumption against a child giving evidence was appropriate.

4.51 Lady Hale, in giving the judgment of the court, emphasised, in setting out leading counsel for the appellant's submissions, that,

> 'All the parties in care proceedings are entitled to a fair hearing in the determination of their civil rights and obligations – the parents who stand to lose their children if allegations of abuse are made out, the children who stand to lose their parents if allegations of abuse are made out, but also stand to suffer abuse or further abuse if they are left at home because those allegations cannot be proved. And it is not only their Article 6 rights which are in play. The civil rights in issue are also Convention rights in themselves – the right to respect for the family lives of the parents and their children but also the right to respect for the private lives of the children, which include their rights to be protected from attacks upon their physical and psychological integrity: *X and Y v The Netherlands* (1985) 8 EHRR 235'[59].

4.52 Her Ladyship set out the key principle or balance that, 'When the court is considering whether a particular child should be called as a witness, the court will have to weigh two considerations: the advantages that it will bring to the determination of the truth and the damage it may do to the welfare of this or any other child'[60]. That is the guiding principle. The essential test remains whether justice can be done to all the parties without further questioning of the child[61].

4.53 When applying that principle in practice, *Re W* provides assistance by setting out the key factors that require attention. It is worth reading the two relevant paragraphs from Lady Hale's judgment in full:

> '25. In weighing the advantages that calling the child to give evidence may bring to the fair and accurate determination of the case, the court will have to look at several factors. One will be the issues it has to decide in order properly to determine the case. Sometimes it may be possible to decide the case without making findings on particular allegations. Another will be the quality of the evidence it already has. Sometimes there may be enough evidence to make the findings needed whether or not the child is cross-examined. Sometimes there will be nothing useful to be gained from the child's oral evidence. The case is built upon a web of behaviour, drawings, stray remarks, injuries and the like, and not upon concrete allegations voiced by the child. The quality of any ABE interview will also be an important factor as will be the nature of any challenge which the party may wish to make. The court is unlikely to be helped by generalised accusations of lying, or by a fishing expedition in which the child is taken slowly through the story yet

59 *Re W (Children) (Abuse: Oral Evidence)* [2010] UKSC 12 at [3].
60 [2010] UKSC 12, [2010] 2 All ER 418 at [24].
61 [[2010] UKSC 12, [2010] 2 All ER 418 at [30].

again in the hope that something will turn up, or by a cross-examination which is designed to intimidate the child and pave the way for accusations of inconsistency in a future criminal trial. On the other hand, focussed questions which put forward a different explanation for certain events may help the court to do justice between the parties. Also relevant will be the age and maturity of the child and the length of time since the events in question, for these will have a bearing on whether an account now can be as reliable as a near-contemporaneous account, especially if given in a well-conducted ABE interview.

26. The age and maturity of the child, along with the length of time since the events in question, will also be relevant to the second part of the inquiry, which is the risk of harm to the child. Further specific factors may be the support which the child has from family or other sources, or the lack of it, the child's own wishes and feelings about giving evidence, and the views of the child's guardian and, where appropriate, those with parental responsibility. We endorse the view that an unwilling child should rarely, if ever, be obliged to give evidence. The risk of further delay to the proceedings is also a factor: there is a general principle that delay in determining any question about a child's upbringing is likely to prejudice his welfare: see Children Act 1989, s 1(2). There may also be specific risks of harm to this particular child. Where there are parallel criminal proceedings, the likelihood of the child having to give evidence twice may increase the risk of harm. The parent may be seeking to put his child through this ordeal in order to strengthen his hand in the criminal proceedings rather than to enable the family court to get at the truth. On the other hand, as the family court has to give less weight to the evidence of a child because she has not been called, then that may be damaging too. However, the court is entitled to have regard to the general evidence of the harm which giving evidence may do to children, as well as to any features which are particular to this child and this case. That risk of harm is an ever-present feature to which, on the present evidence, the court must give great weight. The risk, and therefore the weight, may vary from case to case, but the court must always take into account and does not need expert evidence in order to do so.'

4.54 Helpfully, Lady Hale deals also with the application of the *Re W* principles to private law children cases. Her Ladyship holds that, 'In principle, the approach … should be the same …'[62]. However, it is noted that there are specific risks: allegations are not being asserted by a neutral and expert local authority but rather by a parent seeking to gain a litigation advantage, which increases the risk of 'misinterpretation, exaggeration or downright fabrication'; the child will not routinely have the support of a children's guardian; and, there are many more litigants in person. So, if evidence from a child is required in private law proceedings, the court 'will have to take very careful precautions' to ensure that the process does not cause the child to suffer harm[63].

62 [2010] UKSC 12, [2010] 2 All ER 418 at [29].
63 Ibid.

4.55 Following *Re W* and the request of the President of the Family Division, Wall LJ, who had heard the case in the Court of Appeal, a working party was set up under the leadership of Thorpe LJ, to look at the issue of children giving evidence in family proceedings. The working party produced *Guidelines in Relation to Children Giving Evidence in Family Proceedings*[64] (the 2011 Guidelines). The 2011 Guidelines merit reading in full and are set out in Appendix 1 to this chapter, at para 4.86.

4.56 We can draw the following key points from the 2011 Guidelines:

(a) the question of a child giving evidence should be considered 'at the earliest possible opportunity' and, importantly, must not be left simply to the party intending to apply for it to happen[65];

(b) where, as often, there are concurrent or linked criminal proceedings, there should not only be close liaison between the respective parties and allocated judges, but also 'ideally linked directions hearings' and the view of the police/CPS should be obtained before any decision is made for a child to give evidence in the family proceedings[66].

4.57 The court must carefully consider the possibility of further questions being put to the child on an occasion distinct from the substantive hearing. That option should be considered 'at the earliest opportunity' and 'should be carried out as soon as possible after the incident in question'. It will require careful attention to the following: giving the child the opportunity to refresh her memory; choice of questioner; location of questioning; type and nature of questions, including whether advance judicial approval is required; ground rules; and the recording of the interview[67].

4.58 It must also be remembered that:

(a) the court will not be able to come to a conclusion on whether or not a child should give oral evidence unless it has undertaken an evaluation of the evidence that is otherwise available. Where there has been an ABE interview, and the quality and/or content of that interview is to be challenged, it is likely that the judge will have to view the DVD before being in a position to decide the *Re W* issues[68];

(b) before deciding whether a child should be called, it is good practice for the children's guardian to prepare a written report and the court to hear submissions from the child's solicitor. In *Re E (A Child) (Evidence)*, McFarlane LJ noted, however, that it is 'common-place for guardians to advise that the child should not be called to give evidence on the basis that they will or may suffer emotional harm as a result of doing so. Where such advice is based upon the consideration of harm alone, it is unlikely to be of great

64 June 2011.
65 2011 Guidelines at [7].
66 2011 Guidelines at [11].
67 2011 Guidelines at [12].
68 *Re E (A Child) (Evidence)* [2016] EWCA Civ 473, [2017] 1 FLR 1675 at [58].

assistance to the court which is required to consider not only 'harm' but also the other side of the balance described in the Guidelines, namely the possible advantages that the child's testimony will bring to the determination of truth'[69];

(c) any issue as to a child giving evidence should be raised and determined at the earliest stage[70].

4.59 Going back to the 2011 Guidelines, if a decision is taken that live oral evidence is going to take place, the following pre-hearing practical considerations apply: possible need for an intermediary or other communication specialist as well as a known and neutral supporter; 'special measures', such as video link and screens; advance judicial approval of questions; ground rules, breaks and information about the child's communication abilities; the best time for the child and court to (re-)view any ABE interview, not least for the purpose of refreshing memory; importantly – and often overlooked in family proceedings – admissions of as much of the child's evidence as possible (including locations, times and lay-outs); and, 'save in exceptional circumstances', agreement on the proper form and limit of questions and the identity of the questioner. Additionally, there should be: a familiarisation visit to the court by the child to include a demonstration of any 'special measures'; consideration of how the child will enter and leave the building and where she will wait, with any waiting time limited as much as possible. These matters should normally be sorted by the children's guardian[71].

4.60 During the live evidence itself: the child should be given the chance to meet the judge; the advocates should each introduce themselves; she should be encouraged to say if she has a problem or wants a break; the potential for miscommunication should be monitored; if a video live link is being used, its functioning should be explained and it should be checked to ensure that the child witness cannot see the respondent(s) (often her parents or other family members); and the representative should agree which documents will be referred to and it should be checked that they are situated close to the child for convenience[72].

We discuss advocacy in such situations in more detail at paras 4.64–4.73.

4.61 Subsequent to the 2011 Guidelines is the Supreme Court judgment in *Re LC (Children) (Reunite International Child Abduction Centre intervening)*[73] which addresses, in particular, the way that the voice of a child is heard in proceedings instituted under the Hague Convention 1980. Following that judgment, Sir James Munby P has suggested that it is time to review the 2011 Guidelines[74]. In part, the Children and Vulnerable Witness Working Group (chaired by Russell and Hayden JJ) was set up to deal with that: the group produced two reports, an interim

69 [2016] EWCA Civ 473, [2017] 1 FLR 1675 at [61].
70 See, for example, *Re E (A Child) (Evidence)* at [58].
71 2011 Guidelines at [14]–[15].
72 2011 Guidelines at [18].
73 [2014] UKSC 1, [2014] AC 1038.
74 *12th View from the President's Chambers*, 4 June 2014.

report in July 2014 and a final report in February 2015. Points emphasised in those reports include: the need for the family justice system to provide training to its judiciary and advocates, of which the toolkits in The Advocate's Gateway form a key component; and the extent to which we (in the family justice system) lag behind and can make use of the law, guidance, training and tools that characterise the approach in the criminal justice system.

4.62 Practitioners should also be aware of the Children Act 1989 (CA 1989), s 96. Section 96 is important for two reasons. First, it states that, in any civil proceedings, even where a child does not, in the opinion of the court, understand the nature of an oath, the evidence may be heard if, in the court's opinion 'he understands that it is his duty to speak the truth; and he has sufficient understanding to justify his evidence being heard'[75]. Second, it gave statutory permission for the Lord Chancellor and Lord Chief Justice to make provision for the admissibility of evidence which would otherwise be inadmissible under hearsay rules[76]. That invitation was accepted by way of the Children (Admissibility of Hearsay Evidence) Order 1993[77], which provided that such evidence shall be admissible when 'given in connection with the upbringing, maintenance or welfare of a child' notwithstanding 'any rule of law relating to hearsay'[78].

4.63 Importantly, and as recommended by the Children and Vulnerable Witness Working Group, since 27 November 2017 we now have additions to the FPR 2010: Part 3A of the FPR 2010 and the accompanying PD 3AA, *Vulnerable persons: participation in proceedings and giving evidence*. Notable changes include the automatic use of ground rules hearings where a vulnerable witness, vulnerable party or protected party is to give evidence[79], the expectation of familiarity of all advocates (including litigants in person) with the relevant toolkits of The Advocate's Gateway[80] and the requirement that the court applies the 2011 Guidelines[81]. Practitioners should note that r 3A.4 – which places on the court a duty to consider how a party can participate in the proceedings – does *not* apply to children.

CHILDREN GIVING EVIDENCE IN FAMILY PROCEEDINGS: ADVOCACY

4.64 As the 2011 Guidelines make clear, if the court decides that a child is to give oral evidence in family proceedings, one needs to turn to and use a variety of tools: most importantly, and in addition to the 2011 Guidelines, *Good practice guidance in managing young witness cases and questioning children*[82] and,

75 CA 1989, s 96(2).
76 CA 1989, s 96(3).
77 SI 1993/621.
78 SI 1993/621, Art 2.
79 FPR 2010, PD 3AA para 5.2.
80 FPR 2010, PD 3AA para 5.7.
81 FPR 2010, PD 3AA para 5.1.
82 June 2009.

the Court of Appeal's judgment in *R v Barker*[83]. In addition to that, practitioners should, we strongly suggest, read carefully and familiarise themselves with the relevant toolkits of The Advocate's Gateway[84] and the FPR 2010, Part 3A and the accompanying PD 3AA.

Good practice guidance in managing young witness cases and questioning children

4.65 Following a period of research, published and discussed in *Measuring up? Evaluating implementation of government commitments to young witnesses in criminal proceedings*[85], the *Good Practice Guidance* was published in June 2009 as a joint project of the NSPCC and The Nuffield Foundation.

4.66 The headlines from the reports included that:

- around half of those young people who gave evidence to the study did not understand some questions at court (notably, that was consistent with two previous studies);
- 65 per cent experienced problems of comprehension, complexity, questions that were fast or having their answers talked over; and
- almost half of the children described defence lawyers (those children were prosecution witnesses) as 'sarcastic', 'rude', 'aggressive' or 'cross'[86].

4.67 The *Good Practice Guidance* is helpfully split into pre-trial, at trial, and post-trial and sets out the following guidance:

(a) pre-trial: list cases and avoid adjournments; enquire about the child's level of understanding; consider the full range of special measures; consider the benefits to the child of a trusted supporter – but that supporter should then sit out of the child's line of sight when giving evidence; on the morning that a child will give evidence, ensure the court gives the case a clean start with nothing else instead on the list; agree admissions as far as one can (including locations, layouts and times); conduct a court familiarisation visit; allow the child to remind herself of her statement pre-evidence; and consider access to the building and the waiting room[87];

(b) at trial: advocates should introduce themselves and judges may ask if the child would like to meet pre-evidence; be professionally vigilant to ensure the child lets the court know if she has a problem or needs a break – coloured 'signal' cards can be used; remind the child that, over live link, she can

83 [2010] EWCA Crim 4.

84 For a fuller reading list, one can contact the Council of the Inns of Court: The Inns of Court College of Advocacy which, on its national training programme, *Advocacy and the Vulnerable*, suggests a range of academic texts and practical reports as core reading.

85 Plotnikoff and Woolfson, *Measuring up? Evaluating implementation of government commitments to young witnesses in criminal proceedings* (2009).

86 *Good Practice Guidance* (June 2009) p 6.

87 Ibid, pp 3–4.

always be seen; a demonstration of touching a body part should be on a body outline and not on the child's own body; and, ensure ahead of time that all technology is working[88];

(c) post-trial: thank the child and ensure she is informed of the outcome; and, locally, seek feedback on experiences[89].

Accompanying the *Good Practice Guidance* are two annexes, dealing with good practice questions and special considerations when questioning about intimate touching.

R v Barker

4.68 In *R v Barker*[90], Steven Barker was convicted of anal rape of a child under 13 years old. He had previously been convicted for causing or allowing the death of a child (a child widely known as 'Baby P'), contrary to the Domestic Violence, Crime and Victims Act 2004, s 5. For the latest offence, Steven Barker was sentenced to life imprisonment with a minimum term of ten years. The child in question had been not yet three years old when the offence occurred; by the time of the first instance trial, the child was four and a half. The focus of the appeal was the extent to which a conviction based heavily on the evidence of a child that young could be regarded as safe.

4.69 In the judgment, the Lord Chief Justice made clear that cross-examination in particular must be 'adapted to enable the child to give the best evidence of which he or she is capable'. It is also made clear that: if it is suggested that the child is lying or mistaken, short questions should be put, sufficiently simply to cover the essential elements of the case; aspects of evidence that may or do undermine the child's credibility need not form the subject matter of detailed cross-examination; comment on the evidence should be addressed after the child's oral evidence.[91]

2011 Guidelines

4.70 The 2011 Guidelines go on also to say that questioning should:

— be at the child's pace and consistent with their understanding;

— use simple common words and phrases;

— repeat names and places frequently;

— ask one short question (one idea) at a time;

— let the child know the subject of the question;

88 Ibid, p 5.
89 Ibid, p 6.
90 [2010] EWCA Crim 4.
91 All at [42].

- follow a structured approach, signposting the subject;
- avoid negatives;
- avoid repetition;
- avoid suggestion or leading, including 'tag' questions;
- avoid a criminal or 'Old Bailey' style cross-examination[92];
- avoid 'do you remember' questions;
- avoid restricted choice questions;
- be slow and allow enough time to answer;
- check the child's understanding;
- test the evidence, not trick the witness;
- take into account and check the child's level of understanding;
- not assume the child understands;
- be alert to literal interpretation;
- take care with times, numbers and frequency;
- avoid asking the child to demonstrate intimate touching on his or her own body (if such a question is essential, an alternative method, such as pointing to a body outline, should be agreed beforehand)[93].

Relevant toolkits of The Advocate's Gateway; training

4.71 The various advice is drawn together in the relevant toolkits of *The Advocate's Gateway*. Especially, for present purposes: Ground rules hearings and the fair treatment of vulnerable people in court: Toolkit 1; Planning to question a child or young person: Toolkit 6; Additional factors concerning children under seven (or functioning at a very young age): Toolkit 7; and, most importantly, Vulnerable witnesses and parties in the family courts: Toolkit 13.

4.72 Toolkit 13, given its direct application to the family courts, merits reading in full. It addresses:

- general principles, definitions and context;
- our duties and responsibilities as advocates;
- early identification of possible vulnerability and case management;
- additional measures and other adjustments;
- assistance to vulnerable parties and witnesses;

92 For those who have not observed much criminal or 'Old Bailey' style cross-examination, no guidance is given as to what this might mean.

93 All at [20].

— obtaining evidence and sharing evidence;

— use of experts;

— litigants in person; and

— litigation friends and the Official Solicitor.

4.73 In addition, the Inns of Court College of Advocacy offers at the time of writing, national training that focuses on advocacy – especially ground rules hearings and cross-examination – in relation to vulnerable witnesses, including children. That training is to become mandatory for any advocate wishing to undertake publicly funded work in serious sexual offence cases involving vulnerable witnesses.

CHILDREN MEETING JUDGES

4.74 At the time of writing, the guidance for advocates and courts remains the *Guidelines for Judges Meeting Children who are Subject to Family Proceedings* (April 2010), as produced by the Family Justice Council and approved by the then-President.

4.75 The *Guidelines* should, we suggest, be read in full: they are set out in Appendix 2 to this chapter, at para 4.87. It is a short document, only two pages long, whose purpose is to encourage judges to enable children to feel more involved and connected with proceedings. The fundamental principle is that the meeting is *not* for evidence-gathering (that is the responsibility of the Cafcass officer) but rather it is to enable the child to gain an understanding of what is going on and to be reassured that the judge has understood her[94].

4.76 The *Guidelines* state that:

(a) the lawyer for the child and/or the Cafcass officer should advise the judge whether the child wishes to meet, if so what is the purpose of that meeting for the child, whether it is in the child's welfare interests, and what the purpose is for the child's professional representatives;

(b) the other parties are entitled to make representations before the judge makes her decision;

(c) the child's chronological age is relevant but not determinative: 'some children of seven or even younger have a clear understanding of their circumstances and very clear views'[95];

(d) if the judge declines to have the meeting, she should provide to the child a brief explanation in writing;

94 *Guidelines for Judges Meeting Children who are Subject to Family Proceedings*, April 2010 at [5].
95 *Guidelines for Judges Meeting Children who are Subject to Family Proceedings*, April 2010 at [3].

(e) having heard representations, the following are in the judge's discretion: purpose and proposed contact of the meeting; stage in proceedings at which it takes place; where it takes place; who will bring the child to the meeting; who will prepare the child for it (usually the Cafcass officer); who shall attend – a judge should never see a child alone; by whom a minute shall be taken, how it shall be approved by the judge and how it shall be communicated to the other parties;

(f) if the meeting takes place prior to the conclusion of proceedings, the judge must explain to the child: that the judge cannot hold secrets; that decisions are the judge's responsibility and not that of the child; and, how the judge's decision will be communicated to the child. In addition, there should be an opportunity for the other parties to respond to the content of the meeting, either by oral evidence or submissions[96].

4.77 In the case of *Re KP (A Child)*[97] – an appeal focused on a meeting between Parker J and a subject child in Hague Convention proceedings, in which the Court of Appeal took the opportunity to review the *Guidelines* – it was held that the *Guidelines:*

(a) indicate that there is a firm line to be drawn between a process in which a judge and young person simply encounter each other and communicate in a manner which is not for the purpose of evidence gathering, and a process in which one of the aims of the meeting is to gather evidence[98] – with it being remembered that, where it is considered that a child *should* give evidence in the proceedings (as opposed or in addition to a simple meeting with a judge), any process must respect the ECHR, Art 6 rights of the parties and must accord with the 'overriding objective'[99]; and

(b) are 'no more than they purport to be, namely guidelines', given that 'What is, or is not, the appropriate channel through which a child is heard will differ from case to case, and the matter in which the task is undertaken will depend upon the developing skill and understanding of the judge and other professionals involved' and 'it is to be acknowledged that the courts in this jurisdiction are, rightly, still feeling their way forward in order to determine how best to "hear" the voice of a child who is the subject of an application [there, under the Hague Convention]'[100].

4.78 This illustrates what is a central difficulty inherent in the *Guidelines*: the judge is to meet the child to hear her wishes and feelings – yet at the same time, it is not part of the judicial function to evidence-gather, so the wishes and feelings expressed at the meeting cannot properly be taken into account when making decisions. This is, in the words of the Children and Vulnerable Witness Working Group, 'a difficult concept for any young person to grasp at best; and is

96 *Guidelines for Judges Meeting Children who are Subject to Family Proceedings* (April 2010) at [1]–[6].
97 [2014] EWCA Civ 554.
98 Per McFarlane LJ at [50].
99 Per McFarlane LJ at [51].
100 Per McFarlane LJ at [50].

misleading as it amounts to saying the judge is here to listen to you but cannot take any notice of what you say'[101].

4.79 Following *Re KP (A Child)*, the President directed the Children and Vulnerable Witness Working Group specifically to look at the *Guidelines*, believing it to be 'time to review [them]'[102]. The conclusion drawn in the Working Group's final report was that:

> 'A fresh approach to the evidence of children and young people, including the expression of their wishes and feelings (it needs emphasising that their wishes and feelings are part of the evidence which must be considered by the court as a matter of law and statute) is long overdue'[103].

4.80 It appears that there is, at the time of writing, no easy answer. The *Guidelines* remain just that – but with the central flaw yet to be remedied. The proposal of the Children and Vulnerable Witness Working Group is that 'meeting judges alone will not provide the increased role that should be played by young people and children now the family courts have entered the 21st century' and that, one again, the family justice system lags behind its criminal counterpart, including, for example, the criminal pilot schemes in Leeds, Kingston and Liverpool under the Youth Justice and Criminal Evidence Act 1999, s 28, which includes pre-recording of cross-examination and re-examination[104].

CONCLUSION

4.81 When thinking about ABEs, the *Achieving Best Evidence in Criminal Proceedings, Guidance on interviewing victims and witnesses, and guidance on using special measures*[105] should be at the forefront of practitioners' minds.

4.82 When dealing with children and vulnerable witnesses giving evidence, we need to look at: *Re W (Children) (Abuse: Oral Evidence)*[106]; *Re E (A Child) (Evidence)*[107]; the *Guidelines in Relation to Children Giving Evidence in Family Proceedings* (June 2011); the CA 1989, s 96; and the FPR 2010, Pt 3A and the accompanying PD 3AA, noting that r 3A.4 – which places on the court a duty to consider how a party can participate in the proceedings – does *not* apply to children.

4.83 When conducting advocacy with child witnesses, have with you: *Good practice guidance in managing young witness cases and questioning children*

101 Children and Vulnerable Witness Working Group, final report (February 2015) at [24], endorsing the work of Professor Cooper in this area.
102 *12th View from the President's Chambers*, 4 June 2014.
103 Children and Vulnerable Witness Working Group, final report at [25].
104 Children and Vulnerable Witness Working Group, final report at [21] and [26].
105 (Ministry of Justice, March 2011).
106 [2010] UKSC 12, [2010] 2 All ER 418.
107 [2016] EWCA Civ 473, [2017] 1 FLR 1675.

(June 2009); the Court of Appeal's judgment in *R v Barker*[108]; and, the relevant toolkits of The Advocate's Gateway[109].

4.84 When looking at children meeting judges, the key document is *Guidelines for Judges Meeting Children who are Subject to Family Proceedings* (April 2010), though practitioners should remember that there are criticisms of this document.

4.85 In cross-examining witnesses on ABE evidence, it is vital to ensure that there is sufficient disclosure of the pre-ABE thought process and then to focus on the extent to which the (normally) police officers have complied with the ABE guidance.

4.86 At *Re W* hearings, it is simply a matter of applying the *Re W* test, as amplified by the *Guidelines in Relation to Children Giving Evidence in Family Proceedings* (June 2011). When conducting advocacy with a child, careful thought – and significant planning – is required. It is, for many practitioners, a new skill; it is one that we must work hard to develop.

APPENDIX 1: GUIDELINES IN RELATION TO CHILDREN GIVING EVIDENCE IN FAMILY PROCEEDINGS (24 JUNE 2011)

4.87

1. These Guidelines have been produced by Lord Justice Thorpe's Working Party.

2. This Working Party was set up following a request to the President of the Family Division by the Court of Appeal in *Re W* [2010] Civ 57, a case which considered the issue of children giving evidence in family proceedings.

3. That same case then went to the Supreme Court and is reported as *Re W* [2010] UKSC 12. It is now the leading authority on this issue. The Supreme Court held that there was no longer a presumption or even a starting point against children giving evidence in such cases.

4. Enquiries by this Working Party suggest that the number of applications for children giving evidence since this decision may be increasing.

5. The aim of these Guidelines is to provide those involved in family proceedings with advice as to what matters should be taken into account in such situations.

108 [2010] EWCA Crim 4.

109 For a fuller reading list, one can contact the Council of the Inns of Court: The Inns of Court College of Advocacy which, on its national training programme, *Advocacy and the Vulnerable*, suggests a range of academic texts and practical reports as core reading.

6. Hearsay evidence is of course admissible in family proceedings: Children (Admissibility of Hearsay Evidence) Order 1993 SI 1993/621.

7. The issue of whether a child should be further questioned or give evidence in family proceedings should be considered at the earliest possible opportunity by the court and all the parties and not left to the party intending to so apply.

Legal considerations

8. In light of *Re W*, in deciding whether a child should give evidence, the court's principal objective should be achieving a fair trial.

9. With that objective the court should carry out a balancing exercise between the following primary considerations:

i) the possible advantages that the child being called will bring to the determination of truth balanced against;

ii) the possible damage to the child's welfare from giving evidence ie the risk of harm to the child from giving evidence;

having regard to:

a. the child's wishes and feelings; in particular their willingness to give evidence; as an unwilling child should rarely if ever be obliged to give evidence;

b. the child's particular needs and abilities;

c. the issues that need to be determined;

d. the nature and gravity of the allegations;

e. the source of the allegations;

f. whether the case depends on the child's allegations alone;

g. corroborative evidence;

h. the quality and reliability of the existing evidence;

i. the quality and reliability of any ABE interview;

j. whether the child has retracted allegations;

k. the nature of any challenge a party wishes to make;

l. the age of the child; generally the older the child the better;

m. the maturity, vulnerability and understanding, capacity and competence of the child; this may be apparent from the ABE or from professionals' discussions with the child;

n. the length of time since the events in question;

o. the support or lack of support the child has;

p. the quality and importance of the child's evidence;

q. the right to challenge evidence;

r. whether justice can be done without further questioning;

s. the risk of further delay;

t. the views of the guardian who is expected to have discussed the issue with the child concerned if appropriate and those with parental responsibility;

u. specific risks arising from the possibility of the child giving evidence twice in criminal or other and family proceedings taking into account that normally the family proceedings will be heard before the criminal; and

v. the serious consequences of the allegations ie whether the findings impact upon care and contact decisions.

10. The Court must always take into account the risk of harm which giving evidence may do to children and how to minimise that harm, although that may vary from case to case but the Court does not necessarily need expert evidence in order to assess the risk.

11. Where there are concurrent or linked criminal proceedings there should be close liaison between the respective parties and the allocated judges and ideally linked directions hearings. The Police/CPS should be informed of any proposal that a child give evidence in family proceedings and their views obtained before any such decision is made.

Alternatives to child giving live evidence at a hearing

12. The Court needs to consider seriously the possibility of further questions being put to the child on an occasion distinct from the substantive hearing so as to avoid oral examination. This option would have significant advantages to the child and should be considered at the earliest opportunity and in any event before that substantive hearing. Such further questioning should be carried out as soon as possible after the incident in question. The Court will need to take into account practical and procedural issues including:

a. giving the child the opportunity to refresh his memory;

b. the appropriate identity of the questioner;

c. matching the skills of the questioner to the communication needs of the child;

d. where the questioning should take place;

e. the type and nature of the questions;

f. advance judicial approval of any questions proposed to be put to the child;

g. the need for ground rules to be discussed ahead of time by the judge, lawyers (and intermediary, if applicable) about the examination; and

h. how the interview should be recorded.

Practical considerations pre hearing

13. Once a decision has been made that a child should give evidence at a hearing and be questioned at court, the Court must factor in steps to improve the quality of the child's evidence and minimise the risk of harm to the child.

14. At the earliest opportunity and in any event before the hearing at which the child's evidence is taken, the following matters need to be considered:

a. if 'live' cross examination is appropriate, the need for and use of a registered intermediary [insert details of register of intermediaries] [subject to their availability] or other communication specialist to facilitate the communication of others with the child or relay questions directly, if indicated by the needs of the child;

b. the use of other 'special measures' in particular live video link and screens;

c. the full range of special measures in light of the child's wishes and needs;

d. advance judicial approval of any questions proposed to be put to the child;

e. the need for ground rules to be discussed ahead of time by the judge, lawyers (and intermediary, if applicable) about the examination;

f. information about the child's communication skills, length of concentration span and level of understanding e.g. from an expert or an intermediary or other communication specialist;

g. the need for breaks;

h. the involvement and identity of a supporter for the child;

i. the timetable for children's evidence to minimise time at court and give them a fresh clear start in the morning;

j. the child's dates to avoid attending court;

k. the length of any ABE recording, the best time for the child and the Court to view it (the best time for the child may not be when the recording is viewed by the court);

l. admissions of as much of the child's evidence as possible in advance; including locations, times, and lay-outs;

m. save in exceptional circumstances, agreement as to i) the proper form and limit of questioning and ii) the identity of the questioner.

15. If a child is to give oral evidence at the hearing the following should occur:

a. a familiarisation visit by the child to the court before the hearing with a demonstration of special measures, so that the child can make an informed view about their use;

b. the child should be accompanied and have a known neutral supporter, not directly involved in the case, present during their evidence;

c. the child should see their ABE interview and/or their existing evidence before giving evidence for the purpose of memory refreshing;

d. consideration of the child's secure access to the building and suitability of waiting/eating areas so as to ensure there is no possibility of any confrontation with anyone which might cause distress to the child (where facilities are inadequate, use of a remote link from another court or non-court location);

e. identification of where the child will be located at court and the need for privacy.

16. Where possible the children's solicitor/Cafcass should be deputed to organise these matters.

17. A child should never be questioned directly by a litigant in person who is an alleged perpetrator.

Practical considerations at hearing

18. If the decision has been made that the child should give oral evidence at the hearing the following should occur:

a. advocates should introduce themselves to the child;

b. judges and magistrates should ask if the child would like to meet them, to help to establish rapport and reinforce advice;

c. children should be encouraged to let the court know if they have a problem or want a break but cannot be relied upon to do so;

d. professionals should be vigilant to identify potential miscommunication;

e. the child should be told how the live video link works and who can see who;

f. a check should be made (before the child is seated in the TV link room) to ensure that the equipment is working, recordings can be played and that camera angles will not permit the witness to see the Respondents;

g. the parties should agree which documents the child will be referred to and ensure they are in the room where the child is situated for ease of access.

Examination of children

19. If the Court decides a child should give oral evidence, the Court and all parties should take into account the *Good Practice Guidance in managing young witness cases and questioning children* (part of the NSPCC/ Nuffield Foundation research 'Measuring Up' July 2009 by Joyce Plotnikoff and Richard Woolfson; and the subsequent Progress Report which Guidance has been endorsed by the Judicial Studies Board, the Director of Public Prosecutions, the Criminal Bar Association and the Law Society: http://www.nspcc.org.uk/Inform/research/findings/measuring_up_guidance_w df66581.pdf).

20. Examination of the child should take into account the Court of Appeal judgment in *R v Barker* [2010] EWCA Crim 4, para 42, which called for the advocacy to be adapted 'to enable the child to give the best evidence of which he or she is capable' and which questioning should:

a. be at the child's pace and consistent with their understanding;

b. use simple common words and phrases;

c. repeat names and places frequently;

d. ask one short question (one idea) at a time;

e. let the child know the subject of the question;

f. follow a structured approach, signposting the subject;

g. avoid negatives;

h. avoid repetition;

i. avoid suggestion or leading, including 'tag' questions;

j. avoid a criminal or 'Old Bailey' style cross examination;

k. avoid 'do you remember' questions;

l. avoid restricted choice questions;

m. be slow and allow enough time to answer;

n. check child's understanding;

o. test the evidence not trick the witness;

p. take into account and check the child's level of understanding;

q. not assume the child understands;

r. be alert to literal interpretation;

s. take care with times, numbers and frequency;

t. avoid asking the child to demonstrate intimate touching on his or her own body (if such a question is essential, an alternative method, such as pointing to a body outline, should be agreed beforehand).

Court's overriding duty

21. All advocates have a responsibility to manage the questioning of a child witness fairly. However the ultimate responsibility for ensuring that the child gives the best possible evidence in order to inform the court's decision rests with the tribunal. It should set out its expectations of the advocates and make it clear to the child witness that they can indicate to the court if they feel they are not saying what they want to say or do not understand what is being said to them. The court must be scrupulous in the attention it gives to the case management and control of the questioning process and should be prepared to intervene if the questioning is inappropriate or unnecessary.

22. These Guidelines will be reviewed periodically. Those involved in family proceedings are invited to contact the Family Justice Council with any relevant comments.

APPENDIX 2: GUIDELINES FOR JUDGES MEETING CHILDREN WHO ARE SUBJECT TO FAMILY PROCEEDINGS (APRIL 2010)

4.88

These Guidelines are produced by the Family Justice Council and approved by the President of the Family Division. In these Guidelines:

- All references to 'child' or 'children' are intended to include a young person or young people the subject of proceedings under the Children Act 1989.
- 'Family proceedings' includes both public and private law cases.
- 'Judge' includes magistrates.
- Cafcass includes CAFCASS CYMRU.

Purpose

The purpose of these Guidelines is to encourage judges to enable children to feel more involved and connected with proceedings in which important decisions are made in their lives and to give them an opportunity to satisfy themselves that the Judge has understood their wishes and feelings and to understand the nature of the Judge's task.

Preamble

- In England and Wales in most cases a child's needs, wishes and feelings are brought to the court in written form by a Cafcass officer. Nothing in this guidance document is intended to replace or undermine that responsibility.
- It is Cafcass practice to discuss with a child in a manner appropriate to their developmental understanding whether their participation in the process includes a wish to meet the Judge. If the child does not wish to meet the Judge discussions can centre on other ways of enabling the child to feel a part of the process. If the child wishes to meet the Judge, that wish should be conveyed to the Judge where appropriate.
- The primary purpose of the meeting is to benefit the child. However, it may also benefit the Judge and other family members.

Guidelines

1. The judge is entitled to expect the lawyer for the child and/or the Cafcass officer:

(i) to advise whether the child wishes to meet the Judge;

(ii) if so, to explain from the child's perspective, the purpose of the meeting;

(iii) to advise whether it accords with the welfare interests of the child for such a meeting to take place; and

(iv) to identify the purpose of the proposed meeting as perceived by the child's professional representative/s.

2. The other parties shall be entitled to make representations as to any proposed meeting with the Judge before the Judge decides whether or not it shall take place.

3. In deciding whether or not a meeting shall take place and, if so, in what circumstances, the child's chronological age is relevant but not determinative. Some children of 7 or even younger have a clear understanding of their circumstances and very clear views which they may wish to express.

4. If the child wishes to meet the judge but the judge decides that a meeting would be inappropriate, the judge should consider providing a brief explanation in writing for the child.

5. If a judge decides to meet a child, it is a matter for the discretion of the judge, having considered representations from the parties –

(i) the purpose and proposed content of the meeting;

(ii) at what stage during the proceedings, or after they have concluded, the meeting should take place;

(iii) where the meeting will take place;

(iv) who will bring the child to the meeting;

(v) who will prepare the child for the meeting (this should usually be the Cafcass officer);

(vi) who shall attend during the meeting – although a Judge should never see a child alone;

(vii) by whom a minute of the meeting shall be taken, how that minute is to be approved by the Judge, and how it is to be communicated to the other parties.

It cannot be stressed too often that the child's meeting with the judge is not for the purpose of gathering evidence. That is the responsibility of the Cafcass officer. The purpose is to enable the child to gain some understanding of what is going on, and to be reassured that the judge has understood him/her.

6. If the meeting takes place prior to the conclusion of the proceedings –

(i) The judge should explain to the child at an early stage that a judge cannot hold secrets. What is said by the child will, other than in exceptional circumstances, be communicated to his/her parents and other parties.

(ii) The judge should also explain that decisions in the case are the responsibility of the judge, who will have to weigh a number of factors, and that the outcome is never the responsibility of the child.

(iii) The judge should discuss with the child how his or her decisions will be communicated to the child.

(iv) The parties or their representatives shall have the opportunity to respond to the content of the meeting, whether by way of oral evidence or submissions.

Chapter 5

FORCED MARRIAGE, HONOUR-BASED VIOLENCE AND FEMALE GENITAL MUTILATION

INTRODUCTION

5.1 According to Munby LJ in *Re G*[1], family law will tolerate things which society as a whole may find 'undesirable'. Implicit in this statement is the recognition that there is a range of cultural, social, and religious practices in the UK, and even if they are offensive to some people, they do not constitute 'harm' for the purposes of public child law proceedings.

5.2 However, there are certain practices that are impermissible and illegal, which will not be tolerated in this jurisdiction. These include forced marriage, honour-based violence, and female genital mutilation. Though proponents might claim a cultural, religious or social imperative when justifying these practices, the family court is clear that forced marriage, honour-based violence, and female genital mutilation are all 'barbarous practices' that are 'beyond the pale'[2].

5.3 This chapter will examine what legal remedies the government has put in place to combat forced marriage, honour-based violence, and female genital mutilation, and what family law practitioners in particular need to be aware of when dealing with allegations of the same.

FORCED MARRIAGE

5.4 In 2016, the Forced Marriage Unit[3] (FMU) gave advice and/or support in 1,428 cases related to forced marriage in the UK[4]. Of those cases,

1 [2012] EWCA Civ 1233 at [39].

2 *Singh v Entry Clearance Officer, New Delhi* [2004] EWCA Civ 1075, 68.

3 The Forced Marriage Unit is a joint Foreign and Commonwealth Office and Home Office unit, which was set up in January 2005 to carry out the Government's forced marriage policy, outreach, and casework.

4 *The Forced Marriage Unit Statistics* (Home Office, Foreign and Commonwealth Office, 9 March 2017) 3.

371 (26 per cent) concerned victims under the age of 18[5]. Yet it is important to note that these cases only represent those that have been reported to the FMU; as forced marriage is a 'hidden crime,' these statistics may not reflect the full extent of the abuse, nor the number of potential children affected, both as victims or the children of victims[6].

5.5 Forced marriage is not specific to one country or culture. Since its formation in 2005, the FMU has dealt with cases relating to over 90 countries across the Middle East, Africa, Europe, and North America[7]. In 2016, 157 (11 per cent) of the FMU's cases had no international element.[8] In other words, the forced marriage, or risk thereof, took place entirely within the UK.

5.6 There are a number of reasons why a person, such as a parent, may seek to force another person to marry. Some of the main motives identified include:

(a) controlling sexuality, such as perceived promiscuity or same-sex relationships;

(b) circumscribing unwanted behaviours, such as drinking and drug use, wearing make-up, or behaving in a 'Westernised' manner;

(c) preventing 'unsuitable' relationships, for example, with persons of another religion or caste;

(d) protecting family 'honour';

(e) responding to peer or family pressure;

(f) financial gain;

(g) ensuring that land, property, and wealth remain within the family;

(h) protecting perceived cultural or misguided religious ideals;

(i) ensuring care for the child or vulnerable adult where the existing carers can no longer fulfil that role;

(j) obtaining British citizenship; and

(k) family commitments[9].

5.7 Whilst the above may explain why this practice exists, there is no justification for forced marriage. The UK government views forced marriage as an abuse of human rights and a form of domestic abuse[10]. To that end, forced marriage has been criminalised as a specific offence. Within public law proceedings, where there is a risk of forced marriage or where a child has been forcibly married, it is regarded as a form of abuse and is a child protection issue.

---

5 Ibid, 3.
6 Ibid, 6.
7 Ibid, 3.
8 Ibid, 3.
9 *The Right to Choose: Multi-agency statutory guidance for dealing with forced marriage* (HM Government, June 2014) 8.
10 Ibid, 1.

5.8 Allegations of forced marriage within child protection proceedings raise particular issues – both procedural and practical – that legal and social work practitioners must be live to. For example, family group conferences may not be appropriate where a young person is at risk of forced marriage because of the pressure that family or community members might exercise in such a meeting. Likewise, the court might need to give special consideration to the non-disclosure of documents if said disclosure could pose a risk to the child, for example, by expediting travel to a foreign country to perpetrate the forced marriage. Family lawyers and other professionals working with victims and perpetrators of forced marriage must be familiar with the nuances of this area of law.

Definition of forced marriage

5.9 The government defines 'forced marriage' as a marriage in which one or both spouses do not consent to the marriage but are forced into it. 'Force' may include physical, psychological, financial, sexual, and emotional pressure[11].

5.10 It is important to distinguish between a forced marriage and an arranged marriage. In an arranged marriage, the bride and/or groom's families may take a pivotal role in arranging the marriage, but the choice to marry is ultimately the decision of the parties to the marriage. Conversely, in a forced marriage, one or both of the spouses do not consent to the marriage (or do not have the capacity to consent) and are coerced into it.

Relevant statutes

Anti-Social Behaviour, Crime and Policing Act 2014

5.11 Pursuant to the Anti-Social Behaviour, Crime and Policing Act 2014, s 121(1), forced marriage is a criminal offence. A person commits an offence under this section if he or she:

(a) uses violence, threats or any other form of coercion for the purpose of causing another person to enter into a marriage; and

(b) believes, or ought reasonably to believe, that the conduct may cause the other person to enter into the marriage without free and full consent.

5.12 It is important to note that 'marriage' in this context is not limited to legally binding ceremonies; it is defined under s 121(4) as any religious or civil ceremony of marriage. Further, the marriage need not take place in this jurisdiction. As stated in s 121(3), a person commits an offence under the law of England and Wales if he or she practises any form of deception with the intention of causing another person to leave the UK to be forcibly married pursuant to s 121(1). Likewise, neither the person committing the offence nor the victim of the

11 Ibid, 5.

offence under s 121(1) need to be in England or Wales, provided that at least one of them is habitually resident in England and Wales[12] or is a UK national[13].

5.13 A person found guilty under the Anti-Social Behaviour, Crime and Policing Act 2014, s 121 may face a fine and/or imprisonment for up to twelve months on summary conviction, or up to seven years' imprisonment on conviction on indictment[14].

5.14 In addition to the specific offence of forced marriage, a number of criminal offences might have been perpetrated in the commission of the forced marriage. Perpetrators may have also committed offences such as fear or provocation of violence; actual bodily harm; grievous bodily harm; harassment; common assault; kidnap; abduction; theft (for example, of passport); threats to kill; false imprisonment; and murder[15]. It is the role of the Crown Prosecution Service (CPS) to determine which offences the perpetrators should be charged with[16].

Policing and Crime Act 2017

5.15 Practitioners should also be aware of the Policing and Crime Act 2017, s 173, which came into effect on 31 January 2017. This provision provides lifelong anonymity for victims of forced marriage and applies from the time an allegation is made. From that point onwards, the publication or broadcast of any information likely to result in identification of the victim to members of the public will be prohibited. This includes all forms of publication/broadcasting, from traditional print and broadcast media to social media. Breach of this provision is a criminal offence, the maximum penalty for which is an unlimited fine. In the context of family law proceedings, this protection has implications for, inter alia, reporting restrictions, which is discussed in further detail in Chapter 8.

Forced Marriage Protection Orders

5.16 In addition to the criminalisation of forced marriage under the Anti-Social Behaviour, Crime and Policing Act 2014, s 121, the family court provides relief in the form of Forced Marriage Protection Orders (FMPO), the provisions for which were inserted into the Family Law Act 1996 (FLA 1996), s 63 by the Forced Marriage (Civil Protection) Act 2007, s 1. Prior to 2014, the breach of an FMPO was dealt with as a civil contempt of court, punishable with a fine or a custodial sentence of up to two years' imprisonment. However, pursuant to the Anti-Social Behaviour, Crime and Policing Act 2014, s 120, breach of an FMPO became a criminal offence.

12 Anti-Social Behaviour, Crime and Policing Act 2014, s 121(7)(b).
13 Anti-Social Behaviour, Crime and Policing Act 2014, s 121(7)(c).
14 Anti-Social Behaviour, Crime and Policing Act 2014, s 121(9).
15 *The Right to Choose: Multi-agency statutory guidance for dealing with forced marriage*, supra note 9, 11.
16 Ibid, 11.

5.17 The purpose of an FMPO is twofold:

(a) to protect a person from being forced into a marriage or from any attempt to be forced into a marriage; or

(b) to protect a person who has already been forced into a marriage[17].

It makes provision for the protection of both children and adults, and specific directions for those who lack capacity to consent to marriage.

5.18 As indicated in the FLA 1996, s 63B(1), the court has a wide discretion in respect of the contents of an FMPO: it may contain prohibitions, restrictions, requirements, and/or any other terms that the court feels is appropriate for the purposes of the order. This may include provisions circumscribing conduct both inside and outside of England and Wales, and may be aimed not only at those who conspire or attempt to force the victim into marriage, but also at those who aid, abet, counsel, procure, encourage or assist another person to force, or to attempt to force, a person to enter into a marriage[18]. Some examples include provisions for: handing over passports; forbidding persons from removing the potential victim from the jurisdiction; and prohibiting the potential victim from being left alone with certain persons.

5.19 When deciding whether to exercise its powers under this section and what directions should be included in the order, the court must have regard to all the circumstances of the case, including the need to secure the health, safety, and well-being of the person to be protected[19]. 'Well-being' encompasses, inter alia, the person's wishes and feelings so far as they are reasonably ascertainable and in light of his or her age and understanding[20]. Although the court is required to take account of 'all the circumstances' when deciding whether or not to make an order, the court does not need to apply any given criteria beyond those listed in the FLA 1996, s 63A(2)[21]. In respect of duration, the order may be made for a specified period or until varied or discharged[22].

5.20 The court may make an FMPO of its own volition (including on an ex parte basis) or on application by the person who is to be protected by the order or any 'relevant third party' (a person specified, or falling within a description of persons specified, by order of the Lord Chancellor; for example, a local authority or the police)[23]. Any other person may make an application with the leave of the court[24]. When considering whether to grant leave, the court must have regard to all of the circumstances, including:

(a) the applicant's connection with the person to be protected;

---

17 FLA 1996, s 63A(1).
18 FLA 1996, s 63B(3).
19 FLA 1996, s 63A(2).
20 FLA 1996, s 63A(3).
21 *A Chief Constable v A* [2010] EWHC 3282 (Fam) at 18.
22 FLA 1996, s 63F.
23 FLA 1996, s 63D; s 63C(1)–(2).
24 FLA 1996, s 63C(1)–(3).

(b) the applicant's knowledge of the circumstances of the person to be protected; and

(c) the wishes and feelings of the person to be protected so far as they are reasonably ascertainable and so far as the court considers it appropriate, in the light of the person's age and understanding, to have regard to them[25].

The application for an FMPO may be made as part of existing family law proceedings or as a standalone application[26].

5.21 The court may accept an undertaking in lieu of making an FMPO[27]. However, it may only do so where the respondent has not used or threatened violence against the person to be protected, and where an FMPO is not necessary to secure punishment for breach under the FLA 1996, s 63CA[28].

5.22 As noted above, a breach of an FMPO is a criminal offence, unless the person alleged to have committed the offence has a reasonable excuse[29] or was not aware of the order[30]. Pursuant to the FLA 1996, s 63CA(5), a person guilty of an offence under this section is liable:

(a) on conviction on indictment, to imprisonment for a term not exceeding five years, or a fine, or both;

(b) on summary conviction, to imprisonment for a term not exceeding twelve months, or a fine, or both.

Practitioners should note that a person cannot be convicted of an offence for breach of an FMPO in respect of any conduct that has been punished as a contempt of court[31].

FPR 2010, PD 11

5.23 Practice Direction 11 of the Family Procedure Rules 2010 governs applications under the FLA 1996, Part IVA. Family practitioners should read the practice direction in full when seeking to make or respond to an application for an FMPO (or an application to vary, extend, or discharge an FMPO). The salient points are set out below.

5.24 Pursuant to FPR 2010, r 11.2(1), applications for an FMPO may be made without notice, provided that the application is supported by a sworn statement explaining why notice has not been given. Where an application is on notice, the applicant must serve a copy of the application and a notice of the proceedings on

25 FLA 1996, s 63C(4).
26 FLA 1996, s 63C(5).
27 FLA 1996, s 63E(1).
28 FLA 1996, s 63E(2).
29 FLA 1996, s 63CA(1).
30 FLA 1996, s 63CA(2).
31 FLA 1996, s 63CA(4).

the respondent, the person who is the subject of the proceedings[32] (if different), and any other person directed by the court, at least two days before the date on which the application will be heard[33], though the court may abridge this period if needed[34]. The aforementioned must be served personally; conversely, the court must serve the application if requested to by the applicant[35]. Where the person to be protected is not the applicant and is a child, the court will give directions about who should be served with the application[36].

5.25 As noted above, any person may make an application for an FMPO with the leave of the court pursuant to the FLA 1996, s 63C(3). Where permission from the court is required, the person seeking to make an application must file a Part 18 application notice setting out:

(a) the reasons for the application, for the making of which permission is sought ('the proposed application');

(b) the applicant's connection with the person to be protected;

(c) the applicant's knowledge of the circumstances of the person to be protected;

(d) the applicant's knowledge of the wishes and feelings of the person to be protected; and

(e) a draft of the proposed application, together with sufficient copies for one to be served on each respondent and (if different) the person to be protected[37].

5.26 Once the court has received an application for permission to make an FMPO, it must as soon as possible grant the application or direct that a date be fixed for the hearing of the application and fix that date[38]. It is the responsibility of the court officer to inform the applicant and the respondent, as well as the person to be protected (if different) and any other person directed by the court, of the application for leave and whether the application has been granted or fixed for a hearing date[39].

5.27 Any hearing in respect of an application for an FMPO will be heard in private[40] and the court may direct the non-disclosure of any submissions made or evidence adduced pursuant to the FPR 2010, r 11.7(2) in order to protect the person who is the subject of the proceedings or for any other good reason. When adjudicating non-disclosure, the court must consider both r 11.7(2) and r 21.3. The latter concerns claims to withhold inspection or disclosure of a document.

---

32 FPR 2010, r 11.1.2 defines 'the person who is the subject of the proceedings' as 'the person who will be protected by the forced marriage protection order applied for or being considered by the court of its own initiative, if that order is made, or who is being protected by such an order'.

33 FPR 2010, r 11.4(1).

34 FPR 2010, r 11.4(2).

35 FPR 2010, r 11.4(3).

36 FPR 2010, r 11.5.

37 FPR 2010, r 11.3(1).

38 FPR 2010, r 11.3(2).

39 FPR 2010, r 11.3(3).

40 FPR 2010, r 11.7(1).

5.28 Where the court makes an FMPO of its own initiative under the FLA 1996, s 63C, it must set out in the order a summary of its reasons for making the order and the names of the persons who are to be served with the order[41]. It may also direct that a hearing or further hearing be held to consider any representations made by any of the persons named in, or directed to be served with the order; this applies whether the order is made by application or the court's own initiative[42].

5.29 Finally, FPR 2010, rr 11.13–11.6, which will not be detailed here, set out the procedure for issuing a warrant for arrest if an FMPO is breached, proceedings following arrest, and the enforcement of orders and undertakings.

The Right to Choose

5.30 Whilst it is not a statutory instrument, practitioners should familiarise themselves with the government's statutory guidance for dealing with forced marriage, entitled *The Right to Choose*[43]. A copy of this publication is given to all persons and bodies in England and Wales who exercise public functions in relation to safeguarding and promoting the welfare of children as listed in the Children Act 2004, s 11(1) or s 28(1), including local authorities and the police. It sets out the duties and responsibilities of agencies in respect of protecting children, young people, and adults from forced marriage.

FPR 2010, PD 3AA

5.31 As family law practitioners will be aware, pursuant to the FPR 2010, r 3A.4, the court must consider whether a party's participation in the proceedings (other than by way of giving evidence) is likely to be diminished by reason of vulnerability and, if so, whether it is necessary to make one or more participation directions. Likewise, r 3A.5 stipulates that the court has a duty to consider whether the quality of evidence given by a party or witness is likely to be diminished by reason of vulnerability and, if so, whether it is necessary to make one or more participation directions.

5.32 When considering the vulnerability of a party or witness for the purposes of the FPR 2010, rr 3A.4 and 3A.5, the court must have regard to a number of matters set out in r 3A.7, including, inter alia, any concerns arising in relation to abuse. According to FPR 2010, PD 3AA, para 2.1, 'abuse' in the context of the rule includes any concerns arising in relation to forced marriage (as well as 'honour-based violence' and female genital mutilation). If a party, witness or person to be protected is found to be vulnerable by virtue of concerns relating to forced marriage (or 'honour-based violence' or female genital mutilation), the court will need to consider what role that person should take in the proceedings

41 FPR 2010, r 11.8.
42 FPR 2010, r.11.9.
43 *The Right to Choose: Multi-agency statutory guidance for dealing with forced marriage*, supra note 9.

and whether he or she should give evidence. If the court deems that the vulnerable person must give evidence, then the court will direct a 'ground rules hearing'[44], at which any necessary participation directions will be given.

Common issues in respect of forced marriage

Interim care orders and removal

5.33 As highlighted above, forced marriage is regarded as a form of child abuse and a child protection issue. However, the risk of forced marriage will not automatically meet the threshold for public law orders, particularly where an FMPO in already in place. This may be seen in *London Borough of Camden v RZ*[45]. The case concerned DZ (aged 10) and SZ (aged 6), who had been taken into police protection on 12 August 2015 following the service of an FMPO on their father. The family were of Afghan heritage and the mother, who was in Afghanistan at the time, alleged that the father intended to take DZ to Afghanistan to marry her to her 18-year old paternal cousin.

5.34 The local authority issued an application for interim care orders in respect of both children. Whilst the mother had made a number of additional allegations about the father vis-à-vis domestic violence and neglect, the principal ground of the local authority's application was the risk of removal for the purposes of forced marriage, rather than concerns about the father's parenting. The local authority maintained that the risk of abduction to Afghanistan was so high, and the consequences of that risk so serious, that an FMPO was not sufficient protection.

5.35 In his judgment, Macdonald J was clear that, pursuant to the FLA 1996, s 63R, the making of an FMPO does not preclude the use of other protective measures[46] and there will be cases where the additional relief under the Children Act 1989 (CA 1989) is appropriate[47]. However, the test for the making of an interim care order must be met before such an order can be made; the risk of forced marriage will not ipso facto satisfy the test. In *London Borough of Camden v RZ*, the court held that the FMPO adequately addressed the risk of forced marriage in respect of DZ and removal from the jurisdiction in respect of both children. As such, the children were not at risk of suffering significant harm pursuant to the CA 1989, s 31(2), and continued removal from the father would not be proportionate. There was therefore no basis for continuing the interim care orders.

5.36 Although *London Borough of Camden v RZ* relates specifically to interim care orders, the same reasoning arguably applies to all public law child orders. Further protective measures under the CA 1989 may not be made unless the established test for the making of said order is met.

---

44 FPR 2010, PD 3AA, para 5.2.

45 [2015] EWHC 3751 (Fam).

46 [2015] EWHC 3751 (Fam) at [74].

47 Ibid, [87].

Expert evidence

5.37 Cases of forced marriage, as well as honour-based violence and female genital mutilation, can often involve cultural and legal issues that the court and practitioners will be unfamiliar with. As such, the court may view the appointment of an expert as necessary, either to assess risk, provide a generic report on forced marriage within a certain cultural/regional context, or both[48]. In respect of risk, a Cafcass officer, social worker (as part of a s 47 inquiry) or independent expert may be directed to produce a report assessing risk, provided that he or she has with the relevant expertise and experience of forced marriage.

5.38 For example, *A County Council v SB*[49] concerned the risk of forced marriage and honour-based violence to a 16-year-old girl whose parents disapproved of her relationship with her boyfriend. A number of alleged incidents had occurred that led to public law proceedings being issued, including the girl being found close to her home by a member of the public with her hands tied together, and another occasion when she claimed that her mother locked her in the family home for three days and would not let her out. The child was removed from her parents' home and placed in foster care under an interim care order.

5.39 The court ordered an expert to conduct an honour-related abuse assessment to ascertain the risk to the child of forced marriage. In carrying out the assessment, the expert read all of the papers in the proceedings and interviewed the relevant parties, including the child. The expert concluded that the girl was not at immediate risk of forced marriage, but recommended that the FMPO remain in place, especially as there were related criminal proceedings concerning the child's brothers, who had allegedly kidnapped and threatened the child's boyfriend. A second report was subsequently ordered when it was revealed during the expert's oral evidence that the expert had received information from the interviewees, including the child, that had not been included in the first report; that this information had influenced the expert's conclusions; and that neither this information, nor its source, had been disclosed, as the expert had given assurances of confidentiality to the child.

5.40 Conversely, the court may determine that the appointment of an expert is necessary to ascertain the wishes and feelings of the person who is to be protected by the FMPO. As stated above, when deciding whether to make an FMPO, the court must have regard to all of the circumstances of the case, including the need to secure the health, safety, and well-being (including the wishes and feelings) of the person to be protected[50]. Whilst the statute does not stipulate how the court should make a realistic assessment of the aforementioned criteria, some guidance has been set out by Sir Nicholas Wall (then President of the Family Division) in *A Chief Constable v A*[51].

---

48 Field Court Chambers, 'Honour-based violence and forced marriage in public law children proceedings' (4 January 2017), available at fieldcourt.co.uk/honour-based-violence-forced-marriage-public-law-children-proceedings/.

49 [2010] EWHC 2528 (Fam).

50 FLA 1996, s 63A(2).

51 [2010] EWHC 3282 (Fam).

5.41 *A Chief Constable v A* concerned a 19-year old woman of Pakistani descent who had been born and brought up in the UK. Her parents wanted her to marry a man of their choosing (B), and the Chief Constable of the Police made an ex parte application for an FMPO, which was granted. The woman made an application to set aside the order, which was not successful; however, she subsequently went through a marriage ceremony with B and sought to regularise her marriage (it could not be registered by virtue of the FMPO).

5.42 In order to ascertain the woman's wishes and feelings, as part of the criteria under the FLA 1996, s 63A(2), the court directed that the papers from the proceedings should be disclosed to an expert witness from one of the organisations which specialises in forced marriage and 'honour violence' cases, and that the expert should then meet with the woman to establish whether she genuinely and independently wished the FMPO to be discharged. The Executive Director of the Henna Foundation interviewed the woman, during which she specifically expressed her wish to regularise her marriage to B.

5.43 Discharging the order as sought, Wall P stated that the main reason for this judgment being published was that it was his hope that what happened in the proceedings could be replicated in other cases. In particular, he emphasised that if the court is to make a realistic assessment pursuant to s 63A(2), it is essential that the person to be protected is seen by someone who is aware of the pressures that may be placed on him/her and is an expert in the field[52]. Further, he noted that it is desirable that the person to be protected is separately and independently represented[53].

5.44 *A Chief Constable v A* concerned a legal adult, whose wishes and feelings would arguably hold more weight than those of a child, particularly where the order sought was the discharge of the FMPO. However, the provision is clear that the court must have regard to all of the circumstances of the case, including the need to secure the health, safety, and well-being of the person to be protected[54]. This applies equally to adults and children, though the person's wishes and feelings are evaluated in light of his or her age and understanding[55].

5.45 It appears to be good practice that in proceedings regarding allegations of forced marriage, family law practitioners should consider whether to make an application under the CA 1989, Part 25 for an expert to be appointed to assist the court, and, if granted, to seek directions for some (or all) of the papers to be disclosed to that expert. Care will need to be given to the identification of an appropriate expert, as he or she will need to have particular experience of forced marriage – often within a specific cultural context – as well as giving evidence within legal proceedings. Non-profit organisations, such as Karma Nirvana and the Henna Foundation, may be able to suggest and/or provide appropriate experts.

52 [2010] EWHC 3282 (Fam) at [6].
53 Ibid.
54 FLA 1996, s 63A(2).
55 FLA 1996, s 63A(3).

Disclosure, non-disclosure, and special advocates

5.46 As family law practitioners will be aware, disclosure of documents to parties to the proceedings is the rule, not the exception. As such, the threshold to be met for non-disclosure is high. The reasoning for this is set out by Lord Mustill in *Re D (Minors) (Adoption Reports: Confidentiality)*[56]:

> 'My Lords, it is a first principle of fairness that each party to a judicial process shall have an opportunity to answer by evidence and argument any adverse material which the tribunal may take into account when forming its opinion. This principle is lame if the party does not know the substance of what is said against him (or her), for what he does not know he cannot answer ...'.

5.47 In respect of applications for FPMOs, there will be certain situations in which the disclosure of information given by a witness might put the witness, or the source of the information, at risk. As outlined previously, the court may direct the withholding of any submission made, or any evidence adduced, for or at any hearing concerning an application for an FMPO in order to protect the person who is the subject of said order or for any other 'good reason'. In deciding whether to make such an order, the court must consider the FPR 2010, r 11.7(2) in conjunction with r 21.3 and the ECHR rights of the parties involved, namely the Art 2 (right to life), Art 3 (prohibition of torture and 'inhuman or degrading treatment or punishment'), and Art 8 (right to respect for private and family life) rights of the applicant and/or person to be protected, and the Art 6 (right to a fair trial) and Art 8 rights of the respondent.

5.48 The court's approach to disclosure and the balancing of ECHR rights is set out in *Re B (Disclosure to Other Parties)*[57]. Munby J (as he then was) proffered three propositions:

(a) whilst an entitlement to a fair trial under the ECHR, Art 6 is absolute, this does not mean that a party has an absolute and unqualified right to see all the documents[58];

(b) pursuant to the Human Rights Act 1998, the interests of any person – not just a child – whose Art 8 rights are sufficiently engaged can be relied on to justify non-disclosure[59]; and

(c) a limited qualification of the right to see the documents may be acceptable if directed towards a clear and proper objective. Non-disclosure must be limited to what the situation imperatively demands and is justified only when the case is compelling or strictly necessary, with the court being rigorous in its examination of the feared harm and any difficulty caused to the litigant counterbalanced by procedures designed to ensure a fair trial[60].

56 [1996] AC 593 at 603H–604A.
57 [2001] All ER (D) 22 (Aug).
58 [2001] All ER (D) 22 (Aug) at [56].
59 Ibid, [66].
60 Ibid, [6].

5.49 According to Wall P in *Chief Constable v YK*[61], an FMPO acts in a 'protective capacity', and in doing so may require certain information not to be disclosed to the other parties. As protection is the 'primary' purpose of the FLA 1996, s 63, that purpose is sufficient to justify non-disclosure under the ECHR. Further, Wall P raised doubts about whether a respondent's Art 6 right to a fair trial 'in the determination of his civil rights and obligations' is even engaged by an application for an FMPO, as forcing a person into a marriage is neither a civil right nor an obligation[62]. However, he accepted that an application to set aside an FMPO would likely engage Art 6. Irrespective of whether Art 6 applied or not, Wall P reminded himself that the right to a fair trial does not entitle a party either to see all the documents in the case or to have all the information in the possession of the court, especially information which, if abused, would lead to serious breaches of the rights of the person to be protected[63].

5.50 However, as withholding documents in proceedings is 'exceptional', the court must consider alternatives to non-disclosure. In *A County Council v SB*[64], which is cited above and in which the court considered whether an expert assessment should be disclosed to all of the parties, Wall P suggested that full disclosure should be made to the court of the relevant material, and that the court should then decide whether the Art 6 rights of the parties required disclosure[65]. A different approach is offered in *Re A (A Child) v Chief Constable of Dorset & B*[66], which is a judicial review case and does not concern forced marriage. In *Re A (A Child) v Chief Constable of Dorset & B* the court indicated that a way of dealing with non-disclosure would be for the court to direct the party seeking to withhold information to set out in writing a summary of the harm and the nature of the sensitive and confidential information he or she sought to withhold[67]. If the respondent to the application for non-disclosure agreed that the information could be disclosed to his legal advisors, and not to himself, the legal advisors could then provide the court with a written undertaking that they would not disclose the material to their client[68]. However, this course could only be taken if the court was satisfied that the respondent gave his informed consent freely and voluntarily[69].

5.51 It is incumbent on family law practitioners who are dealing with proceedings concerning forced marriage to be live to issues of disclosure from the earliest stage of any application, to ensure that:

(a) the person to be protected or any alternative source of information is not placed at increased risk by virtue of disclosure to the other parties and that their rights under the ECHR, Art 2 and Art 3 are not infringed by such disclosure; and

(b) the ECHR, Art 6 rights of the respondent(s) are protected where applicable.

61 [2010] EWHC 2438 (Fam) at [91].
62 Ibid, [101].
63 Ibid, [101]–[102].
64 [2010] EWHC 2528 (Fam).
65 [2010] EWHC 2528 (Fam) at [36].
66 [2010] EWHC 1748 (Admin), [2011] 1 FLR 11.
67 Ibid, [16].
68 Ibid, [42].
69 Ibid, [30].

5.52 Finally, it is necessary to add a short note about the court's approach to disclosure and special advocates[70]. In *Chief Constable v YK*[71], it was raised whether the special advocate procedure is appropriate in a forced marriage case to decide any issue of disclosure that may arise. Stating that the use of special advocates is a matter of last resort, Wall P indicated that it is usually inappropriate for special advocates to be appointed in cases concerning FMPOs.

HONOUR-BASED VIOLENCE

5.53 Honour-based violence ('HBV') often goes hand-in-hand with forced marriage. In the first year following the criminalisation of forced marriage, the number of incidents of HBV reported to the police in the UK increased from 3,335 in 2014 to 5,595 in 2015, a spike of 68 per cent[72]. In 2016, the number of cases dropped slightly, to 5,105[73]. According to the Halo Project, a non-profit organisation that supports victims of forced marriage, HBV, and female genital mutilation, there are approximately 12–15 honour killings per year in the UK[74]. Indeed, the problem is so prevalent that 14 July has been named 'Honour Killing Memorial Day', to commemorate Shafilea Ahmed, the 17-year-old British Pakistani woman from Bradford who was killed by her parents in 2003 for rejecting a potential husband. As in the case of forced marriages, these statistics only represent those incidents of HBV that have been reported; it does not, for example, take into account cases where adults and/or children are taken abroad and do not return and whose whereabouts are unknown[75].

5.54 The family court's approach to HBV is set out in *Re B-M (Children) (Care Orders: Risk)*[76], the first case to feature HBV within care proceedings, which reached the Court of Appeal[77]. According to Wall LJ:

> '... the time has surely come to re-think the phrase "honour killings". It is one thing to mock the concept of honour – as, for example, Shakespeare does through Falstaff in I Henry IV Act V, Scene i. It is quite another matter to distort the word "honour" to describe what is, in reality, sordid criminal behaviour ... We should, accordingly, identify [incidents of HBV] as criminal acts and as nothing else ...'[78].

70 A 'special advocate' is a specially appointed lawyer who is instructed to represent a person's interests in relation to material that is kept secret from that person (and his ordinary lawyers) but analysed at an adversarial hearing held in private.

71 [2010] EWHC 2438 (Fam).

72 IKWRO, '53% rise in "honour" based violence cases reported to the police since the criminalisation of forced marriage' (8 November 2017), available at ikwro.org.uk/2017/11/violence-criminalisation-marriage/.

73 Ibid.

74 Halo Project, 'Honour-Based Violence', available at www.haloproject.org.uk/honour-based-violence-W21page-3.

75 Ibid.

76 [2009] EWCA Civ 205.

77 '"Honour" Killings: Re B-M' (2009) Fam Law 455(2).

78 [2009] EWCA Civ 205 at para 117.

5.55 Whilst the court is clear that incidents of HBV are fundamentally criminal acts, family law practitioners must be live to the different cultural contexts in which these offences occur and the particular vulnerability of victims. In doing so, the family law practitioner – as well as the court – will be better placed to consider the risk to the subject children (and parents) and make appropriate decisions about their future care.

Definition of honour-based violence

5.56 The CPS and Association of Chief Police Officers define HBV – also known as 'honour crime' or 'izzat'[79] – as a crime or incident that has or may have been committed to protect or defend the 'honour' of the family and/or community[80]. In other words, it takes place where the victim is perceived to have undermined the family and/or community's code of conduct. HBV includes an array of crimes, including assault, imprisonment, and murder, and is usually (though not exclusively) perpetrated against women[81]. Unlike other forms of abuse, it is often committed with some degree of approval and collusion from family and/or community members[82].

Relevant statutes

5.57 As the above definition intimates, there is no specific offence of 'honour-based violence'; it is an umbrella term to encompass various offences covered by existing legislation. There is no specific statutory relief in the family court, unlike the FMPO or the Female Genital Mutilation Protection Order (discussed in detail below). However, HBV functions as a child protection issue (namely, abuse and domestic violence) in public law proceedings where either the subject child(ren) and/or her carer(s) are at risk of significant harm by virtue of HBV. In those circumstances, the relevant local authority may make an application for public law orders under the CA 1989, s 31 (care and supervision orders) and s 38 (interim orders), relying on HBV as part of the threshold criteria for the making of orders.

5.58 As is the case with forced marriage, the FPR 2010, PD 3AA also applies in respect of proceedings concerning allegations of HBV.

Common issues in respect of honour-based violence

Expert evidence

5.59 Where there are allegations of HBV (or the risk of HBV) within public law proceedings, which are denied, the court may be asked to undertake

79 Originally from the Arabic 'izza' meaning glory, 'izzat' is a Hindi and Urdu word meaning 'honour.'
80 *Honour Based Violence and Forced Marriage – Legal Guidance, Domestic Abuse* (CPS, 21 December 2017), available at www.cps.gov.uk/legal-guidance/honour-based-violence-and-forced-marriage, 8.
81 *The Right to Choose: Multi-agency statutory guidance for dealing with forced marriage*, supra note 9, 5.
82 *The Right to Choose: Multi-agency statutory guidance for dealing with forced marriage*, supra note 9, 5.

a fact-finding exercise to determine whether the allegations are true on a balance of probabilities. It is a well-established principle of law that on all matters in dispute during care proceedings, the standard of proof (balance of probabilities) remains the same regardless of how serious the allegation is or the seriousness of the consequences[83]. This extends to allegations of HBV.

5.60 However, where the allegations concern HBV, the court may take the view that an expert report is necessary to assist with the fact-finding exercise, in order to provide a cultural context for the allegations. This may be seen in the case of *Re S (Findings of Fact)*[84], which concerned an application by a father for a contact order in respect of his three children. The mother opposed contact between the children and the father (or with her own family) and made a number of allegations of domestic violence and HBV against the father and against her own parents, who intervened in the hearing.

5.61 As part of the proceedings, an expert from the Halo Project, Jasvinder Sanghera CBE (founder of Karma Nirvana), gave general evidence about HBV in a report. Whilst the judge was clear that he did not place any weight on specific comments by Ms Sanghera about the likelihood of the mother's account being true, which is a matter for the court and not for a witness, the generic information contained within the report provided the frame of reference for his findings; for example, he accepted the submission made on behalf of the mother that the code of conduct within the culture, described by Ms Sanghera, provided a unifying feature explaining the most striking features of the mother's case.

5.62 Although *Re S (Findings of Fact)* was a private family law matter, it is arguable that obtaining an expert report would be appropriate within the context of a fact-finding exercise in respect of HBV in public law proceedings, especially where there are conflicting accounts of cultural issues. Additionally, or in the alternative, the court may take the view that an expert report is necessary after the fact-finding, where findings of HBV have been made, in order to ascertain the risk to the subject child and/or his parent or other relevant party.

FEMALE GENITAL MUTILATION

5.63 In recent years, the UK government has taken a proactive stance against female genital mutilation (FGM). On 6 February 2014, the International Day of Zero Tolerance for Female Genital Mutilation, the UK government released a declaration signed by a number of leading ministers and officials pledging to end FGM in the UK and abroad[85], and in December 2016, it published 'A Statement

83 *Re BR (Proof of Facts)* [2015] EWFC 41.

84 [2013] EWHC 15 (Fam).

85 'Declaration on FGM' (HM Government, 6 February 2014), available at www.gov.uk/government/publications/female-genital-mutilation-declaration.

Opposing Female Genital Mutilation'[86]. According to the latter, FGM is child abuse and an extremely harmful practice with devastating health consequences for girls and women.

5.64 Unsurprisingly, this sentiment has been echoed in the family court. Summing up the judicial position, Munby P stated the following in *Re B and G (Children) (No 2)*[87]:

> '55. I do not want there to be any doubt. FGM is a criminal offence under the Female Genital Mutilation Act 2003. It is an abuse of human rights. It has no basis in any religion. I repeat what I first said as long ago as 2004 in *Singh v Entry Clearance Officer, New Delhi* [2004] EWCA Civ 1075, [2005] 1 FLR 308, para 68: it is a "barbarous" practice which is "beyond the pale".
>
> 56. In *Fornah v Secretary of State for the Home Department* [2005] EWCA Civ 680, [2005] 2 FLR 1085, Auld LJ (para 1) described it as "an evil practice internationally condemned and in clear violation of Art 3 of the European Convention for the Protection of Human Rights and Fundamental Freedoms 1950". In the same case, Arden LJ (para 58) described it as "a repulsive practice ... deleterious to women's health". I entirely agree.'

5.65 However, the consideration of allegations of FGM in the family law courts is not necessarily straightforward. As explored below, practitioners will need to have a strong understanding of the different types of FGM and appropriate remedies, and the need for expert evidence.

Definition of female genital mutilation

5.66 There are a number of different types of FGM. The World Health Organisation (WHO) identifies the following four categories:

— Type I *Clitoridectomy*: partial or total removal of the clitoris and in rare cases only the prepuce (the fold of skin surrounding the clitoris);

— Type II *Excision*: partial or total removal of the clitoris and labia minora with or without removal of the labia majora;

— Type III *Infibulation*: narrowing of the vaginal opening through the creation of a covering seal. The seal is formed by cutting and repositioning the labia minora or majora with or without removal of the clitoris;

— Type IV *Other*: all other harmful procedures to the genitals for non-medical reasons, for example pricking, piercing, incising, scraping and cauterizing the genital area.

---

86 'A Statement Opposing Female Genital Mutilation' (Home Office, Department for Education, Department for International Development, Department for Health and Ministry of Justice, December 2016), available at www.gov.uk/government/publications/statement-opposing-female-genital-mutilation.

87 [2015] EWFC 3.

Following *Re B and G (Children) (No 2)*[88], discussed in more detail below, the court has utilised the aforementioned categories when considering allegations of FGM.

5.67 It is important for practitioners to note that there is no definition of 'mutilate' in the relevant statutory instruments, as set out in the following paragraphs. In *Re B and G (Children) (No 2)*, the President used the meaning from the *Oxford English Dictionary*, namely 'the action of mutilating a person or animal; the severing or maiming of a limb or bodily organ', 'mutilate' being defined as meaning

> 'To deprive (a person or animal) of the use of a limb or bodily organ, by dismemberment or otherwise; to cut off or destroy (a limb or organ); to wound severely, inflict violent or disfiguring injury on'[89].

Relevant statutes

Female Genital Mutilation Act 2003

5.68 FGM has been a criminal offence in England and Wales since 1985, pursuant to the Prohibition of Female Circumcision Act 1985. The 1985 Act was subsequently repealed and replaced by the Female Genital Mutilation Act 2003 (FGMA 2003), which is the statutory provision that governs both the criminal offence of FGM and the civil remedy, namely the Female Genital Mutilation Protection Order (FGMPO).

5.69 Pursuant to the FGMA 2003, s 1(1), a person is guilty of the offence of FGM if he or she excises, infibulates, or otherwise mutilates the whole or any part of a girl's[90] labia majora, labia minora or clitoris. It is interesting to note that under this provision, Type IV FGM, as defined by the WHO, does not constitute a criminal offence unless it involves actual mutilation. Likewise, no offence is committed where an approved person – namely a medical professional – 'mutilates' a girl's labia majora, labia minora or clitoris when performing a surgical operation on a girl which is necessary for her physical or mental health, or a surgical operation on a girl who is in any stage of labour, or has just given birth, for purposes connected with the labour or birth[91].

5.70 Under the FGM Act 2003, s 2, it is a criminal offence to aid, abet, counsel or procure a girl to excise, infibulate, or otherwise mutilate the whole or any part of her own labia majora, labia minora, or clitoris. Likewise, s 3 contains an extra-territorial provision, which makes it a criminal offence for someone to aid, abet, counsel or procure a person who is not a UK national or UK resident to perform FGM outside of the UK.

---

88 [2015] EWFC 3.

89 [2015] EWFC 3 at [12].

90 'Girl' in the context of the FGM 2003 includes women (s 6).

91 FGMA 2003, s 2.

5.71 The FGMA 2003 not only criminalises the actions of person(s) who played an active role in the exercise of FGM, but also the non-action of those who are deemed to be responsible for the victim and fail to protect her from the risk of FGM[92]. A person is 'responsible' for a girl (or woman) under s 3A(3) if he or she has parental responsibility for and frequent contact with the girl. Additionally, under s 3A(4), a person may be said to be 'responsible' for the girl or woman where the person is over the age of 18 years and has assumed (and not relinquished) responsibility for caring for the girl in the manner of a parent.

5.72 There are two defences against an offence under the FGMA 2003, s 3A, namely:

(a) at the relevant time, the person responsible for the girl did not think that there was a significant risk of a genital mutilation offence being committed against the girl, and could not reasonably have been expected to be aware that there was any such risk[93]; or

(b) the responsible person took such steps as he or she could reasonably have been expected to take to protect the girl from being the victim of a genital mutilation offence[94].

5.73 An offence under the FGMA 2003, ss 1, 2, 3 and 3A can be committed wholly or partly outside the UK by a person who is a UK national or a UK resident[95]. If an offence is committed outside of this jurisdiction, proceedings may be taken, and the offence may be treated as having been committed, in any place in England and Wales or Northern Ireland[96].

5.74 A person guilty of an offence under the FGMA 2003, ss 1, 2 or 3 is liable on conviction on indictment to imprisonment for a term not exceeding 14 years or a fine (or both); or, on summary conviction, to imprisonment for a term not exceeding six months or a fine not exceeding the statutory maximum (or both)[97]. The penalty is slightly different for the offence of failing to protect a girl from FGM under s 3A. A person guilty of an offence under s 3A is liable on conviction on indictment, to imprisonment for a term not exceeding seven years or a fine (or both); or, on summary conviction in England and Wales, to imprisonment for a term not exceeding 12 months or a fine (or both)[98].

5.75 There is a duty on persons who work in a 'regulated profession' (ie a healthcare professional, a teacher, or a social care worker[99]) to notify the chief of police where a girl informs the person that an act of FGM (however described) has been carried out on her[100]. Likewise, the same duty exists where the person in

---

92 FGMA 2003, s 3A.
93 FGMA 2003, s 3A(5)(a).
94 FGMA 2003, s 3A(5)(b).
95 FGMA 2003, s 4(1A).
96 FGMA 2003, s 4(2).
97 FGMA 2003, s 5(2).
98 FGMA 2003, s 5(3).
99 The latter is defined as a 'regulated professional' in Wales only.
100 FGMA 2003, s 5B(1)–(3).

a regulated profession observes physical signs on the girl appearing to show that an act of FGM has been carried out on her, and the person has no reason to believe that the act was, or was part of, a surgical operation. The report to the police is known as an FGM notification and, importantly for professionals, s 5B(7) stipulates that a disclosure made in an FGM notification does not breach any obligation of confidence owed by the person making the disclosure, or any other restriction on the disclosure of information.

5.76 The FGMA 2003, Sch 1 provides for the anonymity of persons against whom an FGM offence is alleged to have been committed.

Female Genital Mutilation Protection Order

5.77 Pursuant to the Serious Crime Act 2015, s 73, the FGMA 2003 was amended to include a civil remedy in the form of an FGMPO. The FGMPO, which is contained in the FGMA 2003, s 5A and Sch 2, is modelled largely on the FMPO (see paras 5.16–5.22) and indeed, many of the provisions are almost identical. However, unlike the FMPO, the person to be protected under an FGMPO is by definition a girl or woman.

5.78 Under the FGMA 2003, Sch 2, Part 1, para 1, the court in England and Wales may make an FGMPO for the purposes of protecting a girl against the commission of a genital mutilation offence, or protecting a girl against whom any such offence has been committed. An FGMPO may be made for a specified period or until varied or discharged[101].

5.79 In deciding whether to make an FGMPO and in what manner, the court must have regard to all the circumstances, including the need to secure the health, safety and well-being of the girl to be protected[102]. However, as HHJ Pearce notes,

> 'in view of the obvious physical nature of the act of genital mutilation and the very serious and long term consequences that result from it, in most cases it is unlikely to be difficult to establish the need for protection where the evidence clearly points to a risk of FGM'[103].

5.80 As per an FMPO, the court has a wide discretion in respect of what provisions to include under an FGMPO, including such prohibitions, restrictions or requirements, and/or any such other terms, as the court considers appropriate for the purposes of the order[104]. This includes provisions relating to conduct outside of England and Wales[105]. However, as clarified in *Re E (Children) (FGM Protection Orders)*[106], the court will only direct those provisions that are designed to protect

101 FGMA 12003, Sch 2, Part 1, para 1(6).
102 FGMA 12003, Sch 2, Part 1, para 1(2).
103 HHJ N Pearce, 'FGM Protection Orders: the new civil remedy' (2015) Fam Law 837.
104 FGMA 2003, Sch 2, Part 1, para 1(3).
105 FGMA 2003, Sch 2, Part 1, para 1(4)(a).
106 [2015] EWHC 2275 (Fam).

the girl who is at risk of or has undergone FGM; any other person who requires protection in proceedings concerning FGM will need to apply for a different statutory remedy, for example, an injunction under the FLA 1996[107].

5.81 Pursuant to the FGMA 2003, Sch 2, Part 1, para 1(4)(b), the terms of an FGMPO may also relate to respondents who aid, abet, counsel, procure, encourage or assist another person to commit, or attempt to commit, a genital mutilation offence against a girl; or who conspire to commit, or to attempt to commit, such an offence, whether within the UK or extra-territorially.

5.82 The court may make an FGMPO on an application being made to it by the girl who is to be protected by the order or a relevant third party; anyone else must seek the leave of the court to make an application[108]. At the time of writing, the only 'relevant third party' identified is a local authority[109]. When deciding whether to grant leave to any other person, the court must have regard to all the circumstances including:

(a) the applicant's connection with the girl to be protected;

(b) the applicant's knowledge of the circumstances of the girl[110].

5.83 Where any other family proceedings are before the court, the court may make the order of its own volition if the court considers that an FGMPO should be made to protect a girl (whether or not she is a party to the proceedings), and a person who would be a respondent to any proceedings for an FGMPO is a party to the current proceedings[111].

5.84 Further, the court before which there are criminal proceedings in England and Wales for an FGM offence may make an FGMPO without an application being made to it if the court considers that an FGMPO should be made to protect a girl (whether or not the victim of the offence in relation to the criminal proceedings), and a person who would be a respondent to any proceedings for an FGMPO is a defendant in the criminal proceedings[112].

5.85 The court may make an ex parte FGMPO where it is just and convenient to do so[113]. When deciding whether to do so, the court must have regard to all the circumstances, including:

— the risk to the girl – or to another person – of becoming a victim of a FGM offence if the order is not made immediately;

— whether it is likely that an applicant will be deterred or prevented from pursuing an application if an order is not made immediately; and

107 [2015] EWHC 2275 (Fam) at [27].
108 FGMA 2003, Sch 2, Part 1, s 2(1)–(2).
109 Female Genital Mutilation Protection Order (Relevant Third Party) Regulations 2015, SI 2015/1422.
110 FGMA 2003, Sch 2, Part 1, para 2(4).
111 FGMA 2003, Sch 2, Part 1, para 2(6).
112 FGMA 2003, Sch 2, Part 1, para 3.
113 FGMA 2003, Sch 2, Part 1, para 5(1).

— whether there is reason to believe that the respondent is aware of the proceedings but is deliberately evading service, and the delay involved in effecting substituted service will cause serious prejudice to the girl to be protected or (if different) an applicant[114].

The court must allow the respondent to an ex parte application the opportunity to make representations about the order made as soon as just and convenient, and at a hearing of which notice has been given to all the parties in accordance with rules of court[115].

5.86 Breach of an FGMPO is a criminal offence, provided that the person who has breached the order is aware of the existence of the FGMPO[116]. Under the FGMA 2003, Sch 2, Part 1, para 4(5), a person guilty of breaching the FGMPO on conviction on indictment is liable to imprisonment for a term not exceeding five years, or a fine, or both; or, on summary conviction, to imprisonment for a term not exceeding twelve months, or a fine, or both.

5.87 Since the introduction of the FGMPO in July 2015, there have only been 163 applications and 145 orders made[117]. This represents merely a fraction of the number of incidents of FGM that take place each year, both in the UK and abroad. Family law practitioners should be vigilant in encouraging their clients to apply for said orders when appropriate.

FPR 2010, PDs 11 and 3AA

5.88 In addition to FMPOs, the FPR 2010, PD 11 also governs the procedure for making an application for an FGMPO. The provisions contained therein apply to protection orders generally. As such, in the rules outlined above (see paras 5.23–5.29) FGMPO may be substituted for FMPO and the full details are not repeated here. However, family law practitioners should note that the application forms for FGMPOs and FMPOs respectively are different.

5.89 As per forced marriage and HBV, FPR 2010, PD 3AA also applies in respect of proceedings concerning allegations of FGM.

Guidance

5.90 Pursuant to the FGMA 2003, s 5C, the Secretary of State may issue guidance to whatever persons in England and Wales the Secretary of State considers appropriate about the effect of any provision in the FGMA 2003, or any other matters relating to FGM. To that end, in 2016 the government

114 FGMA 2003, Sch 2, Part 1, para 5(2).
115 FGMA 2003, Sch 2, Part 1, para 5(4).
116 FGMA 2003, Sch 2, Part 1, para 4(1)–(2).
117 'Family Court Statistics' (2017) Fam Law 1257.

published its *Multi-agency statutory guidance on female genital mutilation* (the *FGM Guidance*)[118]. As the name suggests, the *FGM Guidance* encourages agencies to work together to protect and support girls or women at risk of, or who have undergone, FGM.

5.91 The *FGM Guidance* has three stated purposes:

(a) to provide information on FGM, including on the law on FGM in England and Wales;

(b) to provide strategic guidance on FGM for all persons and bodies in England and Wales who are under statutory duties to safeguard and promote the welfare of children and vulnerable adults; and

(c) to provide advice and support to front-line professionals who have responsibilities to safeguard and support women and girls affected by FGM, in particular to assist them in:

   (i) identifying when a girl or young woman may be at risk of FGM and responding appropriately;

   (ii) identifying when a girl or woman has had FGM and responding appropriately;

   (iii) and implementing measures that can prevent and ultimately help end the practice of FGM[119].

5.92 The *FGM Guidance* is too lengthy to be set out in detail in this chapter; however, it provides comprehensive information about the practice and prosecution of FGM and should be required reading for any legal or social work practitioner.

Common issues in respect of FGM

Leave to apply for an FGMPO

5.93 As noted above, the court may make an FGMPO on an application being made to it by the girl who is to be protected by the order, or by a relevant third party; anyone else must seek the leave of the court to make an application[120]. As may be seen in *Re E (Children) (FGM Protection Orders)*[121], 'anyone else' includes the girl's parent or carer.

5.94 *Re E (Children) (FGM Protection Orders)* concerned one of the first successful applications for an FGMPO. The applicant was the mother of three daughters, ranging between the ages of six and twelve. She was divorced from the father, and alleged that there was a strong risk that he would force the children

118 *Multi-agency statutory guidance on female genital mutilation* (HM Government, April 2016).
119 Ibid, 3.
120 FGMA 2003, Sch 2, Part 1, para 2(1)–(2).
121 [2015] EWHC 2275 (Fam).

to undergo FGM, as he had allegedly done so to the mother. At that time, the Secretary of State had not identified who fell into the category of 'relevant third party' and as such, the mother had to seek leave from the court to make an application for an FGMPO.

5.95 Leave was given at a previous ex parte hearing, but Holman J felt that it was appropriate to further consider her 'status and capacity' at the first 'in-court hearing'[122]. In deciding whether to grant leave, the court considered all the circumstances of the case, as it is required to do pursuant to the FGMA 2003, Sch 2, Part 1, para 2(4), including the applicant's connection with the girl to be protected, and the applicant's knowledge of the circumstances of the girl.

5.96 Unsurprisingly, the court did not hesitate to grant the mother leave to make the application. As Holman J noted, the connection between the applicant and the girls concerned 'could not be a closer one', as she was their parent and primary carer. When seeking an FGMPO on behalf of a client, legal practitioners must ascertain whether leave is required. However, it is worthwhile noting that there has not been a reported case since the introduction of FGMPOs where leave has not been granted, and, indeed, it is hard to imagine a situation where leave would be refused, save where the allegations are ostensibly spurious.

Expert evidence

5.97 As per proceedings in respect of forced marriage or honour-based violence, the court will probably need expert evidence when considering allegations of FGM, whether actual or threatened. This is particularly apposite where FGM has allegedly taken place, as an expert will be needed to ascertain whether there is evidence of FGM and if so, what type under the WHO classifications.

5.98 *Re B and G (Children) (No 2)*[123] highlights the integral role that an expert will play in cases of alleged FGM and the need for that expert to be suitably qualified. *Re B and G (Children) (No 2)* was the first case in which FGM was raised in the context of care proceedings. It concerned two children, B (aged 4) and G (aged 3), whose parents were African Muslims, though the mother was born and brought up in a Scandinavian country. The mother abandoned G in the street and both children were taken into foster care, where they remained at the time of the proceedings. Concerns that G may have been subjected to FGM were raised once the children were in care. In the first instance, blood was found in her nappy when she was at nursery, though the two doctors who examined her stated that there was no sign of damage to her female organs nor any sign of FGM[124]. A year later, the children's foster carer also queried whether G had been subjected to FGM based on her 'irregular genitalia'.

122 [2015] EWHC 2275 (Fam) at [17].
123 [2015] EWFC 3.
124 [2015] EWFC 3 at [13].

5.99 As part of the proceedings, three experts undertook medical investigations into whether G had undergone FGM: Dr Share, a community paediatrician; Dr Momoh MBE, a registered midwife; and Professor Creighton, a consultant obstetrician and gynaecologist. Dr Share and Dr Momoh, who had undertaken physical investigations of G, concluded that she had been a victim of FGM. Professor Creighton, who viewed the video-colposcope recordings of Dr Share's examinations and had access to Dr Share's and Dr Momoh's notes, did not find any evidence of FGM.

5.100 Overall, Munby P preferred the evidence of Professor Creighton and found that it was impossible to reply on Dr Share's or Dr Momoh's evidence that G had been subjected to FGM. He noted that neither Dr Share nor Dr Momoh were able to give a 'clear, accurate or consistent account' of what they observed when examining G[125] and raised particular concerns about Dr Momoh's lack of experience and expertise in examining children who had allegedly undergone FGM.

5.101 Given the difficulties with the experts in the case and guided by the comments of Professor Creighton, Munby P took the opportunity in his judgment to set out some guidance in respect of the appointment and practice of experts in FGM proceedings:

(a) there is a dearth of medical experts in this area, particularly in relation to FGM in young children, and specific training and education is highly desirable;

(b) knowledge and understanding of the classification and categorisation of the various types of FGM is vital. The WHO classification is the one widely used and should be used for forensic purposes (this was reconfirmed in *Re CE (Female Genital Mutilation and Permission to Remove)*[126]);

(c) careful planning of the process of examination is required to ensure that an expert with the appropriate level of relevant expertise is instructed at the earliest opportunity (in particular, he referenced the FGM clinics mentioned by Professor Creighton);

(d) when conducting the examination, the colposcope should be used wherever possible;

(e) it is vital that clear and detailed notes are made during any examination, recording (with the use of appropriate drawings or diagrams) exactly what is observed. If an opinion is expressed in relation to FGM, it is vital that: (a) the opinion is expressed by reference to the specific type of FGM that has been diagnosed, which must be identified clearly and precisely; and (b) that the diagnosis is explained, clearly and precisely, by reference to what is recorded as having been observed.

5.102 Whilst an expert may be appointed to determine whether a girl has undergone FGM, the respondent to allegations of threatened FGM may also wish

125 [2015] EWFC 3 at [48].
126 [2016] EWHC 1052 (Fam).

to rely on expert medical evidence to prove that he and/or his family do not support the practice, for example, by adducing a medical report that concludes that the respondent and/or the female members of his family have not undergone FGM. Though it is not specifically suggested in the case law, legal practitioners who seek expert evidence to support respondents against allegations of FGM should consider following the same guidance for experts as set out by Munby P in *Re B and G (Children) (No 2)*.

5.103 The need for good quality evidence to refute allegations of FGM may be seen in the recent case of *Re X (A Child) (Female Genital Mutilation Protection Order) (Restrictions on Travel)*[127]. In that case, the local authority sought an FGMPO in respect of a 14-month old child, with a ban on travelling to Egypt, following the mother's disclosure to the child's health visitor that she planned to travel to Egypt and was concerned that the child would be subject to FGM from the paternal family. Both the mother and the father opposed the FGMPO.

5.104 As part of the father's case, the paternal grandfather produced an unnotarised, undated letter that purported to be from a doctor who undertook examinations of the paternal aunts and concluded that they had not undergone FGM. The letter consisted of one sentence:

> 'We confirm that the following medical tests on the following people [there follows two names] under the supervision of Dr A, attending doctor in the family clinic of S medical centre, we confirm that there was no female genital mutilation performed on the above-named person [sic] as proven by the medical test'.

5.105 Unsurprisingly, Russell J found the letter to be 'wholly unsatisfactory' and refused to accept it as proof that FGM had not taken place[128]. In her judgment, she set out what information she would have expected to see alongside a more detailed letter of examination, including:

— a CV of the person(s) who carried out the test;

— their qualifications or expertise;

— the nature of the examination;

— the results of the individual examinations; and

— the methodology or the findings on examination.

Though it is not intended as official guidance, family law practitioners should keep this list in mind when seeking expert medical evidence to counter allegations of FGM, as well as the guidance set out by Munby P in *Re B and G (Children) (No 2)*.

5.106 As in cases of forced marriage and HBV, the court will probably need evidence to understand the law, practice, and likelihood of FGM in certain

127 [2017] EWHC 2898 (Fam).
128 [2017] EWHC 2898 (Fam) at [47].

cultural/regional contexts. The court may therefore direct that an appropriate expert provide a generic report on FGM, which will provide a framework in which the allegations of FGM may be assessed. For example, in *Re Z (A Child) (FGMPO: Prevalence of FGM)*[129], the court heard evidence from Dr Schroven, a social anthropologist at the Max Planck Institute of Social Anthropology in Germany, on the practice and prevalence of FGM in Guinea and sub-Saharan West Africa[130]. Similarly, in *Re X (A Child) (Female Genital Mutilation Protection Order) (Restrictions on Travel)*, which is referred to above, the court directed two expert reports from an expert in Egyptian law who was also a consultant on human rights and the civil and criminal law on FGM in Egypt[131].

5.107 As the above demonstrates, family law practitioners dealing with allegations of actual or threatened FGM should give particular consideration as to whether an expert – or experts – are needed in order for the court to make findings of FGM and/or welfare decisions for the child being protected. However, it is perhaps otiose to note that an expert will only be appointed if a party makes an application in accordance with the FPR 2010, Part 25, with the requisite supporting information, and can show that the expert's evidence is necessary in order to assist the court in resolving the proceedings justly.

Threshold and proportionality

5.108 Where there are allegations of FGM in respect of a child, the relevant local authority may choose to apply for public law orders in addition to any remedy under the FGMA 2003. Pursuant to *Re B and G (Children) (No 2)*, the family court has confirmed that FGM – or the risk thereof – falls within the scope of significant harm for the purposes of the CA 1989, s 31. Whilst it might be surprising to some that the categorisation of FGM as significant harm was ever in doubt, this idea was fully scrutinised and ultimately accepted in *Re B and G (Children) (No 2)*. For further discussion on threshold in respect of FGM, see paras 2.26–2.27.

5.109 Having established that the threshold has been met, the court must turn its mind to welfare and proportionality when considering whether making orders under the CA 1989, s 31. As Munby P observed in *Re B and G (Children) (No 2)*, 'arriving at an overall welfare evaluation and identifying the appropriately proportionate outcome is likely to be especially difficult in many FGM cases'[132]. He identified two particular problems:

(a) the risk of further harm; and

(b) the gendered nature of FGM.

In respect of the former, he accepted that once a girl had been subjected to FGM, there was little chance that she would be subjected to it again (though her sisters,

129 [2017] EWHC 3566 (Fam).
130 [2017] EWHC 3566 (Fam) at [48].
131 [2017] EWHC 2898 (Fam) at [27].
132 [2015] EWFC 3 at [75].

if any, might be at risk). Given that the future risk of harm is arguably absent, the court queried how proven FGM was to be considered in any overall welfare evaluation.

5.110 Similarly, the gendered nature of FGM means that where it is the only threshold matter, there will be no statutory basis for care proceedings in respect of any male siblings. Munby P raised the example of a situation where the incident of FGM was so severe that were the girl an only child, the outcome would be adoption. However, if she had a male sibling who was not the subject of proceedings, what would be the best outcome in terms of her welfare: severing the sibling tie? Remaining in the family unit? The court did not provide any answers to the aforementioned welfare considerations; however, Munby P pointed out that local authorities and judges should not be too quick to come to the conclusion that proven FGM should lead to adoption[133].

5.111 Though FGM is now officially accepted as 'significant harm' for the purposes of making orders under the CA 1989, s 31, family law practitioners will need to consider the issues raised by the President when arguing about the best interests of – and long-term plans for – the girl who is at risk or has been subjected to FGM, as well as any relevant siblings.

CONCLUSION

5.112 As this chapter has demonstrated, a number of criminal and civil remedies have been created and amended in recent years to protect persons at risk of forced marriage or FGM. In doing so, the government has sent out a clear message that forced marriage and FGM, as well as HBV, function as forms of abuse and will not be tolerated.

5.113 However, the remedies discussed in this chapter are not exhaustive. Family practitioners should note that the making of an FMPO or an FGMPO does not prevent victims or potential victims from seeking other protective measures from the courts in addition to the said orders. Depending on the specifics of the case, where allegations of forced marriage, HBV, and/or FGM are raised, assistance may also be afforded by:

- orders under the inherent jurisdiction or wardship of the High Court;
- orders under the criminal courts, including the relatively new offence of controlling or coercive behaviour;
- civil remedies under the Protection from Harassment Act 1997;
- injunctive orders under the Family Law Act 1996, Part IV;
- orders under the CA 1989 (both private and public law orders); and/or
- claims in tort.

133 [2015] EWFC 3 at [77].

Chapter 6

CHILD TRAFFICKING

INTRODUCTION

6.1 Child trafficking is a growing global crime, with children trafficked into, out of, and within the UK. Approximately 1.2 million children are trafficked globally each year[1], and the UK government estimates that there are close to 3,000 child victims of trafficking and modern slavery in this jurisdiction alone[2].

6.2 As the definition of 'trafficking' (set out at para 6.6 ff) indicates, child trafficking can take many forms. Children may be trafficked for sexual exploitation, forced labour, domestic servitude, criminal enterprise (such cannabis cultivation, drug trafficking, pickpocketing, begging, and benefit fraud), and inter-country adoption, to name a few.

6.3 There are a number of both domestic and international statutory instruments designed to protect victims of child trafficking. However, in light of the staggering statistics of child trafficking in the UK, it is concerning how rarely trafficked children are identified as such in care proceedings. In his lecture entitled 'The Rights and Representation of Trafficked Children in Care Proceedings'[3], Mark Twomey QC identified four reasons why trafficking is rarely a feature of the Children Act 1989 (CA 1989), s 31 proceedings, namely:

(a) professionals miss the signs of trafficking;

(b) trafficking may be recognised, but the special obligations owed to trafficked children are not known;

(c) trafficked children often go missing within a short time of being found (estimates suggest that up 60 per cent of children who have potentially been trafficked go missing from local authority care in the UK, usually

1 'Every Child Counts: New Global Estimates on Child Labour' (International Labour Office, 2002), available at www.ilo.org/ipecinfo/product/download.do?type=document&id=742.

2 *Modern Slavery Strategy* (Home Office, 2014), available at www.gov.uk/government/uploads/system/uploads/attachment_data/file/383764/Modern_Slavery_Strategy_FINAL_DEC2015.pdf.

3 M Twomey and H Stott, 'The Rights and Representation of Trafficked children in care proceedings' (Coram Chambers, 23 February 2016).

within 48 hours of being placed in care and before being formally recognised as victims)[4]; and

(d) local authorities are not issuing care proceedings in respect of trafficked children and prefer to place the children in s 20 accommodation.

6.4 In respect of professionals missing the signs of trafficking, this is compounded by the fact that victims of child trafficking do not often identify themselves as such. Victims have often been coached into adopting false identities and personal details. They may be unaware of their rights, reticent to confide in professionals about their experiences, and/or unsure of who to trust. Moreover, the identity documents of trafficked persons, if they exist at all, are likely to be false.

6.5 Section 17 of the CA 1989 places a general duty on every local authority to safeguard and promote the welfare of children in need within their area by providing services appropriate to those children's needs. Trafficked children face their own unique challenges, and have special vulnerabilities and concomitant needs. It is therefore incumbent on all legal and social work practitioners to become familiar with the obligations owed to trafficked children and how these should manifest in public law proceedings.

DEFINITION OF TRAFFICKING

6.6 The definition of 'human trafficking' is set out in the Council of Europe Convention on Action Against Trafficking in Human Beings (ECAT)[5], Art 4, which entered into force in respect of the UK on 1 April 2009. Article 4 provides the following definitions, for the purposes of ECAT:

'(a) "trafficking in human beings" shall mean the recruitment, transportation, transfer, harbouring or receipt of persons, by means of the threat or use of force or other forms of coercion, of abduction, of fraud, of deception, of the abuse of power or of a position of vulnerability or of the giving or receiving of payments or benefits to achieve the consent of a person having control over another person, for the purpose of exploitation. Exploitation shall include, at a minimum, the exploitation of the prostitution of others or other forms of sexual exploitation, forced labour or services, slavery or practices similar to slavery, servitude or the removal of organs;

(b) the consent of a victim of "trafficking in human beings" to the intended exploitation set forth in subparagraph (a) of this article shall be irrelevant where any of the means set forth in subparagraph (a) have been used;

4 Group of Experts on Action against Trafficking in Human Beings, 'Report concerning the implementation of the Council of Europe Convention on Action against Trafficking in Human Beings by the United Kingdom: Second Evaluation Round', available at www.coe.int/en/web/anti-human-trafficking/-/uk-urged-to-improve-protection-ofchild-victims-of-human-trafficking.

5 Warsaw, 16.V.2005.

(c) the recruitment, transportation, transfer, harbouring or receipt of a child for the purpose of exploitation shall be considered "trafficking in human beings" even if this does not involve any of the means set forth in subparagraph (a) of this article;

(d) "child" shall mean any person under eighteen years of age;

(e) "victim" shall mean any natural person who is subject to trafficking in human beings as defined in this article'.

6.7 As ECAT, Art 4 makes clear, the definition of 'child trafficking' requires two inter-related parts: there must be movement – 'recruitment, transportation, transfer, harbouring or receipt' – of the trafficked person, whether within or across national borders; and it must be for the purposes of 'exploitation'. Some primary forms of exploitation are identified, but the list is not exhaustive.

6.8 Unlike the trafficking of adults, the consent of persons under 18 years of age is irrelevant regardless of whether any of the 'means' set out in ECAT, Art 4(a) – 'by means of the threat or use of force or other forms of coercion, of abduction, of fraud, of deception, of the abuse of power or of a position of vulnerability or of the giving or receiving of payments or benefits to achieve the consent of a person having control over another person' – are utilised. A child is considered incapable of having the legal capacity to give consent in these circumstances.

RELEVANT STATUTES

6.9 The UK has adopted a number of national and international frameworks on the issue of human trafficking, which set out the legal obligations on the UK concerning the protection of victims, the prosecution of offenders, and the prevention of abuse. The key statutes are as identified below.

ECAT

6.10 ECAT was signed by the UK on 23 March 2007 and came into force on 1 April 2009. As set out in Art 1, the purposes of ECAT are:

(a) to prevent and combat trafficking in human beings, while guaranteeing gender equality;

(b) to protect the human rights of the victims of trafficking, design a comprehensive framework for the protection and assistance of victims and witnesses, while guaranteeing gender equality, as well as to ensure effective investigation and prosecution; and

(c) to promote international cooperation on action against trafficking in human beings.

6.11 In order to meet its obligations under ECAT, the UK government has developed an 'action plan' against human trafficking, which has been set out most recently in *Human Trafficking: the Government's Strategy*[6]. Further, the government established the National Referral Mechanism (NRM), a procedure for identifying victims of trafficking and providing support, including medical support, education, accommodation, translation services, and therapeutic interventions.

6.12 Practitioners should take note that local authorities are regarded as 'first responders' in respect of the NRM. This means that they are one of a select group of professional organisations that can refer individuals (including children) to the NRM. As this is a form of public function, any local authority (or other 'first responder') that refuses to refer an individual to the NRM could be challenged by judicial review in the High Court[7]. It is also important to note that the 'first responder' does not require the consent of the trafficked individual to make a referral to the NRM where that person is a child.

Directive 2011/36/EU

6.13 Directive 2011/36/EU of the European Parliament and of the Council of 5 April 2011 on preventing and combating trafficking in human beings and protecting its victims (the Directive) is a comprehensive piece of legislation that deals with preventing and combating trafficking in human beings and protecting its victims. As a matter European law, certain provisions of directives can have direct effect in domestic law if they are clear, precise, and unconditional, and if the deadline for implementation has passed. Provisions of directives must be incorporated into domestic law regardless, but if they have not, or have not been incorporated properly, persons may rely directly on those effective provisions before domestic courts. Additionally, individuals can bring actions for damages against the government for failing to implement the provisions of a directive that have direct effect.

6.14 The UK initially opted out of the Directive on the basis of its view that it already complies with many of the provisions contained in the draft EU Directive. However, it later applied to opt-in to the Directive, and its application was accepted by the European Commission. The Directive entered into force for the UK on 18 October 2011.

United Nations Convention on the Rights of the Child

6.15 The United Nations Convention on the Rights of the Child (UNCRC) was adopted and opened for signature, ratification, and accession by General Assembly resolution 44/25 of 20 November 1989 and entered into force 2 September 1990. Although the UK has not directly incorporated the UNCRC into domestic law, the principles guide domestic law and practice, and are often referred to by the courts when interpreting obligations imposed by human rights

6 (July 2011). See also the *Modern Slavery Strategy* (HM Government, 2014).
7 Twomey and Stott, supra note 3.

and other legislation[8]. Of particular relevance to victims of child trafficking are the following:

(a) Art 19:

(i) States Parties shall take all appropriate legislative, administrative, social and educational measures to protect the child from all forms of physical or mental violence, injury or abuse, neglect or negligent treatment, maltreatment or exploitation, including sexual abuse, while in the care of parent(s), legal guardian(s) or any other person who has the care of the child.

(ii) Such protective measures should, as appropriate, include effective procedures for the establishment of social programmes to provide necessary support for the child and for those who have the care of the child, as well as for other forms of prevention and for identification, reporting, referral, investigation, treatment and follow-up of instances of child maltreatment described heretofore, and, as appropriate, for judicial involvement.

(b) Art 32:

(i) States Parties recognize the right of the child to be protected from economic exploitation and from performing any work that is likely to be hazardous or to interfere with the child's education, or to be harmful to the child's health or physical, mental, spiritual, moral or social development.

(ii) States Parties shall take legislative, administrative, social and educational measures to ensure the implementation of the present article. To this end, and having regard to the relevant provisions of other international instruments, States Parties shall in particular:

(iii) Provide for a minimum age or minimum ages for admission to employment;

(iv) Provide for appropriate regulation of the hours and conditions of employment;

(v) Provide for appropriate penalties or other sanctions to ensure the effective enforcement of the present article.

(c) Art 34:

(i) States Parties undertake to protect the child from all forms of sexual exploitation and sexual abuse. For these purposes, States Parties shall in particular take all appropriate national, bilateral and multilateral measures to prevent:

(1) the inducement or coercion of a child to engage in any unlawful sexual activity;

---

8 *The UK's compliance with the UN Convention on the Rights of the Child Eighth Report of Session 2014–15* (House of Lords, House of Commons Joint Committee on Human Rights, 2015), available at www.publications.parliament.uk/pa/jt201415/jtselect/jtrights/144/144.pdf.

(2) the exploitative use of children in prostitution or other unlawful sexual practices;

(3) the exploitative use of children in pornographic performances and materials.

(d) Art 36:

(i) States Parties shall protect the child against all other forms of exploitation prejudicial to any aspects of the child's welfare.

(e) Art 39:

(i) States Parties shall take all appropriate measures to promote physical and psychological recovery and social reintegration of a child victim of: any form of neglect, exploitation, or abuse; torture or any other form of cruel, inhuman or degrading treatment or punishment; or armed conflicts. Such recovery and reintegration shall take place in an environment which fosters the health, self-respect and dignity of the child.

European Convention on Human Rights

6.16 The European Convention on Human Rights (ECHR) was ratified in the UK by the Human Rights Act 1998. Article 4 of the ECHR prohibits slavery and forced labour. In *Rantsev v Cyprus and Russia*[9], the European Court of Human Rights held that Art 4 of the ECHR includes the definition of human trafficking set out in Art 4 of ECAT.

Sexual Offences Act 2003

6.17 The Sexual Offences Act 2003, ss 57, 58, and 59 create offences for human trafficking into, within, and out of the UK respectively for the purposes of sexual exploitation.

Modern Slavery Act 2015

6.18 The Modern Slavery Act 2015 (MSA 2015), which came into law on 26 March 2015, criminalises slavery, servitude and forced or compulsory labour, and human trafficking. Of particular relevance to practitioners is that s 52 creates a statutory duty on local authorities to notify the Secretary of State, through the NRM, where there are reasonable grounds to believe that an individual (child or adult) may be a victim of modern slavery or human trafficking.

6.19 It should be noted that the definition of human trafficking set out in the MSA 2015, s 2 is different than that in ECAT; however, it similarly involves movement ('travel') and exploitation.

9 Application No 25965/04 (2010) 51 EHRR 1.

LOCAL AUTHORITY OBLIGATIONS TO TRAFFICKED CHILDREN: GENERAL

6.20 What relevance do the aforementioned instruments on human trafficking have in respect of child protection practices and proceedings? As indicated above, local authorities – along with other professional bodies such as the police – have a statutory duty to refer any potential victim of human trafficking, including children, to the NRM. In 2011, the Department for Education published practice guidance, 'Safeguarding children who may have been trafficked'[10], which provides detailed advice on steps that the local authorities should take in partnership with other agencies to identify and protect child victims of modern slavery, including trafficking, before they become looked after children.

6.21 However, the local authority's obligations to trafficked children extend beyond the identification and referral processes. Local authorities in England and Wales have obligations pursuant to the CA 1989 to safeguard and promote the welfare of children in need in their area, which clearly includes safeguarding and protecting victims of trafficking. In recognition of the particular needs and vulnerabilities of trafficked children, the Department for Education has set out statutory guidance for local authorities in 'Care of Unaccompanied migrant children and victims of modern slavery: Statutory guidance for local authorities' (the DoE Guidance)[11]. Published in November 2017, the DoE Guidance advises on the steps that local authorities should take for the provision of support for looked after children (and care leavers) who are unaccompanied migrant children, unaccompanied asylum-seeking children, or victims of modern slavery, including trafficking.

6.22 The DoE Guidance was issued under the Local Authority Social Services Act 1970, s 7, which requires local authorities to act under the general guidance of the Secretary of State when exercising their social services' duties. As such, the local authorities *must* comply with this DoE Guidance when carrying out their functions, unless there are exceptional circumstances that justify a departure from the guidance[12]. The DoE Guidance details the following local authority responsibilities to trafficked children, some of which are responsibilities to children in care generally and should already be familiar to those working in the field of child protection:

(a) there is a general duty under the CA 1989, s 17 on every local authority to safeguard and promote the children in need within their area by providing services appropriate to those children's needs;

(b) an unaccompanied child, including a trafficked child, will become looked after by the local authority after having been accommodated by the local

10 *Safeguarding children who may have been trafficked* (Department for Education, 2011).

11 'Care of unaccompanied migrant children and victims of modern slavery: Statutory guidance for local authorities' (Department for Education, November 2017).

12 Ibid at 6.

authority under the CA 1989, s 20(1) for 24 hours and are therefore entitled to the same local authority provision as any other looked after child;

(c) assessment and care provisions should commence immediately for any looked after child, including a trafficked child, regardless of whether any immigration claim has been submitted to the Home Office;

(d) the Care Planning, Placement and Case Review (England) Regulations 2010[13], which set out the duties of local authorities with regards to providing for looked after children and care leavers, were amended in 2014 to require that those duties are fulfilled with particular regard to the child's circumstances and needs as an unaccompanied or trafficked child. The Regulations apply to all children, regardless of status, nationality, or documentation;

(e) local authorities must ensure that they have processes in place to monitor their policies and performance in respect of trafficked children;

(f) local authorities should include trafficking concerns on a child's care plan;

(g) there must be a cohesive multi-agency approach to protecting children from trafficking, and the local authority and the police must have a clear understanding of their respective roles in planning for and protecting victims;

(h) the local authority must be aware that trafficked children may require specialist support, including access from a legal representative to assist in any claims for protection (eg asylum); and

(i) those involved in the care of trafficked children should receive appropriate training to recognise and understand the particular issues faced by said children, including recognising the indicators of trafficking, and how to make referrals to the NRM.

The above list is not exhaustive and reference should be made to the DoE Guidance in respect of each individual child/case.

LOCAL AUTHORITY OBLIGATIONS TO TRAFFICKED CHILDREN: PUBLIC LAW PROCEEDINGS

6.23 Both social workers and legal practitioners must be aware of the duties and obligations owed to trafficked children to ensure not only that their needs are being met generally, but also that the applicable legal processes are followed and the correct remedies are sought for any given child. To that end, we have identified a number of key local authority obligations under the DoE Guidance that have particular relevance for public law proceedings, which are described below.

13 SI 2010/959.

Placement

6.24 Though all children in care are entitled to an appropriate placement when accommodated by the local authority[14], trafficked children have specific protection needs in respect of placement. Placement decisions must take particular care in identifying placements that protect the child from any risk of being exploited and from a heightened risk of the trafficked child going missing from care.

6.25 In order to ensure that a placement is safe for a trafficked child, the DoE Guidance stipulates that any placement must be fully risk-assessed, to include consideration of the risks of the child going missing and/or being located by her traffickers[15]. Given the risk of a trafficked child going missing within 48 hours of being taken into care, there must be sufficient supervision and monitoring in any emergency accommodation, and certain types of placements – such as bed and breakfast (B&Bs) and hostels – may not be appropriate. When making placement decisions, local authorities should contemplate whether transfer to another local authority or out of area placement is appropriate to separate the child from her traffickers[16].

6.26 Ideally, a trafficked child should be placed with carers who have an awareness of and training in the needs of trafficked children, even if said carers are not a cultural match to the child(ren) in question. The DoE Guidance highlights that carers should be able to identify possible indicators of mental health issues, which have arisen out of the child's experience of trafficking and exploitation (for example, post-traumatic stress disorder)[17]. Moreover, carers of trafficked children – whether residential home staff, foster carers, or support workers of semi-independent living facilities – must be made aware of the risk of a child going missing and/or any risk from their previous exploiters, and the practical steps to take when a child goes missing[18].

6.27 It is the duty of the local authority to identify the appropriate placement for any child that it accommodates. However, both social work and legal practitioners will need to ensure that the specific needs of the trafficked child are being met in the proposed placement before asking the court to approve any local authority care plan.

Assessment and care planning

6.28 Under the Care Planning, Placement and Care Review (England) Regulations 2010, local authorities must undertake single assessments of any

14 CA 1989, s 22C.
15 'Care of unaccompanied migrant children and victims of modern slavery: Statutory guidance for local authorities' (Department for Education, November 2017), 67.
16 Ibid, 70.
17 Ibid, 76.
18 Ibid, 78.

relevant children as the first step in the care planning process. The local authority must then utilise the assessment to produce a care plan setting out how the relevant child's needs are to be met. The care plan must include, inter alia, a permanence plan, health plan, and educational plan. This is true for any child who is subject to child protection planning. However, in respect of trafficked children, the DoE Guidance prescribes that the child's status as 'trafficked' must be reflected in their care plan. This is to ensure that all of the persons involved in the child's care are aware of the child's specific circumstances and are therefore able to meet any needs arising from them.

6.29 The DoE Guidance is clear that any assessment should make reference to and take account of the child's needs as a trafficked child[19]. Thereafter, the child's care plan should set out how the child's needs in relation to being trafficked are to be met[20]. For example, the Care Planning, Placement and Care Review (England) Regulations 2010, reg 5 stipulates that prior to a child being placed (or by the first review where that is not reasonably practical), the local authority must undertake a health assessment of the child. The health assessment must establish whether the child has any particular physical, psychological, or emotional symptoms arising out of her experience of being trafficked, and should also screen for infectious diseases[21].

6.30 Thereafter, the child's care plan must include a health plan detailing how the local authority intends to meet the (trafficked) child's health needs as identified in the assessment(s). A review of the child's health plan, which includes further assessments, must be conducted at least once every six months for children under the age of five and once per year for children over the age of five[22].

6.31 Likewise, the Care Planning, Placement and Care Review (England) Regulations 2010, reg 5, specifies that the local authority care plan include a personal education plan (PEP) for the child, to ensure that appropriate educational provisions are put in place at the same time as placement. Yet, trafficked children may not have had consistent – or any – formal education. The DoE Guidance therefore suggests that for unaccompanied children, appropriate education may include a period of 'settling in' time during which their educational needs can be assessed more fully and integrated into their PEP[23].

6.32 A trafficked child may need specialist legal advice and support, whether in respect of immigration claims, criminal proceedings, and/or compensation claims. The care plan of a trafficked child must identify when specialist legal support is required and how it will be provided. The social worker must ensure that the child is accompanied to all meetings with legal professionals, though the social worker need not be the person accompanying the child[24].

---

19 Ibid, 44.
20 Ibid, 60.
21 Ibid, 51.
22 Ibid, 51.
23 Ibid, 53.
24 Ibid, 61.

6.33 It is important to note that as a trafficked child in care approaches the age of 18, her chance of going missing from care may increase due to her concerns about immigration status[25]. This risk should be identified in their care plan.

6.34 Whilst the assessments and care plans of the trafficked child fall under the purview of the local authority, legal practitioners in care proceedings should ensure that where a child is identified as 'trafficked', the aforementioned obligations are met in the child's care plan(s).

Alternate carers

6.35 As referenced above, a (trafficked) child's care plan should include a plan for permanence. This may involve the consideration of family reunification or any kinship carers, as well as proposals for contact with family members. Any investigations into family members must be handled sensitively and child protection must be paramount. Care must be taken to ensure that a child is not placed with or made available to family members who were involved in the child's initial trafficking, thus increasing the risk of him/her being re-trafficked and/or re-traumatised. Children should be consulted about family tracing, and their wishes and feelings are important.

6.36 Relatedly, social work professionals must make certain that those persons who identify themselves as relatives of the trafficked child are actually family members, and not traffickers posing as relatives to obtain access to the trafficked child.

Language

6.37 Depending on where she has been trafficked from, English might not be the trafficked child's first language. The child must have access to an interpreter in her involvement with social services, and local authorities should have clear policies on how an interpreter can be obtained for a child who requires one[26]. Interpreters who deal with trafficked children should have additional training to enable them to interpret particular issues that a trafficked child might face, and should be subject to appropriate checks to ensure that they are not linked to the child's traffickers. Care should also be given in the choice of an interpreter, including the interpreter's age, gender, nationality, and community affiliations.

6.38 It is equally important for a child to have an interpreter to enable him/her to participate fully in any CA 1989 proceedings. This may include the translation of documents, interpreting conversations with her guardian, and, in the case of older children, giving oral evidence. Where the trafficked child intends to attend court, provision should be made in every case management order for an interpreter to attend to assist him/her.

---

25 Ibid, 60.
26 Ibid, 46.

COMMON ISSUES IN RESPECT OF TRAFFICKED CHILDREN IN PUBLIC LAW PROCEEDINGS

6.39 There is limited reported case law in respect of trafficked children in public law proceedings. However, two recurring issues may be identified, namely age assessments and jurisdiction. Each of these is discussed in turn below.

Age and age assessments

6.40 As noted above, the identity documents of trafficked children – if they have them at all – are often counterfeit. This can cause difficulties in respect of ascertaining a trafficked child's age and determining whether she is a 'child' pursuant to the CA 1989, s 105(1). For example, older children who have been brought into the country and forced to work as sex workers or domestic labourers may present as older than their biological age. The local authority may undertake an age assessment where it maintains that the child is older than she claims and is not a 'child' for the purpose of the CA 1989. However, the DoE Guidance stipulates that age assessments should only be carried out where there is significant reason to doubt that the individual in question is a child and should not be a routine part of a local authority's assessment of trafficked children[27].

6.41 There is a large body of case law in respect of the processes of age assessment, the starting point of which is *R (on the application of B) v Merton London Borough Council*[28]. This case concerned an unaccompanied asylum-seeking individual from the Ivory Coast who claimed to be 17 years old but had no proof of birth or age to support his assertion. A social worker of the relevant local authority – the London Borough of Merton – undertook an interview by phone with the assistance of an interpreter and determined that the individual was over 18 years old and therefore the local authority did not have any obligations to him under the CA 1989. The asylum-seeker applied for judicial review of that decision and, in the absence of any statutory guidance, both the applicant and the respondent asked the court for guidance on the lawful assessment of age in disputes between the local authority and an unaccompanied asylum seeking child claiming to be under the age of 18 years old.

6.42 The following principles and guidance may be extrapolated from *R (on the application of B) v Merton London Borough Council*:

(a) age assessment is a matter which may be determined informally, provided safeguards of minimum standards of inquiry and of fairness are adhered to; judicialisation of the process is to be avoided[29];

(b) except in clear cases, the decision maker cannot determine age solely on the basis of the appearance of the applicant. The decision maker must

27 Ibid, 22.
28 [2003] EWHC 1689 (Admin).
29 [2003] EWHC 1689 (Admin) at [36].

seek to elicit the general background of the applicant, including his family circumstances and history, his educational background, and his activities during the previous few years. Ethnic and cultural information may also be important[30];

(c) if there is reason to doubt the applicant's statement as to his age, the decision maker will have to make an assessment of his credibility, and will have to ask questions designed to test the applicant's credibility[31];

(d) there is no onus of proof on the applicant [alleged child] to prove her age[32];

(e) there should be no predisposition, divorced from the information and evidence available to the local authority, to assume that an applicant is an adult, or conversely that he is a child[33];

(f) the local authority cannot simply adopt a decision made by the Home Office but must itself decide whether an applicant is a 'child' and 'in need'[34]);

(g) a local authority is obliged to give adequate reasons for its decision that an applicant claiming to be a child is not a child, and who is therefore refused support under the CA 1989[35]; however, the reasons do not need to be long or elaborate[36];

(h) where an interpreter is required in respect of interviews, it is greatly preferable for him or her to be present during the interview and to take a note, though said note does not need to be a verbatim transcript of the conversation[37].

In applying the above principles, the decision of the local authority in *R (on the application of B) v Merton London Borough Council* was found to be unlawful.

6.43 *R (on the application of B) v Merton London Borough Council* has become the standard for age assessment in the UK and age assessments are measured by whether they are 'Merton-compliant'. However, there have been further cases that have refined the guidance therein. A useful summary of the key principles can be found in *R (on the application of BM) v London Borough of Hackney*[38]. Whilst the judgment should be read in full by any legal or social work practitioner who is dealing with a contested age assessment, the principles and case law including and since *R (on the application of B) v Merton London Borough Council* can be found at para 44 and summarised as follows:

(a) the importance of a child's age being properly and lawfully determined was emphasised by the Court of Appeal in *R (on the application of AE) v London Borough of Croydon*[39];

---

30 Ibid at [37].
31 Ibid.
32 Ibid at [38].
33 Ibid.
34 Ibid at [39].
35 Ibid at [45].
36 Ibid at [48].
37 Ibid at [52].
38 [2016] EWHC 3338 (Admin).
39 [2012] EWCA Civ 547.

(b) in carrying out an age assessment, local authorities are primary fact finders;

(c) the decision-makers cannot determine age solely on the basis of the appearance of the applicant, except in clear cases[40];

(d) demeanour can also be notoriously unreliable[41]. It will generally need to be viewed together with other things[42];

(e) if the chronological information derived from the child's oral history is credible, believable and plausible, any observation about physical appearance or demeanour is unlikely to tip the balance against the claimed age[43];

(f) there should be no predisposition, divorced from the available information and evidence, to assume that an applicant is an adult or a child. Any decision must be based on the particular facts of the individual and therefore the decision-maker must seek to elicit the general background of the applicant, including his family circumstances and history, his educational background, and his activities during the previous few years. Ethnic and cultural information may also be important[44];

(g) the assessors must try to establish a rapport with the applicant, and questioning should be open-ended and child-friendly[45];

(h) there is no burden of proof imposed on the applicant to prove his age during the assessment[46];

(i) benefit of the doubt is always given to the child since it is recognised that age assessment is not a scientific process[47]. There should be no assumption that a child is lying;

(j) the child must have an appropriate adult present during the age assessment[48];

(k) the applicant should be given a fair and proper opportunity, at a stage when a possible adverse decision is only provisional, to deal with important points adverse to his case and provide an explanation[49];

(l) the decision must be based on firm grounds. Assessments devoid of details and/or reasons for the conclusion are not compliant with the *Merton* guidelines; the conclusions must be 'expressed with sufficient detail to

---

40 *R (on the application of B) v Merton London Borough Council* [2003] at [37], *R (on the application of NA) v London Borough of Croydon* [2009] EWHC 2357 (Admin) at [27], *R (R) v London Borough of Croydon* [2011] EWHC 1473 (Admin) at [15].

41 *R (on the application of NA) v London Borough of Croydon* [2009] EWHC 939 (Admin) at [28].

42 *A and WK v London Borough of Croydon* [2009] EWHC 939 (Admin) at [56].

43 *R (on the application of AM) v London Borough of Croydon* [2011] EWHC 3308 (Admin) at [44].

44 *R (on the application of B) v Merton London Borough Council* [2003] at [37]–[38].

45 *A and WK v London Borough of Croydon* [2009] EWHC 939 (Admin) at [13].

46 *R(B) v Merton London Borough Council* [2003] at [38], confirming in *R (on the application of CJ) v Cardiff City Council* [2011] EWCA Civ 1590 at [21].

47 *A and WK v London Borough of Croydon* [2009] EWHC 939 (Admin) at [40].

48 *FZ v Croydon* [2011] EWCA Civ 59 at [23]–[25]; *R (on the application of GE) v Secretary of State for the Home Department* [2015] EWHC 1406 (Admin) at [22].

49 *FZ v Croydon* [2011] EWCA Civ 59 at [21]; *R (on the application of NA) v London Borough of Croydon* [2009] EWHC 2357 (Admin).

explain all the main adverse points which the fuller document showed had influenced the decision'[50].

6.44 It is worthwhile noting that in October 2015, the Association of Directors of Children's Services published good practice guidance – *Age Assessment Guidance: Guidance to assist social workers and their managers in undertaking age assessments in England* – aimed at assisting frontline social workers in conducting age assessments of unaccompanied children seeking asylum in the UK, which is also relevant to trafficked children.

6.45 Practitioners should also be aware of the MSA 2015, s 51, concerning the 'presumption about age' and the local authority's duties to a 'presumed child':

> '(1) This section applies where—
>
> (a) a public authority with functions under relevant arrangements has reasonable grounds to believe that a person may be a victim of human trafficking, and
>
> (b) the authority is not certain of the person's age but has reasonable grounds to believe that the person may be under 18.
>
> (2) Until an assessment of the person's age is carried out by a local authority or the person's age is otherwise determined, the public authority must assume for the purposes of its functions under relevant arrangements that the person is under 18.
>
> (3) 'Relevant arrangements' means arrangements for providing assistance and support to persons who are, or who there are reasonable grounds to believe may be, victims of human trafficking, as set out in—
>
> (a) guidance issued under section 49(1)(b);
>
> (b) any regulations made under section 50(1).
>
> (4) "Local authority" has the same meaning as in the Children Act 1989 (see section 105 of that Act)'.

JURISDICTION

6.46 Where public law proceedings concern a trafficked child who has crossed international borders, the court will need to deal with the question of whether it has jurisdiction to make orders. The court's approach to this will depend on whether or not the child originates from a Brussels territory (ie a state that is bound by Council Regulation (EC) No 2201/2003 (BIIa)).

50 *FZ v Croydon* [2011] EWCA Civ 59 at [22]; *A and WK v London Borough of Croydon* [2009] EWHC 939 (Admin) at [12].

Trafficking within the EU

6.47 If the child has been trafficked from a BIIa territory, jurisdiction will be dependent on the child's habitual residence. Pursuant to BIIa, Art 8, the courts of an EU state shall have jurisdiction in matters of parental responsibility over a child habitually resident there at the time when the court is seised. There are exceptions to this rule: Art 12 confers jurisdiction on a state which has other links with the child but only where the parties have accepted its jurisdiction; Art 13 provides that, where a child's habitual residence cannot be established (which means where the child is not habitually resident in any EU state) and where Art 12 does not apply, jurisdiction vests in the courts of the state in which the child is present; and Art 14, entitled 'Residual jurisdiction' provides that, where no court of a member state has jurisdiction under the preceding articles, jurisdiction shall be determined by the laws of each state.

6.48 As highlighted in *Re A (Jurisdiction: Return of Child)*[51], the English courts have now adopted the 'habitual residence' test articulated by the Court of Justice of the European Union in *Mercredi v Chaffe*[52], namely that a child's 'habitual residence' is 'the place which reflects some degree of integration by the child in a social and family environment in the country concerned'[53]. Baroness Hale went on to say in *Re A (Jurisdiction: Return of Child)* that 'the social and family environment of an infant or young child is shared with those (whether parents or others) upon whom he is dependent. Hence it is necessary to assess the integration of that person or persons in the social and family environment of the country concerned'[54]. In respect of older children, Lord Wilson indicated in *Re LC (Children) (Reunite International Child Abduction Centre Intervening)*[55] that the child's state of mind might be relevant in determining whether the child shares the habitual residence of the parents.

6.49 Under this test, defining the habitual residence of a trafficked child raises obvious complications. For example, a child sold into sex slavery or an indentured labourer may be kept out of sight and have no opportunity to integrate into a social or family environment, even if the child has been resident in the state for a number of years. Likewise, it may be difficult to ascertain the child's 'state of mind', as she may have been physically or emotionally pressurised by her traffickers.

6.50 Where the trafficked child is not regarded as habitually resident in the state in which she lives, she will likely be habitually resident in her country of origin[56] and as such, that country will be seised of jurisdiction. However, as Mark Twomy QC points out, there is a potential conflict between the obligation to cede primary jurisdiction to the state of origin and ECAT, Art 16(7), which asserts that

---

51 [2013] UKSC 60.

52 C-497/10 PPU, [2011] 1 FLR 1293 at [56].

53 [2013] UKSC 60 at [54].

54 Ibid.

55 [2014] UKSC 1, [2014] AC 1038 at [37].

56 According to Lord Wilson in *B (A Child)* [2016] UKSC 4 at [45], having no habitual residence is 'conceivable' but 'highly unlikely ...'.

'child victims shall not be returned to a State, if there is indication, following a risk and security assessment, that such return would not be in the best interests of the child'[57]. Recent case law indicates that the risk assessment should look at, inter alia, the risk of the child being 're-trafficked' if returned to her state of origin[58].

Re S (Care: Jurisdiction)

6.51 There are two reported cases that deal with the question of the habitual residence of trafficked children between EU States. *Re S (Care: Jurisdiction)*[59] concerned a Roma child ('S') who had been brought from Eastern Romania to the United Kingdom by her father as part of a child trafficking operation. The child, who was one of 13 found in a property in Slough during a police raid, was forced to sell the Big Issue for up to 12 hours per day on the street. On 31 January 2008, the local authority made an application for a care order and was granted an interim care order for the child under BIIa, Art 20.

6.52 Whilst the interim care order was initially unopposed, it was later contested in July 2008 when the local authority sought its renewal. The child, supported by her parents, expressed the wish to return to Romania. At that time, her father had been arrested and charged with offences related to child trafficking, including of S, and with seeking to pervert the course of justice. He was later convicted of trafficking offences and pleaded guilty to perverting the course of justice. Singer J granted the extension to the interim care order, holding that the risks to S in Romania were too great to allow her return. The issue of jurisdiction was raised but was not pursued.

6.53 Shortly thereafter, also in July 2008, the mother, who was still in Romania, made an application under the Hague Convention on the Civil Aspects of International Child Abduction 1980 (the Hague Convention 1980) through the Central Authority. The hearing took place in November 2008. The court held that the Hague Convention 1980 did not apply for two reasons:

(a) the retention of S by the local authority was not in breach of the mother's rights of custody; and/or in the alternative;

(b) the retention was not wrongful.

The court also found that on 31 January 2008, when the local authority issued proceedings and the English court was seised of the matter, the child was habitually resident in Romania.

6.54 As the Hague Convention 1980 did not apply, the court in those proceedings did not need to turn its mind to Art 13(b) of that Convention[60].

---

57 Twomey and Stott, supra note 3.

58 *Rantsev v Cyprus and Russia* (App No 25965/04) (2010) 51 EHRR 1.

59 [2008] EWHC 3013 (Fam), [2009] 2 FLR 550.

60 The Hague Convention 1980, Art 13(b) states as follows: 'Notwithstanding the provisions of the preceding Article, the judicial or administrative authority of the requested State is not bound

However, the issue of jurisdiction and whether the local authority could seek a final care order in respect of S was subsequently raised in the care proceedings, and forms the basis of the judgment in *Re S (Care: Jurisdiction)*[61]. Charles J authorised the local authority to take interim measures, but held that under BIIa the child should be returned to Romania. The judge's reasoning may be summarised as follows:

(a) regardless of S's habitual residence, the courts and public authorities in Romania were better placed to assess the relevant risks to S and to provide and support the appropriate placements in the best interests of S[62];

(b) S was habitually resident in Romania and the possibility of a change in habitual residence arising out of acquiescence in the English court proceedings did not arise[63];

(c) BIIa, Arts 8, 17, and 20 govern jurisdiction in public law proceedings, and in the case of S, Arts 17 and 20 necessitated a return of S to Romania and the making of interim practical arrangements relating to this return[64];

(d) pursuant to BIIa, Arts 55, 8, 17, and 20, cooperation is required between the two central authorities where there are issues of jurisdiction[65]; and

(e) it would be unusual under BIIa, Art 20 for a court to embark on a fact-finding hearing, though it might be appropriate in respect of any incident that has taken place in the UK. Rather, the court should focus on:

    (i) identifying the range of possible issues and risks for decision by the foreign court; and

    (ii) putting in place appropriate interim measures to minimise harm arising from said risks until decisions are taken by the foreign court[66].

6.55 As is clear from above, the court did not re-examine the issue of habitual residence in the care proceedings, nor did it conduct a risk assessment of the child's return to Romania. Rather, it held that the interim measures under BIIa, Art 20 would be sufficient to safeguard the child whilst the courts and authorities in Romania made decisions about S's longer-term welfare.

London Borough of Barking & Dagenham v SS

6.56 The question of jurisdiction under BIIa in respect of a trafficked child also arose in the case of *London Borough of Barking & Dagenham v SS*[67], with a

---

to order the return of the child if the person, institution or other body which opposes its return establishes that – [...] *b)* there is a grave risk that his or her return would expose the child to physical or psychological harm or otherwise place the child in an intolerable situation'.

61 [2008] EWHC 3013 (Fam), [2009] 2 FLR 550.

62 At [41].

63 At [48], [57].

64 At [48]–[51].

65 At [51].

66 At [63], [67], [82].

67 [2014] EWHC 3338 (Fam), [2015] 2 FLR 181.

markedly different result. *London Borough of Barking & Dagenham v SS* concerned a Romanian child ('SS') who had been 'sold' by her mother in Spain to a Roma man when she was approximately 13 years old (in or around 2012). The man trafficked SS into the UK, via Paris, and subjected her to abuse, including sexual abuse and forcing her to engage in criminal activities. Whilst living with the Roma man, SS formed a relationship with another young man (aged approximately 18/19), whom she went to live with in London.

6.57 On 22 November 2013, SS was arrested for being involved in the stealing of mobile phones and was remanded to the care of the local authority by the Youth Court; however, SS absconded from her foster placement after only a few days. She evaded detection for a number of months but was subsequently apprehended by the Transport Police for alleged fare evasion in April 2014. At that time, care proceedings were initiated and the court utilised its powers under BIIa, Art 20 to make interim care and secure accommodation orders. SS was initially placed in secure accommodation, but later moved to a foster placement when the secure accommodation order expired in July 2014. She settled well with the foster carers and remained in the placement at the time of the hearing.

6.58 Whilst it was evident to the court that at the time that the hearing took place, SS was habitually resident in the UK, the question of her habitual residence at the time when the proceedings were issued, namely 29 April 2014, was problematic. As Cobb J noted, SS 'had not integrated into life here in the conventional or traditional sense in which a 15-year old child might be expected to ...'[68]. However, though her daily life had features which were 'precarious'[69], the court held that there were sufficient factors to establish a significant degree of integration, including the length of time that she had been in the jurisdiction; her work in a restaurant (albeit unlawfully); and her intimate relationship with the young man with whom she previously lived. SS was therefore found, on the balance of probabilities, to be habitually resident in the UK at the time that the court was seised, pursuant to BIIa, Art 8[70].

6.59 The court went on to state that even if SS was not habitually resident in the UK on that date, it was satisfied that she was not habitually resident in either Spain or Romania. As such, the court could find jurisdiction on the alternative basis pursuant to BIIa, Art 13 that SS was physically present in the UK on 29 April 2014[71]. Further, with reference to Article 15 of BIIA, the court held that whilst SS had ties to both Spain and Romania, the UK courts were best placed to determine her future[72].

6.60 As each case is fact-specific, it is important that practitioners are familiar with all of the case law in respect of trafficked children and jurisdiction. However, Cobb J's comments in *London Borough of Barking & Dagenham v SS* are perhaps

68 At [34].
69 At [36].
70 At [5], [36]–[37].
71 At [5], [38].
72 At [5], [44]–[45].

particularly pertinent when considering the relationship between the trafficked child and habitual residence:

> 'The fact that SS's life was in many respects unconventional, occasionally lawless and generally unstructured did not mean that she had not in her own way – and to a significant degree – integrated into that society in which she lived in England. That someone lives on the fringes of society [...] does not mean, in my judgment, that they are not members of that society. Nor does it therefore mean that they cannot acquire habitual residence in the country in which they have settled and made their home'[73].

Trafficking from outside the EU

6.61 Where the child has been trafficked into the UK from a non-EU country and remains habitually resident in that country, then according to *Re M (Children) (Suspected Trafficking – Competent Authority)*[74], there is no duty or power of the court to declare that it has no jurisdiction, as allowed for by BIIa, Art 17, and no duty to transfer the proceedings, as required by Art 15[75]. The court therefore has the right to make a care order on the basis of a child's presence in this jurisdiction, pursuant to the Family Law Act 1986, Part I[76].

6.62 Though not bound by the articles of BIIa where the child is found to be habitually resident in a non-Brussels country, the court must still consider whether the case should be transferred to the child's state of habitual residence under the principle of *forum conveniens*, ie which jurisdiction is the 'convenient forum' for the settlement of the matters at issue. In considering *forum conveniens*, important factors include the children's interests, which jurisdiction is better placed to investigate the contested issues, and the demands of international comity (respect for another jurisdiction's legal system[77].

6.63 A discussion of the aforementioned considerations may be seen in the recent 'trafficking' case of *Re M (Children) (Suspected Trafficking – Competent Authority)*[78], which concerned two children who were brought to the UK from Namibia for a two-week holiday by a woman claiming to be their grandmother. The grandmother maintained that the children's parents lived in Canada and that she held 'parental responsibility' for the children. The UK Border Control had reason to believe that the children might be the victims of human trafficking and a referral was made to the NRM.

6.64 Whilst the grandmother was detained and questioned, the children were placed in local authority foster care under interim care orders. However, the

73 At [37].
74 [2017] EWFC 56.
75 *Re M (Children) (Suspected Trafficking – Competent Authority)* [2017] EWFC 56 at [15].
76 Ibid.
77 See *H V H (Minors) (Forum Conveniens) (Nos 1 And 2)* [1993] 1 FLR 958.
78 [2017] EWFC 56.

court eventually held that the children were habitually resident in Namibia and should be returned there, as Namibia was best placed to undertake the relevant investigations into the children's living situation. Although the case concerned unaccompanied children, rather than trafficked children, it may also be of some relevance to legal practitioners when thinking about jurisdiction.

CONCLUSION

6.65 As indicated throughout this chapter, trafficked children have specific needs and vulnerabilities that legal and social worker professionals must be conscious of when considering child protection measures. Practitioners should be familiar with both the domestic and international instruments, as well as the relevant case law and guidance documents. These will have implications for all aspects of the child protection process, from care plans to public law orders, and knowledge of these measures will assist in securing the trafficked child's best interests and safeguarding her from risk.

Chapter 7

RADICALISATION

INTRODUCTION

7.1 Since 2014 the family court has witnessed a marked increase in the number of children cases where there are allegations or suspicions of 'radicalisation'. In its report 'Study of data held by Cafcass in cases featuring radicalisation concerns', Cafcass identified 54 cases concerning 128 children between January and December 2015 that featured some evidence, risk, or allegation of radicalisation[1]. Of those, 24 were categorised as public law cases, 15 as private law cases, and 15 as inherent jurisdiction cases.

7.2 Each case is decided on its own facts, and the courts have warned that a comparison between the facts and conclusions of one case with another case is of limited value[2]. However, radicalisation in the context of family law proceedings has generally fallen into three types:

(a) where children, with their parents or on their own, are at risk of travelling to ISIS (Islamic State)-held territories;

(b) where children have been or are at risk of being radicalised; and

(c) where children have been or are at risk of becoming involved in terrorist activities, whether domestically or abroad[3].

7.3 'Radicalisation' cases will often involve the collaboration of multiple agencies – from the police to Border Control – and it is vital that any legal practitioner undertaking this type of work understands the important role that the family courts play in safeguarding children that have been affected by 'radicalisation'.

---

1 'Study of data held by Cafcass in cases featuring radicalisation concerns' (Cafcass, July 2016) 1.

2 See *Re X (Children) and Y (Children) (Emergency Protection Orders)* [2015] EWHC 2265 (Fam), [2015] 2 FLR 1487.

3 'Radicalisation cases in the Family Courts', guidance issued by Sir James Munby President of the Family Division on 8 October 2015, available at www.judiciary.gov.uk/wp-content/uploads/2015/10/pfd-guidance-radicalisation-cases.pdf, para 1.

DEFINITION OF RADICALISATION

7.4 The government's definition of 'radicalisation', as set out in the *Prevent* Strategy[4], is 'the process by which a person comes to support terrorism and forms of extremism leading to terrorism'[5]. Section 1 of the Terrorism Act 2000 defines terrorism as

> 'the use or threat of action ... designed to influence the Government or to intimidate the public or a section of the public ... for the purpose of advancing a political, religious or ideological cause'.

The *Prevent* Strategy defines 'extremism' as 'the vocal or active opposition to our fundamental values, including democracy, the rule of law, individual liberty, and the mutual respect and tolerance of different faiths and beliefs'.

7.5 In respect of public law proceedings, the meaning of 'radicalisation' is not defined in statute. However, the definition that is most commonly adopted is that of Holman J in *Re M (Children)*[6], namely: 'negatively influencing [a child] with radical fundamentalist thought, which is associated with terrorism'.

PRESIDENT'S GUIDANCE

7.6 When faced with a case where there are potential issues of radicalisation, the starting point for any legal practitioner is 'Radicalisation cases in the Family Courts', the guidance issued by Munby P in October 2015. 'Radicalisation cases in the Family Courts' sets out the procedure that should be undertaken and the issues that the allocated judge should be live to when hearing cases where radicalisation is identified as a potential issue. Both of these will be discussed in turn.

Procedure

7.7 Where there are allegations or suspicions of radicalisation raised in a family law application or during the course of proceedings, the following procedure must be adhered to:

(a) the Designated Family Judge must be alerted immediately;

(b) he must notify the Family Division Liaison Judge, who should liaise with the President of the Family Division; and

(c) urgent steps must be taken, in consultation with the Family Division Liaison Judge, to allocate the case to a High Court Judge of the Family Division[7].

---

4 *Prevent* Strategy (TSO, June 2011).

5 *Roots of violent radicalisation* (Home Affairs Committee, 6 February 2012), available at publications.parliament.uk/pa/cm201012/cmselect/cmhaff/1446/144603.htm.

6 [2014] EWHC 667 (Fam) at [23].

7 'Radicalisation cases in the Family Courts', supra note 3, para 5.

7.8 'Radicalisation cases in the Family Courts' is clear that any case concerning radicalisation must be heard by High Court Judges of the Family Division, which does not include a judge or other person authorised to sit as a High Court Judge under the Senior Courts Act 1981, s 9. In 'exceptional' cases, a case may be heard by a Designated Family Judge, or a judge authorised to sit as a High Court Judge under the Senior Courts Act 1981, s 9, but only if this has previously been authorised in relation to that particular case by the President of the Family Division or the Family Division Liaison Judge[8].

7.9 It is important to note that a Designated Family Judge, or a judge authorised to sit as a High Court Judge under the Senior Courts Act 1981, s 9 will not normally be permitted to adjudicate a 'radicalisation' case where:

— there are issues of public interest immunity (PII);

— there is a need for a closed hearing or use of a special advocate; and

— electronic tagging is proposed[9].

'Live issues'

7.10 Where a judge is hearing a case and radicalisation is potentially a concern, 'Radicalisation cases in the Family Courts' highlights a number of issues that the judge must be live to. They are set out in paras 7 and 8 and can be summarised as follows:

(a) the need to protect the European Convention on Human Rights (ECHR), Art 6 (right to a fair trial) rights of all the parties (para 7);

(b) that much of the information gathered by the police and other agencies will not be relevant to the issues before the court, which is concerned solely with the relevant child(ren) (para 7);

(c) that some of the information gathered by the police and other agencies is highly sensitive such that its disclosure may damage the public interest or even put lives at risk (para 7);

(d) the need to avoid inappropriately wide or inadequately defined requests for disclosure of information or documents by the police or other agencies (para 7);

(e) the need to avoid seeking disclosure from the police or other agencies of information or material which may be subject to PII, or the disclosure of which might compromise on-going investigations, damage the public interest or put lives at risk, unless the judge is satisfied that such disclosure is 'necessary to enable the court to resolve the proceedings justly' (para 7);

(f) the need to safeguard the custody of, and potentially limit access to, sensitive materials provided to the court by the police or other agencies (para 7);

8 Ibid para 6.

9 Ibid.

(g) the need to consider any PII issues and whether there is a need for a closed hearing or use of a special advocate (para 7);

(h) the need to safeguard the custody of, and potentially limit access to, the tape or digital recordings of the proceedings or any transcripts (para 7);

(i) the need to ensure that the operational requirements of the police and other agencies are not inadvertently compromised or inhibited either because a child is a ward of court or because of any order made by the court (para 7);

(j) the assistance that may be gained if the police or other agencies are represented in court, including, in appropriate cases, by suitably expert counsel (para 7); and

(k) whether in any particular case there is a need to: (i) exclude the media; (ii) make a reporting restriction order; or (iii) make an 'anti-tipping-off' order (para 8).

7.11 Although 'Radicalisation cases in the Family Courts' dictates that judges must be live to the above issues, it is clear that legal practitioners also must bear these issues in mind and be prepared to argue them in court proceedings on behalf of their respective clients.

COMMON ISSUES IN RESPECT OF RADICALISATION IN PUBLIC LAW PROCEEDINGS

7.12 Due to the highly sensitive nature of the evidence in 'radicalisation cases' and the concomitant risks to those involved, there is a whole body of case law that has not been reported, particularly in respect of those proceedings that engage ECHR, Art 2 (the 'right to life')[10]. However, in the proceedings that have been reported, a number of common issues have arisen, for which the courts have provided guidance. Each of these is discussed in turn.

Wardship

7.13 As stated previously, 'radicalisation cases' generally fall into three categories within the context of family law proceedings:

(a) where children, with their parents or on their own, are at risk of travelling to ISIS (Islamic State)-held territories;

(b) where children have been or are at risk of being radicalised; and

(c) where children have been or are at risk of becoming involved in terrorist activities, whether domestically or abroad[11].

10 D Fottrell QC. 'Radicalisation in the Family Courts: Prevention or Cure?' (ALC Conference, 2017).

11 'Radicalisation cases in the Family Courts', supra note 3, p 1.

Whilst types (b) and (c) have mostly been dealt with through public law proceedings, type (a) cases have usually involved the court invoking its wardship jurisdiction[12].

7.14 Derived from the delegated performance of the duties of the Crown to protect its subjects, wardship vests parental responsibility of a child solely with the High Court[13]. Whilst day-to-day care and control of the ward is given to an individual or to a local authority, no important step can be taken in the child's life without the court's consent when she is a ward of the court[14]. In other words, the High Court adopts a *parens patriae* jurisdiction over the relevant child. In the appropriate circumstances, the High Court can make any child under the age of 18 who has British citizenship and is either physically present in England and Wales, or has 'habitual residence' in England and Wales, a ward of the court.

7.15 One of the benefits of invoking wardship jurisdiction, especially in the context of the risk of travel to ISIS-held territories, is its immediacy: once the originating summons is issued, the child becomes a ward of the court and no important step may be taken without the agreement of the court. As noted in *White, Carr and Lowe: The Children Act in Practice*, issuing the originating summons functions as a unique 'quasi-administrative mechanism' by which the child's legal position can be 'immediately frozen'[15].

7.16 It is important to note that the power of the High Court to invoke wardship jurisdiction is not limitless. Section 100 of the CA 1989 sets out the restrictions on the use of wardship jurisdiction. In particular, as stated in s 100(4), and as highlighted in the Family Procedure Rules 2010 (FPR 2010), PD 12D, 'such proceedings should not be commenced unless it is clear that the issues concerning the child cannot be resolved under the Children Act 1989'.

7.17 The three principal cases setting out the court's use of wardship to address issues of radicalisation are:

(a) *Re Y (A Minor: Wardship)*;

(b) *London Borough of Tower Hamlets v M*; and

(c) *Re M (Children)*.

7.18 *Re Y (A Minor: Wardship)*[16] concerned an application by the local authority for a 16-year-old male, Y, to be made a ward of the court or, alternatively and/or in addition, to seek protection under the inherent jurisdiction of the High Court. A number of Y's family members, including his brothers, were involved in fighting for the jihadists in Syria. The local authority was concerned that Y might wish to follow in his brothers' footsteps and that his mother would be unable to

12 FPR 2010, PD 12D, para 1.3.

13 *Re Y (A Minor: Wardship)* [2015] EWHC 2098 (Fam) 12.

14 FPR 2010, PD 12D, para 1.3.

15 *White, Carr and Lowe: The Children Act in Practice* (4th edn, LexisNexis, 2008) para 12.14.

16 [2015] EWHC 2098 (Fam).

put in place protective measures to prevent him from travelling abroad. At the time of the hearing, it was clear that Y's mother was depressed, Y had regularly been leaving school without anyone knowing where he was going, and there was a plan for him to travel to Dubai, notwithstanding that Y was on police bail in relation to an allegation of causing grievous bodily harm.

7.19 Referring to the 'Channel: vulnerability assessment framework' used by the Sussex Police to guide decisions about whether an individual needs support to address their vulnerability to radicalisation, Hayden J noted that a number of the features applied to Y. Y was considered susceptible to indoctrination and there was real concern that he would be influenced by family and friends involved in extremism. The local authority did not seek care proceedings and, in light of Y's age, the court queried how effective such proceedings would be in any event. The court held that wardship was the 'proportionate' response because it was 'ideally fitted to the very specific nature of the risk contemplated'[17]. It would prevent Y from being removed from the jurisdiction without an order of the court, and enable the police to assist if Y was removed without permission.

7.20 *Re Y (A Minor: Wardship)* highlights the effective use of wardship, a somewhat antiquated mechanism, in modern child protection where extreme circumstances exist. Moreover, it notes the greater 'protective obligation' that must be accorded to a child versus an adult and, in the case of Y, the need to protect him 'from himself'[18].

London Borough of Tower Hamlets v M

7.21 In *London Borough of Tower Hamlets v M*[19], two local authorities brought ex parte applications for protective measures to prevent children in their respective areas travelling to ISIS-controlled territories, in particular Syria. The first local authority made a wardship application whist the second local authority was invited by the court to consider whether they wished to issue a wardship summons. Pursuant to wardship jurisdiction, the court made orders relating to the retrieval of the passport of each of the young people concerned to prevent them leaving the United Kingdom.

7.22 Hayden J used his judgment to distill a number of core principles that practitioners must be aware of when making ex parte applications relating to 'radicalisation':

(a) prior to attending court, the lawyers should take care to draft, at very least in outline, the scope and ambit of the orders they seek and in respect of whom they seek them (at [18(i)]);

(b) thought should be given, from the very outset, as to how quickly the case can be restored on notice (at [18(ii)]);

17 [2015] EWHC 2098 (Fam) at [13].
18 Ibid.
19 [2015] EWHC 869 (Fam).

(c) such cases require the instruction of senior and experienced lawyers even if brought on an urgent basis (at [18(iii)]);

(d) the welfare of the individual child is paramount and cannot be eclipsed by wider considerations of counterterrorism policy or operations, though the court must have a full picture of the 'wider canvas' of the case (at [18(iv)]);

(e) verbal assurance that the police, security forces or those involved in counter terrorism, are aware of and support the application are not sufficient: there must always be 'hard' evidence placed before the court and capable of being subject to appropriate scrutiny (at [18(v)]);

(f) interference with the ECHR, Art 8 rights of a minor will always require public scrutiny at some stage in the process and accredited press representatives may attend court hearings (though they may be asked to withdraw at sensitive stages) (at [18(vi)]);

(g) prior to the hearing, consideration should be given to the need for reporting restrictions (at [18(vii)]);

(h) consideration of reporting restrictions should also extend to non-conventional media outlets (for example, social media) (at [18(viii)]); and

(i) it is crucial that there is a coordinated strategy – and on-going dialogue – between all the safeguarding agencies involved.

The aforementioned principles are key guidance for both legal practitioners and local authorities to follow when considering issues of wardship and ex parte hearings.

Re M (Children)

7.23 *Re M (Children)*[20] concerned four children (aged between 20 months and seven years) who were at risk of being removed by their parents to Syria to join the Islamic State. On or around 7 April 2015, the parents had left their home in the UK with the children, without warning and without informing friends or extended family. They were reported missing to the police on 16 April, and on 19 April the police made a public appeal for information. By that date, the family were in the process of crossing the border into Turkey. The Turkish authorities detained them on 20 April, and on 5 May the family were voluntarily deported to, and subsequently detained in, Moldova, returning to the UK by 8 May.

7.24 Whilst the family was in transit, the local authority made applications for ex-parte wardship orders in respect of all four children on the basis that it had reasonable grounds to believe that the family were intending to join the Islamic State in Syria. The court granted the applications, holding:

(a) that this was an appropriate case in which the court could proceed in the parents' absence;

20 [2015] EWHC 1433 (Fam).

(b) that unless the court made protective orders, significant harm was likely to come to the children; and

(c) that their welfare would be best served if they remained in detention in Turkey pending assessment by the local authority or, at the least, an on-notice hearing (at [9]).

The matter was re-listed for an on-notice hearing on 8 May.

7.25 When the case came before Munby P on 8 May, he held that the local authority should be given leave to make an application for the court to exercise its inherent jurisdiction, as it was clear that the result which the authority wished to achieve could not be achieved through the making of any other order and there was reasonable cause to believe that if the court's inherent jurisdiction was not exercised with respect to the children, they were likely to suffer significant harm[21]. He then went on to consider whether he should exercise said powers and in what way(s).

7.26 The judgment raises and/or reiterates a number of salient points in respect of the use of wardship jurisdiction in radicalisation cases, which may be summarised as follows:

(a) the Crown's protective duty in relation to a child who is a British subject means that the court may make said child a ward of court even if the child, at the time the order is made, is outside the jurisdiction (at [30]–[31]);

(b) the court must exercise 'extreme circumspection' when deciding whether to invoke wardship jurisdiction (at [32]);

(c) wardship jurisdiction is useful to meet the 'ever emerging needs of an ever changing world,' particularly in cases of harm that might engage ECHR, Arts 2 or 3 (ie risk to life or risk of degrading or inhuman treatment) (at [32]);

(d) it is the role of the court to prevent damage being done to children, rather than risk incurring damage which it cannot repair (at [35]);

(e) ex parte applications are appropriate where there are 'compelling reasons to believe that the child's welfare will be compromised if the parents are alerted in advance to what is going on' (at [36]); and

(f) the child's welfare is paramount and this cannot be 'eclipsed' by wider considerations of counter terrorism policy or operations, though the court requires an 'informed understanding of that wider canvas' (at [37]).

7.27 As outlined above, FPR 2010, PD 12D states that wardship proceedings 'should not be commenced unless it is clear that the issues concerning the child cannot be resolved under the Children Act 1989'. In deciding whether to issue an application for wardship jurisdiction or public law proceedings, Deidre

---

21 See CA 1989, s 100(4).

Fottrell QC notes that the local authority must ask itself what the purpose of the application is[22]. If there are significant issues proving threshold and significant harm, then consideration should be given to public law proceedings[23]. If the issues are limited to passport orders, it may be that wardship proceedings are more appropriate[24].

Wardship and security services

7.28 As previously stated, proceedings that raise issues of radicalisation will often require a multi-agency approach. Whilst disclosure from other agencies may inform public law proceedings, there are also cases where the evidence of the subject child in family proceedings is integral to the larger inquiries of officers of investigatory, enforcement and/or regulatory agencies. The latter scenario highlights two potentially conflicting principles of wardship law: on one hand, no 'important' or 'major' step in the life of a ward can be taken without first obtaining the approval of the wardship judge; and on the other, the wardship court cannot exercise its powers, however wide they may be, so as to intervene on the merits in an area of concern entrusted by law to another public authority[25].

7.29 Munby P faced this dilemma in *Re A (A Child) (Ward of Court)*[26]. Little is known of the facts of this case, save that it involved a teenager who was the subject of proceedings brought by a local authority due to issues of radicalisation. The case number, dates of the hearings (which were themselves not listed) and the names of counsel and those who instructed them were all concealed. The court was being asked to adjudicate a narrow issue, albeit one with far-reaching implications for officers of investigatory, enforcement, and regulatory agencies, namely: does the Security Service need to obtain the permission of the court to fulfil its statutory functions in accordance with the Security Service Act 1989 when those actions relate to a ward of court[27]?

7.30 Munby P held that there is not (and never has been) any principle or rule that judicial consent is required before the police can interview a ward of court[28]. Wardship 'does not privilege a ward over a child who is not a ward and does not give immunity not available to other children' (at [15]). Legal practitioners should be live to this decision and note that, according to Munby P, FPR 2010, PD 12D, which at para 5.2 suggests that police must make an application to interview a ward of the court, is 'simply wrong' (at [48]).

---

22 Fottrell, supra note 10, 3.
23 Ibid.
24 Ibid.
25 *Re A (A Child) (Ward of Court)* [2017] EWHC 1022 (Fam), [2017] 3 WLR 593 at [8].
26 [2017] EWHC 1022 (Fam), [2017] 3 WLR 593.
27 Ibid at [3].
28 Ibid at [45].

Threshold

7.31 As indicated above, a significant number of cases where radicalisation is raised as an issue are dealt with through public law proceedings, namely applications for care or supervision orders. The threshold criteria for the making of care or supervision orders is set out in the CA 1989, s 31(2): the court must be satisfied that the child concerned is suffering, or is likely to suffer, significant harm attributable to the care given to the child not being what it would be reasonable to expect a parent to give to him; or the child being beyond parental control. The threshold remains the same whether there are allegations of radicalisation or not. As such, it will be the role of the court to determine whether the allegations of radicalisation satisfy the threshold criteria, if found to be proven.

7.32 Leading on from that, it is perhaps otiose to add that not all extreme beliefs will correlate to significant harm for the purpose of meeting the threshold criteria. In *Re A (A Child)*[29], the court considered care and placement orders in respect of a young boy, A. The local authority opposed placement of A with his father for a number of reasons, including that the father had had some involvement with the English Defence League (EDL). The President was highly critical of the local authority for seeking to rely on the father's alleged affiliation with the EDL as a basis for satisfying the legal threshold. He reiterated that 'membership of an extremist group such as the EDL is not, without more, any basis for care proceedings' (at [71]).

7.33 Thus, when pleading the legal threshold, practitioners must only seek to rely on facts where there is an established link between the fact and the conclusion that the child has suffered or is at risk of suffering significant harm.

The burden of proof and the balance of probabilities

7.34 In the event that the local authority seeks to rely on allegations of radicalisation and those allegations are denied, the court will have to undertake a fact-finding exercise. As McDonald J noted in *A Local Authority v HB (Alleged Risk of Radicalisation and Abduction)*[30], 'radicalisation' cases can bring with them 'certain additional challenges' when seeking to determine the issues before the court by means of considering the evidence in its totality. However, the principles remain the same for any fact-finding hearing.

7.35 The principles in respect of fact-findings are well established and, in the context of radicalisation, were reiterated by Munby P in *Re X (Children) (No 3)*[31]. The case concerned allegations that a mother, her uncle, and her grandmother were travelling to Syria via Turkey with the mother's four children, with the intention of joining ISIS. Though suspicious of the mother's motivations,

29 [2015] EWFC 11.
30 [2017] EWHC 1437 (Fam) at [70].
31 [2015] EWHC 3651 (Fam).

Munby P was unable to conclude on the basis of all the evidence (and each piece of evidence in the context of all the other evidence) that the local authority had proved any part of the core findings sought in the Scott Schedule and consequently dismissed the care proceedings.

7.36 At para 20 of his judgment, Munby P reiterated eight principles in relation to fact-finding hearings as extrapolated from the judgment of Baker J in *Re L and M (Children)*[32]:

(a) the burden of proof lies at all times with the local authority;

(b) the standard of proof is the balance of probabilities;

(c) findings of fact in these cases must be based on evidence, including inferences that can properly be drawn from the evidence and not on suspicion or speculation;

(d) when considering cases of suspected child abuse the court must exercise an overview of the totality of the evidence;

(e) the opinion of experts needs to be considered in the context of all the other evidence;

(f) the court must be careful to ensure that each expert keeps within the bounds of her own expertise;

(g) the evidence of the parents and any other carers is of the utmost importance. It is essential that the court forms a clear assessment of their credibility and reliability; and

(h) a witness may lie for many reasons; the fact that a witness has lied about some matters does not mean that he or she has lied about everything else.

7.37 He added a further three principles in respect of fact-findings:

(a) the legal concept of proof on a balance of probabilities 'must be applied with common sense' (at [22]);

(b) the court can have regard to the inherent probabilities, though this does not affect the legal standard of proof (at [23]); and

(c) the fact that the respondent fails to prove on a balance of probabilities an affirmative case that she has chosen to set up by way of defence, does not of itself establish the local authority's case (at [24]).

7.38 The aforementioned principles have been reiterated, albeit with slightly different wording, in *A Local Authority v T*[33]; *Re C, D and E (Children) (Radicalisation: Fact-Finding)*[34]; and *A Local Authority v HB (Alleged Risk of Radicalisation and Abduction)*[35]. Whilst legal practitioners should already be familiar with these

32 [2013] EWHC 1569 (Fam).
33 [2016] EWFC 30.
34 [2016] EWHC 3087 (Fam).
35 [2017] EWHC 1437 (Fam).

principles, it is important to review the relevant case law to be able to understand their application within radicalisation cases.

DISCLOSURE

Disclosure out of public law proceedings

7.39 As legal practitioners will be aware, proceedings under the CA 1989 are to be held in private save where the FPR 2010 allows or where the court otherwise directs[36]. 'Publication'[37] of information relating to proceedings held in private is therefore a contempt of court[38]. However, there are exceptions to this rule, and it is within the court's discretion to disclose documents from privately heard proceedings. When doing so, the value of disclosure must be balanced against the confidentiality of family proceedings and the parties' ECHR, Art 6 and Art 8 rights.

7.40 These competing interests may be seen in *Re X, Y and Z (Disclosure to the Security Service)*[39]. In this case the Metropolitan Police Service (the 'Met') made an application to disclose documents in the family proceedings to the Security Service; the court had previously disclosed the documents to the Met with the stipulations that it could not be disclosed onwards, and that no information could be placed in the public domain which would lead to the identification of the family and/or child. The Security Service had not requested this information and remained neutral as to the Met's application.

7.41 None of the parties actively opposed the Met's application; however, they argued that the same stipulations identified in the previous paragraph should apply. The Met sought disclosure without any conditions. The court allowed disclosure of the documents to the Security Service, with the condition that the documents not be disclosed outside the Security Service, albeit it was not necessary to impose conditions on the handling of the documents by the Security Service internally.

7.42 Within his judgment, McDonald J helpfully set out the factors the court should consider when deciding whether public law documents should be onwardly disclosed and any conditions of permission, which derive from *Re EC (Disclosure of Material)*[40]. These may be summarised as follows:

(a) the welfare interests of the child concerned in the care proceedings, and whether the child is likely to be adversely affected by the order in any serious way;

36 FPR 2010, r 27.10.

37 In *Re B (A Child) (Disclosure)* [2004] EWHC 411 (Fam), [2004] 2 FLR 142, Munby J held that 'publication' for the purposes of the Administration of Justice Act 1960, s 12, includes 'most forms of dissemination, whether oral or written' (at [68]–[73]).

38 Administration of Justice Act 1960, s 12(1)(a)(ii).

39 [2016] EWHC 2400 (Fam).

40 [1996] 2 FLR 725.

(b) the welfare interests of other children generally;

(c) the need for confidentiality in children's cases;

(d) the importance of promoting frankness in children's cases;

(e) the public interest in the administration of justice;

(f) the public interest in the prosecution of serious crime and the punishment of offenders and the making available of material to the police that is relevant to a criminal trial;

(g) the gravity of the alleged offence and the relevance of the evidence to it;

(h) the desirability of co-operation between various agencies concerned with the welfare of the children;

(i) a witness cannot be excused from answering incriminating questions in proceedings under the CA 1989; however, any statement of admission will not be admissible against him or her in criminal proceedings;

(j) any other material disclosure that has already taken place.

7.43 Where the court is considering onward disclosure, the court must also consider all of the relevant human rights of the parties under the ECHR (particularly Arts 6 and 8) and, where there are issues of radicalisation, Munby P's guidance in 'Radicalisation cases in the Family Courts'[41]. The court must balance all of the aforementioned factors when making a decision about disclosure and, as such, legal practitioners must be mindful of these factors when making submissions on behalf of their respective clients.

Disclosure into public law proceedings

7.44 It can also transpire that information obtained during the course of public law proceedings may be important to investigatory agencies. Munby P has made clear in 'Radicalisation cases in the Family Courts' that this must be a 'two-way process' and there must be 'reciprocity'[42]. However, the nature of the evidence is such that investigatory agencies may be reticent to disclose sensitive details into public law proceedings. This can cause particular difficulties where the local authority seeks to rely on information provided by investigatory agencies but does not have access to the evidence itself.

7.45 This dilemma may be seen in *Re C (A Child)*[43], where the local authority issued a care application in respect of a child, after learning from the Counter Terrorism Command Special Operations Branch that his father had previously been engaged in terrorism in Syria and was likely to travel there again in the near future to fight for ISIS. The evidence included that the father had been denied

41 See supra note 3.

42 'Radicalisation cases in the Family Courts', supra note 3, p 11.

43 [2016] EWHC 3171 (Fam).

a replacement passport. As the information was critical to the legal threshold, Pauffley J made a disclosure order against the Secretary of State for the Home Department (SSHD) for all information related to any extremist or radicalised conduct by adults in the family.

7.46 The SSHD sought to discharge the order on three bases:

(a) the local authority's approach to disclosure did not accord with Munby P's 'Radicalisation cases in the Family Courts' guidance, with specific reference to the local authority's wide request for information, insufficient notification as to issues, and the order being made without notice (at [20]);

(b) the local authority sought disclosure on an erroneous basis, namely that it would 'assist' the court (at [26]–[27]); and

(c) the order for disclosure against the Passport Office seeking the underlying assessment that formed the basis of the Secretary of State's decision to refuse to issue a replacement passport to the father was wrong because the assessment was made on the basis of expert advice (at [36]). Moreover, the expert advice could be challenged in the administrative court, would likely damage national security if disclosed, and should be respected by the family court.

7.47 Pauffley J rejected the arguments of the SSHD and refused to discharge the order. She held that the information upon which the decision was based could be highly relevant to the fundamental question of whether there was a likelihood that the child would suffer significant harm if an order were not made (at [41]). However, the judge reflected that, in light of some of the submissions made on behalf of the SSHD, she would likely make a claim for PII (at [44]–[47]). This was later pursued and upheld in *Re C (A Child) (Application for Public Interest Immunity)*[44], discussed below.

Disclosure: PII

7.48 Where the disclosure of sensitive information is sought or ordered, the Secretary of State for the Home Department can seek to claim PII or a Closed Material Procedure to prevent or limit disclosure. In *Re C (A Child) (Care Proceedings: Disclosure)*, Pauffley J very helpfully included in her judgment the key stages involved in the SSHD's decision-making process:

— firstly, legal advisers must consider whether the material sought or held is relevant or material to the proceedings (at [14]);

— secondly, officials must undertake a more detailed assessment of the sensitivity of the information sought, with particular emphasis on whether there is a real risk that disclosure would cause substantial harm to an important public interest. If disclosure would not cause substantial harm to the public interest,

44 [2017] EWHC 692 (Fam), [2017] 2 FLR 1342.

it should be made, but if it would, the disclosure sought 'attracts' PII and a claim must be considered (at [15]);

— finally, the SSHD must decide whether to claim PII or make an application under the Justice and Security Act 2013 (the JSA 2013), such as an application for a closed materials hearing (at [16]).

7.49 If the SSHD determines that PII should be claimed, she must finalise and sign a 'PII Certificate,' which is the SSHD's statement of her own judgment as to the likely harm to the public interest caused by disclosure and the weight to be given to competing public interests. As noted in *Re C (A Child) (Care Proceedings: Disclosure)*, the 'Certificate' will generally contain an open and a closed part and a sensitive schedule (at [17]).

7.50 Thereafter, it will be for the court to make the final decision as to whether the material should be disclosed in the public interest, though considerable weight will be given to the SSHD's view as to where the balance of the public interest lies (at [18]). To do so, the court embarks on the balancing exercise set out in *R v Chief Constable of the West Midlands Police, ex p Wiley*[45], which is very similar to that of the SSHD in her decision-making process. This involves consideration of:

(a) whether the material is relevant;

(b) whether the nature of the disclosure would cause 'real damage' or 'serious harm' to the public interest; and

(c) whether the public interest in non-disclosure outweighs the public interest in disclosure for the purpose of doing justice in the proceedings.

If a claim for PII is made and upheld, the material is excluded from the proceedings.

7.51 The consideration of PII may be seen in *Re C (A Child) (Application for Public Interest Immunity)*[46], the follow-up to Pauffley J's decision in *Re C* (discussed above). As noted at para 7.47, in *Re C*, the court refused the SSHD's application to discharge the disclosure order for all information related to any extremist or radicalised conduct by adults in the family. The SSHD failed to comply with the disclosure order and eventually issued a PII application. After a closed hearing, the SSHD disclosed her Certificate, submissions, and a document setting out the facts and the chronology leading to the refusal of the father's application for a passport. Thereafter, the court heard submissions from all of the parties in respect of the *Wiley* balancing exercise, and upheld the SSHD's PII claim.

Disclosure: closed materials

7.52 If, in considering disclosure of sensitive documents, the SSHD determines that the materials in question are highly relevant and the public interest in

45 [1995] 1 AC 274.

46 [2017] EWHC 692 (Fam).

disclosure so pressing that it is inappropriate to claim PII, she may make an application for a declaration that the proceedings are 'proceedings in which a closed material application may be made to the court'[47]. 'Closed materials' are materials which cannot be disclosed because it would damage national security, for example, by alerting suspects. The JSA 2013 therefore sets out how 'closed materials' can be disclosed whilst still protecting the public interests.

7.53 Pursuant to the JSA 2013, s 6(4) and (5), the court may make such a declaration if it considers that the following two conditions are met:

> '(4) The first condition is that—
>
> (a) a party to the proceedings would be required to disclose sensitive material in the course of the proceedings to another person (whether or not another party to the proceedings), or
>
> (b) a party to the proceedings would be required to make such a disclosure were it not for one or more of the following—
>
> (i) the possibility of a claim for public interest immunity in relation to the material,
>
> (ii) the fact that there would be no requirement to disclose if the party chose not to rely on the material,
>
> (iii) section 17(1) of the Regulation of Investigatory Powers Act 2000 (exclusion for intercept material),
>
> (iv) any other enactment that would prevent the party from disclosing the material but would not do so if the proceedings were proceedings in relation to which there was a declaration under this section.
>
> (5) The second condition is that it is in the interests of the fair and effective administration of justice in the proceedings to make a declaration'.

7.54 If the court agrees to make the declaration under the JSA 2013, s 6, the SSHD is joined as a party (if not one already), and the court thereafter directs a hearing of the closed material application, using special advocates[48]. When doing so, the court may make provision for the following:

— the mode of proof and about evidence in the proceedings;

— enabling or requiring the proceedings to be determined without a hearing;

— legal representation in the proceedings;

— enabling the proceedings to take place without full particulars of the reasons for decisions in the proceedings being given to a party to the proceedings (or to any legal representative of that party);

47 JSA 2013, s 6(1).

48 CPR Pt 82, Closed Material Procedure.

- enabling the court concerned to conduct proceedings in the absence of any person, including a party to the proceedings (or any legal representative of that party);
- guidance about the functions of a person appointed as a special advocate; and/or
- enabling the court to give a party to the proceedings a summary of evidence taken in the party's absence[49].

7.55 However, an application for closed materials in the family courts is not necessarily straightforward, as noted by the court in *Re X, Y and Z (Disclosure to the Security Service)*[50]. Whilst *Re X, Y and Z (Disclosure to the Security Service)* did not require the use of the closed material procedure, McDonald J raised it as a possibility should the security services make an application to the court for permission to disclose the material onwards. He noted in his judgment that applications pursuant to the JSA 2013, s 6(1) must be made to the High Court; there is no provision for such applications to be heard by the family court (at [92]). Moreover, the Civil Procedure Rules 1998, Part 82 – Closed Material Procedure, which governs the determination of an application under s 6(1), does not apply to family proceedings nor has it been incorporated into the FPR 2010 (at [92]). As such, there are at present no procedural rules or express statutory provision for determining a s 6 application or any subsequent closed material application in the context of family proceedings.

7.56 Notwithstanding, McDonald J highlights that special advocates have been utilised on a small number of occasions in family proceedings to deal with issues of disclosure of sensitive material, and 'Radicalisation cases in the Family Courts' and the President's Guidance on Special Advocates[51] envision the use of closed hearings and special advocates in family proceedings (at [94]). The court therefore advises that at any initial hearing of an application by the Security Service for permission to disclose, the court will need to consider, inter alia:

> 'whether the application is appropriate to be dealt with by means of the use of a closed procedure utilising special advocates having regard to the guidance set out in *Re T (Wardship: Impact of Police Intelligence)* [2010] 1 FLR 1048, *A Chief Constable v YK and Others* [2011] 1 FLR 1493 *BCC v FZ, AZ, HZ and TVP* [2013] 1 FLR 974, the President's Guidance entitled Radicalisation Cases in the Family Courts dated 8 October 2015 and the President's Guidance entitled The Role of the Attorney General in Appointing Advocates to the Court of Special Advocates in Family Cases dated 26 March 2016'[52].

49 JSA 2013, s 11(2).

50 [2016] EWHC 2400 (Fam).

51 'The Role of the Attorney General in Appointing Advocates to the Court of Special Advocates in Family Cases' President's Guidance (26 March 2016).

52 At [95(iii)].

Reporting restrictions and media exclusion orders

7.57 The issue of reporting restrictions is considered in greater detail in Chapter 8. However, it is worthwhile looking briefly at reporting restrictions within the context of radicalisation cases. As Munby P advises in 'Radicalisation cases in the Family Courts', judges hearing cases where there are allegations of radicalisation need to consider whether it is necessary to exclude the media, make a reporting restriction order, or make an 'anti-tipping-off' order (at para 8). The exclusion of the media is regarded as a 'last resort' and only to be used if there is reason to believe that the situation cannot be adequately protected by a reporting restriction order or 'anti-tipping-off' order' (at para 8).

7.58 The judicial view of media exclusion as a 'last resort' may be seen in the case of *Re M (Children)* (see paras 7.23–7.27 above). Whilst the family were en route to Moldova from Turkey, Munby P conducted a hearing in private to consider, inter alia, whether the relevant children should be made wards of the court. Munby P held that there should not be any reporting either of the fact that there were court proceedings underway or of the terms of any order he was being asked to make (at [15]). However, the court held that there was no reason to exclude the Press Association's reporter provided that he understood that the court was imposing a reporting restriction (at [15]).

7.59 In *London Borough of Tower Hamlets v M*[53], Hayden J considered the issue of reporting restrictions and media exclusion. The following of his 'core principles' applicable to ex parte applications for protective measures to prevent children in their area travelling to ISIS-controlled areas are relevant:

(a) transparency, including the attendance of accredited press officials in court, remains the presumption in all aspects of the work of the family justice system (at [18(vi)]);

(b) attention should be given in advance of the hearing as to whether reporting restrictions are needed to protect the child from publicity and what form they should take (at [18(vii)]); and

(c) when considering reporting restrictions, attention should be paid to non-conventional media outlets such as social media.

Indeed, Hayden J noted that in the instant case the press had attended and

> 'it was only necessary for them to withdraw on one occasion, at the request of a very senior police officer present in court, supported by the local authority. The request was made because sensitive issues of policy and national security arose'[54].

7.60 Hayden J also examined the tension between the need for transparency and the protection of children in *Re S*[55]. *Re S* concerned a child who had been

53 [2015] EWHC 869 (Fam).

54 At [18(vi)].

55 [2015] EWHC 4159 (Fam).

arrested by the police in connection with terrorist offences. Two national newspapers printed articles, both online and in hard copy, identifying the child and his school, which contravened a previous reporting restriction order that the court had made. The Associated Newspapers Ltd subsequently argued that the reporting restriction order was wrongfully made and should be set aside. Though Hayden J expressed concern at limiting public scrutiny, he ultimately held that the protection of vulnerable children will 'always be given considerable weight in a mature, democratic society' (at [3]) and ordered that the reporting restriction order should continue as drafted.

CONCLUSION

7.61 Allegations of radicalisation are a relatively new facet of child protection law. Though the statutory provisions and practice directions that apply remain the same – for example, with respect to wardship and CA 1989 proceedings – family law practitioners must be familiar with the growing body of case law and, in particular, Munby P's 'Radicalisation cases in the Family Courts', in order to understand the unique issues that this area of law raises.

Chapter 8

REPORTING RESTRICTIONS

INTRODUCTION

8.1 In 2008, *The Times* ran a family justice campaign pressing for more transparency in the family courts. In a leading article, it stated that it was 'impossible to know the extent to which miscarriages of justice may be occurring, because the whole system is shrouded in secrecy'.[1] In response, the then-President of the Family Division and Head of Family Justice, Sir Mark Potter, acknowledged that the system was 'far from perfect', but that there was a distinction to be made between privacy and secrecy[2].

8.2 This tension between 'open justice' and privacy lies of the heart of reporting restriction orders. On one hand, there is the parties' right to privacy, enshrined in the European Convention on Human Rights (ECHR), Art 8 (as incorporated into UK law by the Human Rights Act 1998 (HRA 1998)). On the other, there is freedom of expression and the public interest in the machinations of the family court, which is protected by Art 10. In recent years, there has been a greater emphasis on the latter, with changes to the rules and guidance regarding media attendance at private proceedings and the publication of judgments. This chapter explores the current approach to privacy and reporting restrictions in the family law courts, and the movement towards greater transparency in the family court.

RELEVANT STATUTES, REGULATIONS AND GUIDELINES

Family Procedure Rules 2010

8.3 As highlighted in *Re W (Children)*[3], any presumption or principle in favour of open justice that applies generally to court proceedings does not apply

1 T Jarrett, 'Confidentiality and openness in the family courts: current rules and history of their reform' (Briefing Paper Number 07306: 23 September 2015).
2 Ibid.
3 [2016] EWCA Civ 113.

to proceedings held in private and that relate to children. This position is reflected in the statutory law. Pursuant to the Family Procedure Rules 2010 (FPR 2010), r 27.10, family law proceedings are to be held in private; in other words, the general public has no right to be present. Rule 27.11(2) sets out the persons who are permitted attend private proceedings, namely

(a) an officer of the court;

(b) a party to the proceedings;

(c) a litigation friend for any party, or legal representative instructed to act on that party's behalf;

(d) an officer of the service or Welsh family proceedings officer;

(e) a witness;

(f) duly accredited representatives of news gathering and reporting organisations; and

(g) any other person whom the court permits to be present.

8.4 However, under the FPR 2010, r 27.11(3), any of the aforementioned persons may also be excluded from the proceedings where the court is satisfied that this is necessary:

(a) in the interests of any child concerned in, or connected with, the proceedings;

(b) for the safety or protection of a party, a witness in the proceedings, or a person connected with such a party or witness; or

(c) for the orderly conduct of the proceedings.

Conversely, the named persons may also be excluded if the court determines that their attendance will impede or prejudice justice.

8.5 This emphasis on the confidentiality of private proceedings extends to the disclosure of information contained therein. The FPR 2010 permit the communication of information concerning private proceedings between specified individuals in limited circumstances, whereby the communication will not amount to a contempt of court. Pursuant to FPR 2010, r 12.73(1)(a), the information from private proceedings may be communicated where the communication is to:

(a) a party;

(b) the legal representative of a party;

(c) a professional legal adviser;

(d) an officer of the service or a Welsh family proceedings officer;

(e) the welfare officer; the Legal Services Commission;

(f) an expert whose instruction by a party has been authorised by the court for the purposes of the proceedings;

(g) a professional acting in furtherance of the protection of children; and/or

(h) an independent reviewing officer appointed in respect of the subject child.

Further, pursuant to r 12.73(1)(b), the court may give permission for the disclosure of information concerning private proceedings to any person not named in r 12.73(1).

Administration of Justice Act 1960

8.6 As the aforementioned rules indicate, the prima facie position is that information from proceedings conducted in private may not be publicised. This is set out in the Administration of Justice Act 1960, s 12(1), which states that the publication of information from proceedings where the court is sitting in private is an offence (contempt of court) where the proceedings:

(a) relate to the exercise of the inherent jurisdiction of the High Court with respect to minors;

(b) are brought under the Children Act 1989 (CA 1989) or the Adoption and Children Act 2002; or

(c) otherwise relate wholly or mainly to the maintenance or upbringing of a minor.

This includes judgments in proceedings, unless either the judgment has been delivered in public or, where delivered in private, the judge has authorised publication.

Children Act 1989, s 97(2)

8.7 Further protection to the subject child(ren) of proceedings is provided by the CA 1989, s 97(2). Section 97(2) makes it an offence to publish – to the public at large or to any section of the public – any material which would identify, or which would be likely to identify, a child as being involved in family court proceedings (unless a specific order has been made dispensing with this provision).

8.8 As the wording of the statute makes clear, s 97(2) is not an absolute prohibition on publishing material about a child. Moreover, it should be noted that the ban in s 97(2) is limited to the duration of the proceedings[4]. However, in proceedings to which s 97(2) applies, FPR 2010, PD 27B states that the court should continue to consider at the conclusion of the proceedings whether there are any outstanding welfare issues which require a continuation of the protection afforded during the course of the proceedings by that provision. Furthermore, the limitations imposed by the Administration of Justice Act 1960, s 12 on publication of information relating to certain proceedings in private apply during and after the proceedings.

4 FPR 2010, PD 27B, para 2.5.

Children and Young Persons Act 1933

8.9 Additional statutory protection is offered by the Children and Young Persons Act 1933, s 39, which provides the court with the power to prohibit publication of certain matter in newspapers:

> '39(1) In relation to any proceedings in any court other than criminal proceedings the court may direct that the following may not be included in a publication—
>
> (a) the name, address or school of any child or young person concerned in the proceedings, either as being the person by or against or in respect of whom the proceedings are taken, or as being a witness therein;
>
> (aa) any particulars calculated to lead to the identification of a child or young person so concerned in the proceedings;
>
> (b) a picture that is or includes a picture of any child or young person so concerned in the proceedings;
>
> except in so far (if at all) as may be permitted by the direction of the court'.

Contravening s 39(1) is an offence and punishable by a fine on summary conviction[5].

Contempt of Court Act 1981

8.10 Under the Contempt of Court Act 1981, s 11, in any case where a court (having power to do so) allows a name or other matter to be withheld from the public in proceedings before the court, the court may give such directions prohibiting the publication of that name or matter in connection with the proceedings as appear to the court to be necessary for the purpose for which it was so withheld. Under the Contempt of Court Act 1981, s 14, a superior court may impose a prison sentence of up to two years, or an unlimited fine or both; and an inferior court may impose a prison sentence of up to one month, or a fine not exceeding £2,500, or both.

Children Act 1989, s 8

8.11 The court may also consider making a prohibited steps order pursuant to the CA 1989, s 8 preventing the disclosure of information. A s 8 order would be appropriate where there is a risk of the parent(s) (or other parties) disclosing information from the proceedings.

---

5 Children and Young Persons Act 1933, s 39(2).

REPORTING RESTRICTION ORDERS

Definition

8.12 Where the aforementioned instruments do not provide adequate protection to a child who is the subject of CA 1989 proceedings, one or more of the parties may seek a reporting restriction order (RRO).

8.13 An RRO is an injunctive order made on the basis of an individual's right to privacy under the ECHR, Art 8. As such, the court's jurisdiction to make such an order arises out of Convention rights under the ECHR, rather than its inherent jurisdiction[6].

8.14 The purpose of an RRO is to protect the subject child; it is not to confer anonymity on other individuals or organisations[7]. That being said, an RRO may include restrictions on identifying or approaching specified family members, carers, professionals or organisations in cases where the absence of such restriction is likely to prejudice their ability to care for the child or where identification of such persons might lead to the identification of the child and defeat the purpose of the order.

8.15 As highlighted in the Cafcass Practice Note of 18 March 2018[8], situations in which an RRO may be required include where:

(a) the need for protection is not linked to particular court proceedings;

(b) the statutory provisions do not prevent publication of all kinds of information; or

(c) an injunction is needed to prevent approaches to family, doctors or carers.

LEGAL PRINCIPLES

8.16 When considering an application for an RRO, the principal provisions that the court will consider – and balance against one another – are the ECHR, Art 8 (right to respect for private and family life) and Art 10 (freedom of expression). Whilst all family law practitioners should be familiar with these articles, they are worth setting out in full:

> '**Article 8 Right to respect for private and family life**
>
> 1. Everyone has the right to respect for his private and family life, his home and his correspondence.

6 For a discussion of the relevance of inherent jurisdiction to the court's jurisdiction to make RROs, see *Re S* [2004] UKHL 47, paras 22 and 23.

7 *CAFCASS Practice Note* (18 March 2005) [2005] 2 FLR 111 (amended 25 March 2015).

8 Ibid.

2. There shall be no interference by a public authority with the exercise of this right except such as is in accordance with the law and is necessary in a democratic society in the interests of national security, public safety or the economic well-being of the country, for the prevention of disorder or crime, for the protection of health or morals, or for the protection of the rights and freedoms of others'.

'**Article 10 Freedom of expression**

1. Everyone has the right to freedom of expression. This right shall include freedom to hold opinions and to receive and impart information and ideas without interference by public authority and regardless of frontiers. This Article shall not prevent States from requiring the licensing of broadcasting, television or cinema enterprises.

2. The exercise of these freedoms, since it carries with it duties and responsibilities, may be subject to such formalities, conditions, restrictions or penalties as are prescribed by law and are necessary in a democratic society, in the interests of national security, territorial integrity or public safety, for the prevention of disorder or crime, for the protection of health or morals, for the protection of the reputation or rights of others, for preventing the disclosure of information received in confidence, or for maintaining the authority and impartiality of the judiciary'.

8.17 Practitioners should be aware that there is no automatic precedence as between Arts 8 and 10, and both are subject to qualification where the rights of others are engaged[9]. However, the HRA 1998, s 12, highlights further factors that the court must take into account when considering a restriction of the ECHR, Art 10:

'**12 Freedom of expression**

(1) This section applies if a court is considering whether to grant any relief which, if granted, might affect the exercise of the Convention right to freedom of expression.

(2) If the person against whom the application for relief is made ("the respondent") is neither present nor represented, no such relief is to be granted unless the court is satisfied—

(a) that the applicant has taken all practicable steps to notify the respondent; or

(b) that there are compelling reasons why the respondent should not be notified.

(3) No such relief is to be granted so as to restrain publication before trial unless the court is satisfied that the applicant is likely to establish that publication should not be allowed.

---

9 Ibid, 5.

(4) The court must have particular regard to the importance of the Convention right to freedom of expression and, where the proceedings relate to material which the respondent claims, or which appears to the court, to be journalistic, literary or artistic material (or to conduct connected with such material), to—

(a) the extent to which—

(i) the material has, or is about to, become available to the public; or

(ii) it is, or would be, in the public interest for the material to be published;

(b) any relevant privacy code'.

8.18 As such, the HRA 1998, s 12(4) requires the court to have particular regard to the importance of freedom of expression. It must also consider the extent to which material has or is about to become available to the public, the extent of the public interest in such material being published, and the terms of any relevant privacy code or regulation[10].

8.19 In considering which article should take precedence, the court will undertake what was described in *Re S* as the 'ultimate balancing test'[11]. This test consists of four prepositions:

(a) as stated above, neither article has, as such, precedence over the other;

(b) where the value of two articles are in conflict, an intense focus on the comparative importance of the specific rights being claimed in the individual case is necessary;

(c) the justifications for interfering with or restricting each right must be taken into account; and

(d) the proportionality test must be applied to each.

Re S remains good law and has been re-affirmed more recently in *Z v News Group Newspapers Ltd* (Judgment 1)[12]; *Surrey County Council v ME*[13]; *North Somerset Council v LW (Care and RRO)*[14]; and *London Borough of Waltham Forest v AD*[15], to name a few.

PROCEDURE – APPLYING FOR AN RRO

8.20 The procedure for applying for an RRO is governed by the FPR 2010, PD 12I and the *Cafcass Practice Note*[16].

10 Ibid, 5.
11 [2004] UKHL 47 at [17].
12 [2013] EWHC 1150 (Fam).
13 [2014] EWHC 489 (Fam).
14 [2014] EWHC 1670 (Fam).
15 [2014] EWHC 1985 (Fam).
16 18 March 2005 (as amended on 25 March 2015).

FPR 2010, PD 12I

8.21 As set out in the FPR 2010, PD 12I, para 1.1, the Practice Direction applies to any application in the Family Division founded on Convention rights for an order restricting publication of information about children or incapacitated adults. RROs may only be made in the High Court and are usually dealt with by a judge of the Family Division (see para 2.1). If the need for an RRO arises in family proceedings in the lower court, the matter should be transferred to the High Court or the judge of the lower court should liaise with her Family Division Liaison Judge (see para 2.1).

8.22 Paragraph 3 of PD 12I sets out how an application for a reporting restriction is to be served on the national media. As detailed above, the HRA 1998, s 12(2), stipulates that an injunction restricting the exercise of the right to freedom of expression must not be granted where the person against whom the application is made is neither present nor represented, unless the court is satisfied:

(a) that the applicant has taken all practicable steps to notify the respondent; or

(b) that there are compelling reasons why the respondent should not be notified.

8.23 Service of applications for RROs on the national media can be made via the Press Association's CopyDirect service, to which national newspapers and broadcasters subscribe as a means of receiving notice of such applications[17]. The service works as follows: an applicant (or his solicitor) telephones the Press Association's CopyDirect service on a dedicated number, which is listed in PD 12I, confirming that he wishes to apply for an RRO in the Family Division[18]. The applicant (or his solicitor) must then send the documentation identified in para 8.28 below by fax or email to CopyDirect, which is provided when the applicant calls the service. CopyDirect will, on receipt of the documentation, send via either email or fax the documentation to the subscribing media organisations, and will call the media organisations to ensure the material has been received. Once notification is sent, subscribing organisations are regarded as being 'served' for the purposes of legal proceedings.

8.24 Use of CopyDirect should be 'the norm' according to FPR 2010, PD 12I, para 3.3; however, family practitioners must bear in mind that CopyDirect only provides a notification of an application for a reporting restricting order to those organisations that subscribe to the Press Association Service. Of the major presses, *The Financial Times* and *Sky News* do not participate in the CopyDirect service. These two companies need to be served directly with the notice of application. Similarly, local and regional newspapers or magazines are not served with notice of an application by the CopyDirect service[19]. It is vital that orders are properly served; otherwise, they may be unenforceable.

---

17 FPR 2010, PD 12I, para 3.2.

18 See Media Lawyer, 'This Service' at www.medialawyer.press.net/courtapplications/notification system.jsp.

19 *Cafcass Practice Note* (18 March 2005) [2005] 2 FLR 111 (amended 25 March 2015).

8.25 It is also worth noting that the court retains the power to make without notice orders, but such cases will be exceptional, and an order will always give persons affected liberty to apply to vary or discharge it at short notice[20]. PD 12I indicates that legal advisors to the media are used to participating in hearings at very short notice where necessary, and are able to differentiate between information provided for legal purposes versus information for editorial use[21].

Cafcass Practice Note

8.26 The Official Solicitor and the Deputy Director of Legal Services issued the Cafcass Practice Note jointly. It details the recommended practice in relation to any application in the Family Division founded on Convention rights for an order that restricts freedom of expression and includes information about:

— the statutory provisions;

— the application and evidence;

— the service of the application;

— the scope of the order; and

— the service of any orders made.

8.27 In respect of the application for an RRO, para 3 of the Cafcass Practice Note states that the application may be a freestanding claim brought under the procedure in the CPR Pt 8, or it may be made within existing proceedings to which either the CPR or FPR apply. When making an application, it may be appropriate to seek a direction under CPR 39.2(4) that the identity of a party or witness should not be disclosed, and for documents to be drafted identifying individuals by initials.

8.28 The application for a reporting order must be prepared by the applicant and should include:

(a) the application/claim form;

(b) a witness statement justifying the need for an order;

(c) any legal submissions;

(d) a draft order; and

(e) an explanatory note.

Models of (d) and (e) are provided in the Cafcass Practice Note, which practitioners can amend as needed. In particular, if the application is made without notice, the explanatory note should explain why it could not be provided.

---

20 FPR 2010, PD 12I, para 3.4.

21 FPR 2010, PD 12I, para 3.3.

8.29 If the applicant is unable to draft the aforementioned documentation in the time available before the hearing, the court is likely to require the applicant to file a statement at the earliest opportunity, setting out the information placed orally before the Court; however, failing to provide the documentation in advance should be the exception, rather than the rule.

8.30 Paragraph 6 of the Cafcass Practice Note also very helpfully sets out the scope of an RRO. As stated above, the persons protected by the order should be the child or incapacitated adult, rather than other individuals or organisations. However, the order may include restrictions on identifying or approaching specified family members, carers, doctors or organisations in cases where the absence of such restriction is likely to prejudice their ability to care for the child or patient, or where identification of such persons might lead to identification of the child or patient and defeat the purpose of the order. It should be noted that the identity of an expert who provides expert evidence in proceedings is not normally subject to restriction.

8.31 Once an order has been granted, the details of those protected by the order should normally be contained in the Schedule. In rare cases where it is not appropriate for details to be given, a description by reference to the facts of the case should be contained in the Schedule to enable those reading the order to identify whether a person is likely to be the subject of the order[22].

8.32 RROs will not usually prohibit publication of material that is already in the public domain, other than in exceptional cases[23].

8.33 Finally, para 6 of the Cafcass Practice Note also provides guidance as to the duration of an RRO. The duration of an order is case-specific and orders should last for no longer than is necessary to achieve the purpose for which they are made. This is discussed further below.

COMMON ISSUES IN RESPECT OF RROs IN PUBLIC LAW PROCEEDINGS

Duration

8.34 As stated above, the Cafcass Practice Note suggests that RROs should last for no longer than is necessary to achieve the purpose for which they are made. In practice, the maximum extent of an order in a children case will usually be the child's 18th birthday. However, in some cases the order may go beyond the child's minority to protect her safety or welfare, or the anonymity of other children who are named in the order and who are still under age; or to maintain the anonymity of doctors and/or carers after the death of a patient.

22 See *Leeds NHS Trust v A & B* [2003] 1 FLR 1091.

23 See *Venables and Thompson v News Group Newspapers Ltd* [2001] Fam 430.

8.35 The court's approach to extended or even lifelong RROs may be seen in the two linked cases of *Birmingham City Council v Riaz* [2014][24] and *Birmingham City Council v Riaz* [2015][25]. In both cases, the court was concerned with AB, a 17-year-old woman who had been a victim of child sexual exploitation by at least ten older men. The police concluded that there was insufficient evidence to secure criminal convictions against the ten men; however, findings were made in the family court and reported in *Birmingham City Council v Sarfraz Riaz* [2014].

8.36 In *Birmingham City Council v Sarfraz Riaz* [2014], the court considered, inter alia, whether the interim RROs made at a previous hearing should be varied or discharged. There had been two interim reporting restrictions directed: the first afforded anonymity to the respondent men; and the second, which had been unopposed by the parties at the time that it was made, restricted the reporting of the details of AB's identity until her 18th birthday.

8.37 In respect of the first RRO, some of respondent men[26], supported by the Chief Constable of the West Midlands Police, sought an extension of the RROs, which would afford them either full or partial anonymity. Submissions in support of extending the RRO not only relied on the respondents' ECHR, Art 8 rights to privacy, but also on Art 2 (the right of every person to their life) and Art 3 (the prohibition of torture and 'inhuman or degrading treatment or punishment'). It was argued that the men were at high risk of harm, including reprisal attacks by right wing racist organisations or by members of the local community. The Press Association, *The Times*, and the BBC opposed the extension of the RRO in respect of the respondents.

8.38 The court held that the risk to the respondents if there was publicity about the case was, at best, speculative, and that there was no credible evidence that there was risk to the life of any respondent to these proceedings. As such, their Art 2 and 3 rights were not engaged; or, in the alternative, if they were engaged, they should be afforded little weight due to the lack of credible evidence of risk. Whilst the court considered that the respondents' Art 8 rights to privacy was engaged, when balancing their Art 8 rights against Art 10 rights of the press and the broadcast media, the balance fell clearly and decisively in favour of the Art 10 rights. The RROs were therefore discharged in respect of the men.

8.39 In respect of the second RRO, the local authority and AB sought for the reporting restriction in respect of AB to continue past her 18th birthday to give her lifelong protection. It was argued that had the men been found guilty in the criminal courts, AB would automatically have had lifelong anonymity under the Sexual Offences Act 2003. However, the court was not satisfied that this was one of the 'rare' and 'extreme' circumstances where lifelong anonymity

---

24 [2014] EWHC 4247 (Fam).

25 [2015] EWHC 1857 (Fam). See, for example, *Re C (Adult Patient: Publicity* [1996] 2 FLR 251; *Venables and Thompson v News Group Newspapers Ltd* [2001] Fam 430; and *X (formerly known as Mary Bell) v Y* [2003] EWHC (QB) 1101.

26 It should be noted that only four of the respondent men made submissions in respect of the extension of the RRO (see [131]).

should be granted, and Keehan J therefore adjourned the matter until prior to AB's 18th birthday.

8.40 Following on from the first judgment, *Birmingham City Council v Riaz* [2015] was concerned solely with the issue of whether the RRO to prevent the identification of AB should continue past her 18th birthday and give her lifelong protection. As in the previous hearing, Birmingham City Council and AB sought a lifelong RRO and the Press Association and *Times Newspapers* opposed such an order.

8.41 Balancing AB's Art 8 rights against the Art 10 rights of the press, the court accepted the high importance accorded to the principles of open justice and that it is plainly in the public interest for the media to be able to report on proceedings in cases of child sexual exploitation. However, Keehan J held that there was little public interest in identifying AB as a victim of child sexual exploitation and that publicity about AB as a victim of child sexual exploitation would likely have a serious detrimental effect on her emotional and psychological well-being. As such, the court found that there were compelling reasons why AB's history should remain confidential and private to her, and the balance was decisively in favour of granting the lifelong RRO sought.

8.42 As the aforementioned case indicates, the granting of lifelong anonymity under RROs will be 'truly exceptional'[27]. However, the court will consider doing so where the Art 8 rights of an individual necessitate it.

RROs and the foreign press

8.43 Complications can arise where an applicant seeks to restrict information being published in the foreign press. The approach of the court is set out in *Re E (A Child)*[28]. That case concerned a Slovakian child, who was the subject of care and wardship proceedings. The mother of the child enlisted the support of various media outlets in Slovakia and the local authority sought an RRO that included a provision to prevent publication of information about the child in the foreign press.

8.44 According to Munby P in *Re E (A Child)*, it is a general principle that the English court cannot attempt to control foreign media, whether directly or indirectly. It is ultimately a matter for the foreign state whether information should be restricted, and for the English court to attempt to do so would involve an exercise of jurisdiction that is 'plainly exorbitant, not least as involving interference in the internal affairs of the other State' (at [56]). Moreover, such an order would likely be an exercise in futility, as it would not be enforced. The court therefore made an RRO that prohibited the mother from publishing in the English print or broadcast media only; she could publish whatever she wanted in the foreign print or broadcast media.

27 *Birmingham City Council v Riaz* [2015] EWHC 1857 (Fam) at [15].
28 [2014] EWHC 6 (Fam).

8.45 However, as illustrated in *Re J (A Child)*[29] and *Re E (A Child)*, a different approach may be taken where the RRO is sought against an internet provider outside of the jurisdiction that has no legal, physical, or commercial presence and/or no assets in the UK (ie where their only connection with the UK is that the websites that they host are accessible from the UK through the internet). As Munby P noted in *Re E (A Child)*, the nature of the internet is such that it has an 'extra-territorial effect': regardless of where the service provider and/or the service provider's servers are located, the information is accessible around the world (at [57]). As such, an RRO against a certain provider does not interfere with the jurisdiction of a particular State.

8.46 Munby P provides guidance in respect of injuncting foreign internet providers in *Re J (A Child)*[30]. In that case, an aggrieved father repeatedly published details about the care proceedings of his children on the internet, including a covert video on Facebook of the youngest child being removed from his parents' care under an Emergency Protection Order. In his judgment, Munby P indicated that the prima facie position is that an English court can grant injunctive relief against a foreign-based internet provider (at [46]). However, such orders can only properly be made where: (i) the person who is to be injuncted is amenable to the court's jurisdiction; and (ii) the order will be effective, not 'idle and ineffectual' (at [52]). In other words, the court must have 'jurisdiction' and 'discretion' (at [63]).

8.47 An applicant for an RRO against a named foreign service provider must therefore provide evidence that there has been service on the service provider in accordance with the laws of the State in which the service provider is located ('jurisdiction'); and evidence of whether the foreign court would be likely to enforce the injunction ('discretion'). Evidence of the foreign jurisdiction's approach to freedom of speech may also be necessary if applicable.

8.48 Family practitioners should note that injunctions sought against foreign-based bodies such as internet website providers will require proper service regulated by the FPR 2010, r 6.41 and r 6.43(3), which apply by virtue of r 6.1 and r 12.1(1)(d). Conversely, where the applicant seeks a *contra mundum* injunction ('against the world'), it may be appropriate to follow the procedure used for worldwide freezing (Mareva) orders instead[31].

RROs and criminal proceedings

8.49 As family law practitioners will be aware, public law cases may also involve related criminal law proceedings. In considering whether to apply a reporting order restriction to the criminal process, the starting point of the court, as highlighted in *Re S*[32], is that there is a 'general and strong rule' in favour

29 [2013] EWHC 2694 (Fam).
30 [2013] EWHC 2694 (Fam).
31 *Re J (A Child)* [2013], 64.
32 [2004] UKHL 47.

of unrestricted publicity of any proceedings in a criminal trial (at [15]), which may only be displaced by 'unusual or exceptional circumstances' (at [18]). The burden of proof on the applicant in seeking to restrict the publication of criminal proceedings is therefore a heavy one[33].

8.50 This is particularly true where an injunction is sought restricting the identification of the defendant in criminal proceedings, as may be seen in *Surrey County Council v ME*[34]. The case concerned five children who were the subject of care proceedings. The father of the three youngest children had been murdered and criminal proceedings had been commenced in respect of his death. The local authority sought an RRO preventing the identification of the children and family members by the media in their reporting of the criminal trial.

8.51 In undertaking its balancing exercise between the competing Art 8 and Art 10 rights of the individuals involved, the court noted that a restriction on the reporting of the identity of a defendant in criminal proceedings will only be considered where there is an 'absolute necessity' and the circumstances are 'exceptional' (at [23]). In *Surrey County Council v ME*, the court was not satisfied on the facts of the case that an RRO was either necessary or proportionate, much less an 'absolute necessity', and declined to make the orders as sought.

8.52 Yet, there will be 'exceptional circumstances' where the court will be minded to make an RRO in relation to on-going criminal proceedings. For example, in *A Council v M (No 3) (Reporting Restriction Order; Adoption; Artificial Insemination)*[35], the court was concerned with three adopted children whose adopted mother was subject to criminal proceedings for artificially inseminating one of the children. The contentious issue was not whether a RRO should be made, but what its scope should be, and in particular whether it should exceptionally prevent the naming of the defendant in the criminal proceedings.

8.53 The court concluded that *A Council v M (No 3) (Reporting Restriction Order; Adoption; Artificial Insemination)* was a unique case where the claims of Art 8 outweighed those of Art 10, as the probable consequences for the children (and grandchild) if the mother's identity were publicised 'would at best be harmful and at worst disastrous' (at [85]). It therefore made the RRO, to expire in 2029 when the grandchild would be 18 years old.

8.54 It is important to note that the stage of the criminal proceedings may affect whether the court is willing to contemplate an RRO. In *Z v News Group Newspapers Ltd (Judgment 1)*[36], the applicant father applied for an injunction, as the mother of his five children was being tried in the Crown Court for serious benefit fraud relating to claims made by her in respect of the children and their half-siblings. Though the fraud was based on their alleged disabilities, the children were not regarded as defendants, victims, or witnesses for the purposes of the

33 *Z v News Group Newspapers Ltd (Judgment 1)* [2013] EWHC 1150 (Fam) 56.
34 [2014] EWHC 489 (Fam).
35 [2012] EWHC 2038 (Fam).
36 [2013] EWHC 1150 (Fam).

criminal proceedings and were therefore not protected by the Children and Young Persons Act 1933, s 39.

8.55 At the particular stage that the trial had reached, Cobb J held that the father had discharged the burden of proof for the making of a RRO; however, he raised the possibility that if the mother were convicted, the balance between Art 8 and Art 10 may be tipped in favour of the latter. As such, he invited the parties to make further representations before him at the point at which the trial judge started summing up, in order that he could make a further decision in time for the verdict.

8.56 The matter was restored and it was accepted that no party sought variation of the reporting restriction if the mother were to be acquitted. However, the respondents sought variation in the event of a conviction. In *Z v News Group Newspapers Ltd*[37], Cobb J gave a short judgment indicating that whilst the case was 'exceptional', the conviction of the mother would tip the balance in favour of freedom of expression. In other words, the Art 10 right to publish her name as a convicted person would prevail over the right of the whole family to anonymity in the press (at [26]). However, Cobb J emphasised that the right to publish the mother's name in the press did not eradicate the 'enduring and valuable' Art 8 rights of the children and the family (at [29]). He therefore varied the RRO to allow for the mother's name to be published, but retained a number of provisions to protect the identity of the children and the family.

8.57 Family practitioners should note that the court would not be receptive to arguments that an RRO should be made because publication will prejudice a party's criminal appeal and re-trial. In Re C *(A Child)*[38], Guardian News and Media Limited successfully appealed against the decision of Pauffley J that the publication of her judgment concerning the surviving sibling of Ellie Butler should not be published on the ground that publication could prejudice a criminal appeal and any future retrial sought by the parents, who had been convicted of her death. The court held that under the relevant domestic and foreign jurisprudence, as set out by Munby P in *Practice Guidance (Family Courts: Transparency)*[39] (which is further discussed below), publication of the judgment would not prejudice any appeal and/or retrial.

8.58 Further, the first instance judge had failed to take into account the three factors that would reduce the risk of prejudice to any retrial, namely:

> '(i) the fact that the jury would be directed to ignore anything they read or heard outside the trial and that it should and would be trusted to follow the directions given by the trial judge;
>
> (ii) the fact that broadcasting and newspaper editors should be trusted to behave responsibly; and

37 [2013] EWHC 1371 (Fam).

38 [2016] EWCA Civ 798.

39 [2014] 1 WLR 230.

(iii) the fade factor (it would be many months and possibly more than a year before a retrial would take place)'[40].

The Court of Appeal therefore permitted the publication of the judgment with approved redactions.

8.59 Likewise, the risk of 'jigsaw identification', whereby persons involved in public law proceedings may be identified by using information in the public domain as a result of the criminal proceedings, is not considered a reason in itself to withhold publication. As McDonald J noted in *H v A (No 2)*[41], 'jigsaw identification' is a possibility in every case where the family court publishes a judgment in proceedings where there has been reporting of related criminal proceedings. As in any application for an RRO, the question is whether the interference with Art 8 rights arising out of the risk of 'jigsaw identification' outweighs the interference in the Art 10 rights caused by withholding publication.

RROs and aggrieved parents

8.60 According to Munby P in *Re J (A Child)*[42], there is a public interest in the workings of the family justice system and the views about the system of the parents caught up in it (at [36]). He indicated that in a free society, parents who feel 'aggrieved' at their experiences of the family justice system should be able to express their views publicly about what they conceive to be 'failings on the part of individual judges or failings in the judicial system,' as well as the failings of local authorities and other professionals (at [36]). As such, the court will be hesitant to grant widely drafted RROs that prevent an aggrieved parent from legitimately discussing issues about herself or the child, unless publication was prejudicial to the child.

8.61 This may be seen in the case of *Re J (A Child)*[43] which, as discussed above, concerned an aggrieved father who repeatedly published details about the care proceedings of his children on the internet, including a covert video on Facebook of the youngest child being removed from his parents' care. The local authority in that case initially sought a widely drafted *contra mundum* RRO, which included, inter alia, a provision that prohibited the publication of the identities of the local authority and its employees. The court was critical of the local authority and held that the risk that the naming of the local authority and its employees would lead to the child being identified was 'merely fanciful' (at [70]).

8.62 Likewise, the court could see no justification for a provision preventing any person from seeking 'any other particulars or information relating to the child', which in practice would prevent the father from obtaining any information

40 At [34].
41 [2015] EWHC 2630 (Fam).
42 [2013] EWHC 2694 (Fam).
43 [2013] EWHC 2694 (Fam).

relating not only to the child but also to himself (at [71]). Highlighting the right of an aggrieved parent to air their concerns, Munby P commented as follows:

> 'The father wishes to share such information with others and, so long as he keeps within the confines of section 12 of the 1960 Act, why should he not be able to do so? And why should those who may wish to hear his views not be permitted to approach him? On one view this is in effect, if not intention, a means of indirectly gagging the father so that what from the local authority's perspective are his unpalatable views are less likely to see the light of day. It is one thing to say that something shall not be published if and insofar as it is prejudicial to J; this is very different and far more sweeping'[44].

8.63 A more balanced approach by a local authority may be seen in *Tickle v Council of the Borough of North Tyneside*[45]. Ms Tickle, a journalist, sought the permission of the court to analyse and write about a mother's experiences with her various children in the care system for a 5,000-word report in a broadsheet newspaper. The mother supported Ms Tickle's application and had herself published articles on social media about her experiences. Whilst the local authority issued a cross application for an RRO, the parties were able to agree the wording for a *contra mundum* injunction[46]. The court approved the agreed RRO and noted that it appropriately balanced '(a) the public interest in the media being able to report care proceedings as against (b) the interests of the privacy of those whose lives are intimately involved' (at [5]). The order, which is attached to the judgment, provides a useful precedent for family law practitioners to adapt as necessary.

THE SHIFT TOWARDS GREATER TRANSPARENCY

8.64 As stated at the outset of this chapter, there has been a greater shift towards transparency in the family courts in recent years. The astute reader will have noticed that the FPR 2010, r 27.11(2), which is set out in para 8.3, allows for duly accredited representatives of news gathering and reporting organisations to attend private proceedings. Prior to the introduction of this legislation on 27 April 2009, the media had been able to attend family court cases only in family proceedings courts, not in the county courts or High Court[47]. The only exception to this rule is that the media may not attend placement or adoption proceedings, proceedings related to the Human Fertilisation and Embryology Act 2008, s 54 (ie parental orders), or any conciliation or financial dispute resolution appointments[48].

8.65 A further move towards greater transparency in the family courts may be seen in the publication of 'Practice Guidance: Transparency in the Family

44 At [71].

45 [2015] EWHC 2991 (Fam).

46 It should be noted that a *contra mundum* injunction cannot be made by a consent order; it must be directed by the court.

47 Jarrett, supra note 1, para 2.2.

48 FPR 2010, r 27.11(1).

Courts – Publication of Judgments'[49] (the Transparency Practice Guidance). The purpose of the Transparency Practice Guidance is to encourage more family law judgments being made available to the public, with a view to increasing public understanding of the court process and confidence in the court system (para 2).

8.66 The Transparency Practice Guidance, which applies to judgments delivered by Circuit Judges, High Court Judges and persons sitting as judges of the High Court (including where the High Court is exercising inherent jurisdiction), sets out those judgments that the judge *must* ordinarily allow to be published and those that *may* be published (para 15). In respect of the first category, the guidance indicates that permission to publish a judgment should always be given where the judge concludes that it is in the public interest, regardless of whether a request has been made by one of the parties or the media.

8.67 Further, the President indicated that the following types of judgment should be reported if a written judgment already exists in a publishable form, or if the judge has already ordered that the judgment be transcribed:

(a) judgments arising from a substantial contested fact-finding hearing at which serious allegations have been determined (for example, sexual abuse);

(b) judgments arising from the making or refusal of a final care order or supervision order, or any order for the discharge of any such order, unless the matter is not contested;

(c) judgments arising from the making or refusal of a placement order or adoption order under the Adoption and Children Act 2002, or any order for the discharge of any such order, unless the matter is not contested;

(d) judgments arising from the making or refusal of any declaration or order authorising a deprivation of liberty;

(e) judgments arising from any application for an order involving the giving or withholding of serious medical treatment; and

(f) judgments arising from any application for an order involving a restraint on publication of information relating to the proceedings (see para 17).

8.68 In all other cases, the starting point is that permission may be given for the judgment to be published whenever a party or an accredited member of the media applies for an order permitting publication, and the Judge concludes that permission for publication should be given (see para 18). In deciding whether to give permission for publication, the judge must have regard to all the circumstances, including the rights arising under any relevant provision of the ECHR and the effect of publication upon any current or potential criminal proceedings. Where permission for publication is given, the Transparency Practice Guidance also sets out which persons should and should not be named in judgments and who should bear the cost of transcribing the judgment.

49 Issued on 16 January 2014 by Sir James Munby, President of the Family Court.

8.69 All family law practitioners must familiarise themselves with the Transparency Practice Guidance. Moreover, as the guidance makes clear, it is incumbent on practitioners to consider whether the judgment of any case in which they are acting should be published.

CONCLUSION

8.70 The approach of the court to considering applications for RROs is now well established in the case law, but may be difficult to navigate in practice in light of the competing rights engaged. As Tom Wilson points out, arguments in favour of greater transparency rest on a 'simple paradox: it is those attributes of the family justice system that may justify stringent restrictions on public access that also give rise to a compelling, legitimate and irrefutable public interest in its effective operation'[50]. It remains to be seen whether the family court can strike the right balance between the desire for greater transparency and the need to protect vulnerable children, which lies at the core of the family justice system.

50 T Wilson, 'Greater Transparency in Children Proceedings: A Note of Caution' (9 July 2015) Family Law Week, available at www.familylawweek.co.uk/site.aspx?i=ed145745.

Chapter 9

DEPRIVING CHILDREN OF THEIR LIBERTY: SECURE ACCOMMODATION ORDERS AND THE INHERENT JURISDICTION

INTRODUCTION

9.1 Depriving anyone of their liberty is a serious step: be that adults or children. In relation to children, their liberty is, to varying degrees, restricted on a daily basis, most obviously by parents, teachers and other adults, dependent on their age and behaviour. The power of the State, however, to deprive a child of her liberty is one that is appropriate only in rare circumstances. Those circumstances include: where a child is serving a prison sentence, where she has been sectioned under the Mental Health Act 1983 and where her liberty is deprived by a family court either under the Children Act 1989 (CA 1989) or the inherent jurisdiction.

9.2 The deprivation of a child's liberty involves interference with her rights under the European Convention on Human Rights (ECHR), Arts 5 (liberty) and 8 (respect for private and family life). In the family law context, it cannot (with limited exception) take place without the approval of a court and it attracts a number of procedural safeguards.

9.3 Despite the importance of the issues at stake, such applications are often made urgently and require a quick response from practitioners who may be less than used to this area of law. Particular issues include:

(a) the impact of the ECHR rights on the domestic test under the CA 1989, s 25;

(b) the interplay between s 25 and the inherent jurisdiction: the children for whom and the circumstances in which each will be appropriate;

(c) the ability of courts to authorise the deprivation of the liberty of older children; and

(d) the possibility of claims in damages against local authorities.

9.4 This chapter addresses, in turn:

(a) secure accommodation orders;

(b) the use of the inherent jurisdiction;

(c) recent changes to the law;

(d) claims in damages.

SECURE ACCOMMODATION ORDERS

9.5 In the family law context, the most common way of depriving a child of her liberty is by placing her in secure accommodation under the CA 1989, s 25 (or, in Wales, under the equivalent provision, the Social Services and Well-being (Wales) Act 2014, s 119). We need to remember, however, that secure accommodation orders can be used only for certain children and to place them in a set kind of accommodation. For those that do not fall into the secure accommodation categories, we need instead to use the inherent jurisdiction.

9.6 The first step, then, for any given child is to examine what we call the 'gateway criteria' – ie those three criteria that must be satisfied for the case to be a secure accommodation-type case as opposed to an inherent jurisdiction-type case.

The child must be 'looked after'

9.7 A secure accommodation order cannot be made in relation to a child who is not 'looked after' by a local authority. Note, however, that a local authority can and in many cases will apply for an (interim) care order at the same time as the application for the secure accommodation order.

9.8 We need to be clear, though, what 'looked after' does and does not mean in this context:

(a) it does mean: subject to a (full or interim) care order (the CA 1989, s 25(1)) or accommodated (for at least 24 hours) under s 20;

(b) except that it does not include children who are over 16 and are accommodated in a community home under the CA 1989, s 20(5).

So, the child must be 'looked after' for a secure accommodation order to be made in relation to her – and, that includes being accommodated under the CA 1989, s 20, unless the child is 16 or over and accommodated under s 20(5).

9.9 Anecdotally, there remains confusion about whether, when the subject child is 16 or 17, she can be made subject to a secure accommodation order. There need be no confusion. She can. Equally, the statement of law recorded by Hayden J in *London Borough of Barking & Dagenham v SS*[1], must be taken as incorrect. That statement in full is:

> '*The court does not have the power to make an order under s. 25 in respect of a young person over the age of 16*, but the order may be made prior to a child becoming 16, even if it extends beyond the child's 16th birthday' (emphasis added).

It is the italic clause that is incorrect.

9.10 It is incorrect for a simple reason. We know that a child will, unless discharged, remain subject to a care order until her 18th birthday; equally there is no reason that accommodation under s 20 must come to an end before that point. On either basis, a secure accommodation order can be made to protect a child who is 16 or 17. The only bar is that, if 16 or 17 and accommodated under s 20, she must be accommodated under s 20(3) and not under s 20(5). The difference is not always easy to spot. It is helpful to look at the difference in statutory provision under those two sub-subsections of the CA 1989:

> **'20 Provision of accommodation for children: general**
>
> '(3) Every local authority shall provide accommodation for any child in need within their area who has reached the age of sixteen and whose welfare the authority consider is likely to be seriously prejudiced if they do not provide him with accommodation'.
>
> '(5) A local authority may provide accommodation for any person who has reached the age of sixteen but is under twenty-one in any community home which takes children who have reached the age of sixteen if they consider that to do so would safeguard or promote his welfare'.

9.11 Identifying which applies to a given child will require a little thought. That is because it will not (or is very unlikely to) be set out on any s 20 consent document. Instead, we have to look at the essential difference between the two sub-sections: s 20(3) imposes a mandatory duty on a local authority and is triggered by a child whose welfare would otherwise be 'seriously prejudiced'; s 20(5) imposes a discretionary duty on a local authority and is triggered by a child whose welfare would be 'safeguard[ed] or promote[d]'. The difference, then, is severity of need, depending on the vulnerability and the precariousness of the child's situation.

9.12 The question, then, to ask, is this: is the accommodated child we are concerned with one who would be 'seriously prejudiced' without that accommodation, or simply one for whom the accommodation is 'safeguard[ing] or promote[ing]' welfare? We suggest the following rule of thumb: if a child is one

---

1 [2014] EWHC 4436 (Fam), at [2(7)].

for whom a secure accommodation order is envisaged, she is more likely than not to be 'seriously prejudiced' without any form of accommodation. Therefore, the starting point can be that she falls within s 20(3) and that a secure accommodation order can be made in relation to her.

9.13 As a related point, it should be noted that a child under the age of 13 cannot be placed in a secure children's home without the prior approval of the Secretary of State[2].

The purpose of the proposed accommodation: it must be for restricting liberty

9.14 The second and third criteria focus not on the child, but on the type of accommodation proposed. The second looks at the *purpose* of the proposed accommodation: the accommodation must be designed for or have as its primary purpose the restriction of the child's liberty. What it must not be is accommodation that, whilst depriving a child of her liberty, does so only incidentally to a different design or primary purpose[3]. Whilst that may sound slightly fiddly in theory, in practice it is less so. The obvious example of accommodation in which the deprivation of liberty is incidental as opposed to designed is a hospital: there, the primary purpose is to provide medical treatment, with the child not being able to leave a necessary but incidental component of that.

9.15 An example of that is set out in the following factual scenario. A girl, aged 15, suffers from anorexia nervosa. She has done since she was 12. She has attended private hospitals and at times been held under the Mental Health Act 1983. More recently, she is admitted to a NHS clinic. She absconds four times within a month; her behaviour is disturbed, aggressive and at times suicidal. The medical director of the clinic and the consultant psychiatrist say that they will not re-admit the child without a court order. The local authority seeks an order that she can be detained in the clinic for such treatment as prescribed, with the use of force if necessary. This is similar to the facts of *Re C (Detention: Medical Treatment)*[4]. In such a case, the deprivation of liberty is *incidental to* the primary purpose of the clinic: to treat her. So, the second gateway criterion would not be satisfied: a secure accommodation order could not be made.

It must, if a children's home, have been approved by the Secretary of State as secure accommodation

9.16 The third gateway criterion again focuses on the type of accommodation proposed – but here the question is simple and with a clear 'yes' or 'no' answer.

---

2 Child (Secure Accommodation) Regulations 1991, SI 1991/1505, reg 4, as amended.

3 *Re C (Detention: Medical Treatment)* [1997] 2 FLR 180, at 193, with Wall J here considering and adopting a more nuanced view that Cazelet J had earlier the same year, in *A Metropolitan Borough Council v DB* [1997] 1 FLR 767.

4 [1997] 2 FLR 180.

Has the accommodation been approved by the Secretary of State as secure accommodation? Given the increasing pressure on secure beds – a large number are now in the gift of the criminal justice system – this is an increasingly important question. Readers should note that (in England, but not in Wales because of differences in the drafting of the regulations) a complexity creeps in here. Arguably, a placement that is not classified as a children's home need not be approved as secure accommodation for it to be used as secure accommodation, given that reg 3 of the Children (Secure Accommodation) Regulations 1991 says only that it is a 'children's home' (as defined by reg 2) that must be approved by the Secretary of State. That might be thought to be counterintuitive and concerning, yet appears to be the effect of the regulations. It is to be hoped that this complexity (amongst others) will be considered by the Court of Appeal in July 2018 when hearing the appeals in *A Local Authority v T (No 1)*[5] and *A Local Authority v T (No 2)*[6].

9.17 A common example of non-approved secure accommodation is a residential placement that, whilst not officially 'secure', is capable of imposing significant restrictions on a child's liberty, in particular through additional resources bought in by a local authority. In that example, a secure accommodation order could not be made.

Secure accommodation orders: what is the test?

9.18 Having established that the case is one that is capable of having a secure accommodation order made, the next question is: what is the test for making it? The first point to note is that the child's welfare here is *not* paramount. Indeed, it would arguably be inconsistent with the statutory criteria for the making of the order if the paramountcy principle did apply[7].

9.19 Traditionally, one turned simply to the CA 1989. That made clear that, where either of the s 25 criteria is met, the making of an order is mandatory[8], with any discretion vested not in the court but in the local authority in determining whether or not to effect that order. The statutory test itself has two limbs. They are disjunctive – ie either can be satisfied and there is no need to establish both. They are:

First limb:

'(a) that –

(i) he has a history of absconding and is likely to abscond from any other description of accommodation; and,

(ii) if he absconds he is likely to suffer significant harm;'

5 [2018] EWHC 576 (Fam).
6 [2018] EWHC 816 (Fam).
7 *Re M* [1995] 1 FLR 418.
8 CA 1989, s 25(4): 'If a court determines that any such criteria are satisfied, it shall make an order authorizing the child to be kept in secure accommodation and specifying the maximum period for which he may be so kept'.

Second limb:

'(b) that if he is kept in any other description of accommodation he is likely to injure himself or other persons'[9].

For ease, we refer to the first as the 'absconding criteria' and the second as the 'injury criterion'.

9.20 The meaning of 'likely' is the same as in the threshold criteria in the CA 1989, s 31: that is to say, there must be a real possibility – one which cannot sensibly be ignored having regard to the nature and gravity of the feared harm in the particular case.

9.21 The definition of 'absconding' was considered in 2016 by the Court of Appeal in *Re W (A Child)*[10]. In doing so, Macur LJ overruled the judgment (and definition) provided by Keehan J at first instance. Her Ladyship held that 'absconding' means 'escaping indefinitely from an imposed regime, as opposed to deliberately absenting herself for a limited period, knowingly and disdainfully in breach of the night-time curfews imposed'[11]. This, then, is a useful working definition. However, her Ladyship also noted that 'Miss Judd QC's arguments in relation to the judge's definition of "absconding" ... did not persuade us that it is necessary to attempt to define the term beyond its ordinary meaning' and that Munby J 'relied on the definition of "abscond" as found in the Concise Oxford Dictionary. This accords with the usual application of the term to connote the element of "escape" from an imposed regime'.

9.22 Interestingly, her Ladyship dealt also the 'injury criterion', appearing to adopt what, to many, would appear a very strained definition. On the facts of the case[12], she found that the child, W, satisfied the 'injury criterion' because, 'Placed in any accommodation other than that which could "contain" her, she was in danger of serious harm'[13]. That, we suggest, is not immediately reconcilable with a statutory test that focuses on 'likely to injure himself or another person'[14], which holds the child as the protagonist of the injury as opposed to the victim (say, a child who was at risk from physical, emotional or sexual harm from an adult).

9.23 The case of *Re W* is important also for another reason: it makes clear that, whilst a secure accommodation order had to date been thought as mandatory on the satisfaction of either the 'absconding criteria' or the 'injury criterion', in fact it requires a judicial evaluation of the necessity and proportionality of the proposed order. Interestingly, this change has – academically at least – attracted little attention. It came, in fact, from a concession made by leading counsel for

9 CA 1989, s 25(1)(a)–(b).

10 [2016] EWCA Civ 804 at [22].

11 At [22].

12 W's presentation included disruptive, abusive and sexually promiscuous behaviour, including the use of alcohol and illegal drugs: see *Re W (A Child)* [2016] EWCA Civ 804 at [7].

13 At [22].

14 In s 25(1)(b).

the appellant, which was adopted by Macur LJ. It is a helpful and important argument for practitioners to deploy if opposing an application for a secure accommodation order in circumstances in which it is clear that the court will find that the 'absconding criteria' or the 'injury *criterion*' is met.

Secure accommodation orders: procedure; time limits and review; challenge

9.24 The applicant for a secure accommodation order is, where a local authority is looking after a child, that local authority. Where a health authority, the NHS trust or a local authority is providing accommodation for the child, any of those may apply, unless the child is looked after[15].

9.25 The respondents are:

(a) the child;

(b) every person believed to have parental responsibility for the child; and

(c) every person believed to have parental responsibility before any care order[16].

9.26 The application is made to the Family Court in Form C1 and Supplement Form C20. Service must be effected on the respondent(s) at least one day in advance of the date of the hearing.

9.27 Importantly, a secure accommodation order may not be made unless the child is legally represented or has been told of the right to apply for funding under the Legal Aid, Sentencing and Punishment of Offenders Act 2012, is given the opportunity to do so, and has failed or refused to apply[17].

9.28 It is worth bearing in mind also that:

(a) a clear record of facts as found by the court is required, with sworn evidence necessary;

(b) the identification of an appropriate placement is not a pre-requisite to the making of an order[18];

(c) an interim secure accommodation order may be made only where the application is adjourned, with there being no such thing as a freestanding interim application[19].

9.29 Without a court order, a local authority (or other authority) may keep a child in secure accommodation for a total period of 72 hours, whether or not

---

15 Child (Secure Accommodation) Regulations 1991, reg 8; Child (Secure Accommodation) (No 2) Regulations 1991, reg 2(1)–(2).

16 FPR 2010, r 12.3.

17 CA 1989, s 25(6).

18 *Re A (A Child)* [2015] EWHC 1709 (Fam) at [11].

19 CA 1989, s 25(5). See also *Birmingham City Council v M* [2008] EWHC 1085 (Fam) at [23].

consecutive, in any 28-day period[20]. The maximum period for which a court can make a secure accommodation order, except where a child has been remanded to local authority care by a criminal court, is three months on the first application and six months on each subsequent application[21].

9.30 Note, however, that the time runs from the date of the court order and *not* the date when the child is actually placed in secure accommodation – so, if an order is made but a placement is not immediately available, the start and end date of the order relates to the order's date not the date of placement[22].

9.31 The local authority must review the placement within one month of it commencing and at least every three months thereafter. At least three persons – one of whom is independent of the local authority – must be appointed to conduct this review. Equally, the local authority must itself remain satisfied that the 'absconding criteria' or the 'injury criterion' remains satisfied – if not, the child must be released from the secure placement[23]. It is a permissive order, ie it entitles (as long as the criteria remain satisfied) but does not oblige the local authority to place the child in secure accommodation.

9.32 Any party may appeal a secure accommodation order in the normal way. There is no need to apply for permission to appeal in such cases[24]. Where it is asserted that, despite the order continuing in force, neither the 'absconding criteria' nor 'injury criterion' applies, and the local authority does not release the child, the appropriate application is to the High Court for a writ of habeas corpus to challenge the lawfulness of the continued detention. If, of course, an aspect of that claim is that the local authority has failed property to carry out its duties of review or has come to an unreasonable decision, it is possible to apply also for judicial review.

DEPRIVATION OF LIBERTY UNDER THE INHERENT JURISDICTION

9.33 Given that, to make a secure accommodation order, the three 'gateway criteria' – the child being 'looked after', the purpose of the accommodation, and the type of accommodation – must all be met, there are many instances in which a local authority or a court wants to assist or protect a child by significantly restricting her liberty, but is unable to satisfy some or all of the 'gateway criteria' so as to place her in secure accommodation. In short, the option of secure accommodation is not available. Equally, it is never open to a local authority without the authorisation of the court to place a child in a placement that would breach her rights under the ECHR, Art 5. It is in these cases that the inherent jurisdiction is deployed.

20 Child (Secure Accommodation) Regulations 1991, reg 10.
21 Child (Secure Accommodation) Regulations 1991, regs 11–12.
22 *Re B (A Minor) (Secure Accommodation)* [1994] 2 FLR 707 at 711.
23 Child (Secure Accommodation) Regulations 1991, regs 15–16.
24 FPR 2010, r 30.3(2)(b).

9.34 The relevant parts of the ECHR, Art 5 read:

> **'Right to liberty and security**
>
> 1. Everyone has the right to liberty and security of person. No one shall be deprived of his liberty save in the following cases and in accordance with a procedure prescribed by law:
>
> (d) the detention of a minor by lawful order for the purpose of educational supervision ...
>
> 2. –
>
> 3. –
>
> 4. Everyone who is deprived of his liberty by arrest or detention shall be entitled to take proceedings by which the lawfulness of this detention shall be decided speedily by a court and his release ordered if the detention is now lawful'.

9.35 The concept of 'deprived of his liberty' in the terms of ECHR, Art 5.1, has been examined and defined by the European Court of Human Rights (ECtHR) in the leading cases of *Storck v Germany*[25] and *Stanev v Bulgaria*[26], the application of which was explicitly endorsed in our national law by *P (by his litigation friend, the OS) v Cheshire West and Chester Council*[27]. The concept has three components. They are:

(a) the objective component of confinement in a particular restricted place for a not negligible period of time ('confinement');

(b) the subjective component of a lack of valid consent;

(c) the attribution of responsibility to the State.

Where those three components are met, the child (or adult) is deprived of her liberty.

9.36 With the exception of the scheme under the CA 1989, s 25 (and that under the Mental Capacity Act 2005 (MCA 2005) in the Court of Protection for those young persons who are aged 16 or over, and fall within the MCA 2005 provisions), there is no statutory scheme to authorise a child's deprivation of liberty in this context. in other words, there is no statutory scheme to place a child in a non-secure-accommodation placement that deprives her of her liberty. As is well known, however, the High Court retains an inherent power to come to the rescue of subjects of the Crown – what we call the inherent jurisdiction. In circumstances in which some or all of the 'gateway criteria' to the CA 1989, s 25 are

25 [2005] ECHR 406.

26 [2012] ECHR 46.

27 [2014] UKSC 19 at [37].

not met, it is to the inherent jurisdiction and the High Court that we turn to authorise a deprivation of liberty.

9.37 This theme has been explored, in characteristic detail, by Munby P in a lengthy judgment handed down by the Court of Appeal in autumn 2017 and a judgment given at first instance in early 2018. Those cases are, respectively, *Re D (A Child)*[28] and *Re A-F (Children)*[29]. They now form the cornerstone of the jurisprudence in this area and are required reading for practitioners. In addition to those two cases, and as noted at para 9.16, above, the complexities of this difficult area are due to be examined in full by Court of Appeal in July 2018 when hearing the appeals in *A Local Authority v T (No 1)*[30] and *A Local Authority v T (No 2)*[31].

9.38 In practical terms, the two most common scenarios in which we turn to the inherent jurisdiction are when a child is deprived of her liberty, but the *purpose* of the accommodation is not that deprivation or confinement, rather it is an incidental effect, or where the accommodation is not approved for 'secure' use by the Secretary of State, but the accommodation nevertheless effects that deprivation of liberty.

Deprivation of liberty incidental to design or primary purpose

9.39 This is the same as para 9.14, above, and the case study set out at para 9.15. In such cases – say, a hospital – the placement must be approved under the inherent jurisdiction and cannot be sanctioned under the CA 1989, s 25.

Non-approved placement

9.40 This is an increasingly common phenomenon. The problem is simply stated: there are a limited number of registered, secure beds in England and Wales. A proportion of those are in use by the criminal justice system. And, of those that are available in family cases (ie for children who have not committed a crime), it is not uncommon that a particular child's difficulties will mean that registered secure placements are unwilling or unable to take that particular child.

9.41 It is a problem that has recently made headlines in a line of cases in which High Court judges have complained, in public judgments, of the shortage of suitable placements. Perhaps most infamously, and in the context of a clinical placement, were the chilling words of Sir James Munby P in the *Re X* cases that, without an appropriate bed being found, we would have '*blood on our hands*'[32]. The line was picked up on and widely quoted by the national press.

28 [2017] EWCA Civ 1695.
29 [2018] EWHC 138 (Fam).
30 [2018] EWHC 576 (Fam).
31 [2018] EWHC 816 (Fam).
32 *Re X (A Child) (No 3)* [2017] EWHC 2036 (Fam) at [39].

9.42 At that point, the local authority becomes stuck. It needs to protect the child. But there is no registered secure placement available, so the local authority (and the court) must think creatively. It must place the child in a non-registered secure placement: that is to say, a placement, perhaps one with services bought in by the local authority, that significantly restricts a child's liberty, but that is not official secure accommodation. The approval for that regime must be secured by an application to the court for an order under the inherent jurisdiction.

9.43 An example is as follows:

- a local authority is caring for a 'looked after' adolescent boy presenting with severely disruptive and predatory sexual behaviour. Following an extensive search, the local authority is unable to locate a registered secure placement that is able to care for the boy given its duties to other children already in placements;
- the local authority is advised that, such is the boy's behaviour and risk of harm both to himself and others, an appropriate placement must quickly be found for him;
- the local authority is compelled to create and finance a 'bespoke' secure placement. The local authority commissions a small residential children's home so that the child becomes the only child or young person placed in it and buys in resources and staff so as to make the unit 'secure'. The child either cannot or does not consent to the significant restrictions imposed on her liberty;
- such a placement would require authorisation under the inherent jurisdiction.

Using the inherent jurisdiction: what amounts to a confinement

9.44 A difficult and important question is determining what does and what does not amount to a confinement so as to trigger *Storck* component (a) (as to which see para 9.35). It is difficult because children and young persons are restricted in their liberty, all the time and by a range of family members, other adults and institutions: whether that is not being alone for any waking moment (very young children), to not being left home alone and not permitted a mobile phone or unrestricted internet use (say, pre-teenagers), to having curfews imposed (say, teenagers). That applies as strongly to children in the care of local authorities as it does to children living without State intervention. Not all of those situations amount to a confinement that would, in the event of the satisfaction of the *Storck* components (b) and (c), require the sanction of the High Court.

9.45 Equally, it is important precisely for that reason: where the restrictions are such that, taken in conjunction with a child's age and development, there is a deprivation of liberty, not only does that require the authorisation of the High Court but, without that approval, such deprivation is likely to amount to an unlawful breach of the child's rights under inter alia ECHR, Art 5, leading to a possible claim for declarations and perhaps damages under the Human Rights Act 1998 (HRA 1998).

9.46 What we are left with is, we suggest, a spectrum. At one end of that spectrum (say, a toddler being subject to continuous supervision and control and not permitted to wander off), the confinement is not only acceptable in legal terms but also required socially and culturally. At the other end (say, an adolescent in a secure unit subject to monitoring every five minutes, with bars on the windows and locked outer doors, not permitted to leave and not permitted to use a mobile phone or money) we have a clear case in which the confinement falls within *Storck* component (a) so as to risk requiring court approval. Between those two points a grey zone exists, which can be clarified and evaluated only on a case-by-case, fact-specific basis[33].

9.47 The test for the point along the spectrum at which restriction tips into confinement was set out by the President of the Supreme Court, Lord Neuberger, in the well-known Court of Protection case of *P (by his litigation friend, the OS) v Cheshire West and Chester Council*[34]. His Lordship drew on Strasbourg authority and described the test as, 'continuous supervision and control and lack of freedom to leave' (at [63]) – what has become known as the acid test. Subsequently, that test has been applied to the deprivation of liberty of children in a number of cases.

9.48 A definition of 'lack of freedom to leave' was given by Munby J in *JE v DE*[35] as meaning 'leaving in the sense of removing [themselves] permanently in order to live where and with whom one chooses'.

9.49 More recently, the difficult question – the character of *Storck* component (a) – has been analysed by Munby P in *Re D (A Child)*[36] and *Re A-F (Children)*[37]. The following important points can be extracted from those cases:

(a) almost by definition, a child's life is characterised by a 'lack of freedom to leave' (as defined by Munby J in *JE v DE*) meaning that the forensic focus will be on 'continuous control and supervision'[38];

(b) whether a child satisfies the *Cheshire West* acid test for confinement requires a comparison between the restrictions to which the child in question is subject and the restrictions which would apply to a child of the same age, station, familial background and relative maturity, who is free from disability. The comparator child is not one who is subject to a care order[39];

(c) a 'rule of thumb': a child aged under 10, even if under fairly constant supervision, is unlikely to be confined in *Storck* component (a) terms. A child aged 11, if under constant supervision, may be so confined, though the court should be astute to avoid coming too readily to such a conclusion. Once a

33 In the context of the Court of Protection (for those without capacity who are 16 or over), The Law Society has produced a helpful and lengthy guide: *Identifying a deprivation of liberty: a practical guide* (1 April 2015).
34 [2014] UKSC 19.
35 [2006] EWHC 3459 (Fam) at [115].
36 [2017] EWCA Civ 1695.
37 [2018] EWHC 138 (Fam).
38 *Re A-F (Children)* [2018] EWHC 138 (Fam), at [31].
39 *Re A-F (Children)* [2018] EWHC 138 (Fam), at [33] and [44].

child who is under constant supervision has reached the age of 12, the court will more readily come to the conclusion that he is confined[40].

9.50 Given the highly case-by-case and fact-specific nature of the exercise, it is not possible with any precision to set out the facts that will mark the tipping into a *Storck* component (a)-qualifying restriction of liberty – but what one can do is look at the hallmarks from reported case-law and apply them to future cases. Key questions to ask are:

- Do the staff know the child's whereabouts at all times? Is she supervised at all times?
- Is she left alone with other residents? Is she allowed in other residents' bedrooms?
- Are the internal and/or external doors of the placement locked (although note that 'lockability' has explicitly been held by the ECtHR not to be determinative, ie one can be confined even on, say, an open ward[41])? Is this constant or behaviour-dependent?
- What happens when the child goes 'off site' (eg whilst at school or in other educational resource)? How does she get there? Is she permitted on public transport?
- To what extent is she permitted to use a mobile phone and the internet?
- Are other residents subject to the same restrictions?

Using the inherent jurisdiction: subjective component of lack of consent (Storck component (b)) and attribution of responsibility to the State (Storck component (c))

9.51 The case law of the ECtHR and the domestic courts provides some, but limited, guidance to the proper understanding of consent in this context. Again, this is an area will be considered Court of Appeal in July 2018 when hearing the appeals in *A Local Authority v T (No 1)* and *A Local Authority v T (No 2)*. From current domestic case law, it is possible to make the following observations:

(a) it is necessary that the child is: (1) capable in law of providing that consent (ie competent to do so); and (2) does, in fact, provide it[42];

(b) as for who is best placed to make that assessment, there is divergence in judicial thought. Whilst it is the view of Keehan J that this evaluation can be undertaken by a social worker, children's solicitor or guardian (the latter two often, anecdotally at least, being in the best place to do so), Munby P has held *obiter* that, where a child who finds herself subject to such confinement is said to give a valid consent to it, the evidence of a child

40 *Re A-F (Children)* [2018] EWHC 138 (Fam), at [33].

41 *HL v United Kingdom* (2004) 40 EHRR 761, at [92].

42 See, for example, *Re C (A Child)* [2016] EWHC 3473 (Fam) at [52]–[60].

and adolescent psychologist or psychiatric would normally be required in support[43];

(c) that consent must be 'full and genuine' – it must not be a consent that is, on the evidence, short-lived or changeable. That leaves open, however, a thorny question: should the judge, in evaluating an explicitly subjective consent, take account of his view on whether the consent will endure? As it stands, there is conflicting High Court authority on this point. On the one hand, Keehan J has held, in *Trust A v X*[44] that no or little account should be taken of this, drawing on the analogy of the Mental Capacity Act 2005. In contrast, Mostyn J has found that the court *should* take strong account of the likelihood that consent may not endure and, in circumstances in which the court finds that it may not, hold that the consent is insufficient and therefore does trigger *Storck* component (b)[45];

(d) occasional breaches of 'house rules' or obvious expressions of discontent with certain restrictions do not remove that consent[46];

(e) for the avoidance of doubt, a foster carer does not have parental responsibility enabling the carer to provide a valid consent in this context[47].

9.52 Turning, then to *Storck* component (c):

(a) where a child is subject to a care order (whether interim or final) there is involvement and responsibility of the State (both through the local authority and the court). So '*obvious*' is this proposition that, per Munby P, it requires no authority[48];

(b) for the avoidance of doubt, we note that, where a child is not 'looked after' she may well be subject to 'continuous supervision and control and lack of freedom to leave'. That parental decision does not – of course – require the authorisation of any court. Indeed, in a case in which a 15-year-old young person was accommodated by a local authority in a hospital and due to be moved to a residential unit (without, it appears, any order under the CA 1989, Part IV), it has been held that significant restrictions amounting to confinement can be consented to by parents where that consent is a decision within 'the proper exercise of parental responsibility' taking account of the child or young person's behaviour and needs[49]. That conclusion is supported by ECtHR authority, which holds that the extent of parental responsibility here is 'extensive', albeit not 'unlimited'[50].

---

43 Respectively, *Re C (A Child)* 2016] EWHC 3473 (Fam) at [44] and *Re A-F (Children)* [2018] EWHC 138 (Fam), at [53].

44 [2015] EWHC 992 (Fam), sub nom *Re D (A Child) (Deprivation of Liberty)*.

45 *A Local Authority v T (No 1)* [2018] EWHC 576 (Fam) and *A Local Authority v T (No 2)* [2018] EWHC 816 (Fam).

46 *Re C (A Child)* [2016] EWHC 3473 (Fam) at [61].

47 *Re A-F (Children)* [2018] EWHC 138 (Fam) at [12].

48 *Re A-F (Children)* [2018] EWHC 138 (Fam) at [10].

49 *Trust A v X* [2015] EWHC 992 (Fam), sub nom *Re D (A Child) (Deprivation of Liberty)*.

50 *Re A-F (Children)* [2018] EWHC 138 (Fam) at [11], citing *Nielsen v Denmark* 11 EHRR 175.

Using the inherent jurisdiction: what is the test?

9.53 Firstly, a local authority applicant must come within the CA 1989, s 100(3)–(5) for leave to apply for an order under the inherent jurisdiction:

> **'100 Restrictions on use of wardship**
>
> (3) No application for any exercise of the court's inherent jurisdiction with respect to children may be made by a local authority unless the authority have obtained the leave of the court.
>
> (4) The court may only grant leave if it is satisfied that—
>
> (a) the result which the authority wish to achieve could not be achieved through the making of any order of a kind to which subs (5) applies; and
>
> (b) there is reasonable cause to believe that if the court's inherent jurisdiction is not exercised with respect to the child he is likely to suffer significant harm.
>
> (5) This subsection applies to any order—
>
> (a) made otherwise than in the exercise of the court's inherent jurisdiction; and
>
> (b) which the local authority is entitled to apply for (assuming, in the case of any application which may only be made with leave, that leave is granted)'.

9.54 The effect of that is clear and two-fold: the order sought (here, deprivation of liberty) must not be one that could be achieved outside of the inherent jurisdiction (ie the case cannot be a secure accommodation-type one) and without the making of that order there is reasonable cause to believe that the child is likely to suffer significant harm.

9.55 Secondly – and unlike when making an order under the CA 1989, s 25 – the paramountcy principle *does* apply to the making of an order under the inherent jurisdiction[51].

9.56 Thirdly, given the interference with the ECHR, Arts 5 (liberty) and 8 (respect for private and family law), the orders must fall within the permissible exceptions to those ECHR rights. In other words, for a deprivation of liberty to be lawful, it must fall within the exceptions at Art 5(1)(d) and Art 8(2). The exception at Art 5(1)(d) is that a child may be deprived of her liberty for 'the purpose of educational supervision'. It has been held authoritatively that

---

51 *Re C* [1997] 2 FLR 189 at 197–198.

depriving a child of her liberty in a children's home falls within that exception[52]. The Art 8(2) exception permits interference with Art 8 rights 'for the prevention of disorder or crime, for the protection of health or morals, or for the protection of the rights and freedoms of others'. There is no obvious difficulty with the satisfaction of that.

9.57 More contentious is whether there is a fourth principle or limb to the test. Namely, should we import the CA 1989, s 25 'absconding criteria' and 'injury criterion' and apply them by analogy? Whilst there is no requirement under the ECHR to impose such a test, the question is whether the domestic law analogy with secure accommodation orders requires it. In logical terms, there is, we suggest, much to commend that approach. After all, the inherent jurisdiction and the CA 1989, s 25 are, in this context, deployed to achieve the same end: authorising the deprivation of a child's liberty. The degree of imposition that the State is visiting on the child is the same. Surely, the level of safeguards before this imposition can take place must be the same too. Further, we know that Parliament has decided in secure accommodation cases that it is not enough to say that, 'the child's welfare requires her to be deprived of her liberty'. Something more and something different is needed. That something more and different is the 'absconding criteria' and the 'injury criterion', which are set out in the CA 1989, s 25.

9.58 The inherent jurisdiction is judge-made law. Must it take account here of Parliament's law in the analogous area of secure accommodation orders? Can it be right that, if a young person is accommodated under s 20(5) as opposed to s 20(3), or if the local authority has no registered secure places available to it and therefore has to create a bespoke placement, the test that the local authority must satisfy before depriving that child of her liberty be any less? That, if you cannot persuade a court that the statutory test is met to place a child in a registered secure placement, you can instead place them, under exactly the same conditions, in the non-registered children's home next door, still without satisfying the statutory test?

9.59 Support for that view – that the 'absconding criteria' and 'injury criterion' must by analogy be imported and applied – can be found in a number of High Court (or judges sitting in the High Court) authorities[53].

9.60 There is, however, an opposing view. It works on the basis that there is no test above that of the three categories of principle (the CA 1989, s 100(3)–(5), paramountcy principle and ECHR, Art 5 and 8 exceptions) already set out. An example of a case proceeding on that basis is *Re D (A Child) (Deprivation of Liberty)*[54]. For now, there is a divergence of opinion in the High Court.

---

52 *Re K (A Child) (Secure Accommodation Order: Right to Liberty)* [2001] 2 All ER 719, for example at [42], [64] and [114].

53 That includes *Re B (Secure Accommodation: Inherent Jurisdiction) (No 1)* [2013] EWHC 4654 (Fam) at [21] and *(No 2)* [2013] EWHC 4655 (Fam) at [21 7].

54 [2015] EWHC 922 (Fam).

9.61 It is additionally important to note that, where orders are made under the inherent jurisdiction to deprive a child of her liberty, the President has held that the use of the inherent jurisdiction must comply with the substantive and procedural requirements of the ECHR, Art 5[55]. Close regard should also, we suggest, be had to *Re A-F (Children)*[56], which functions as a detailed procedural guide for the management of these orders.

CHILDREN AND SOCIAL WORK ACT 2017

9.62 On 27 April 2017, the Children and Social Work Act 2017, s 10 and Sch 1 came into force. The Act introduces a number of changes to secure accommodation orders. An important one is that the bar on English and Welsh courts placing children in secure accommodation in Scotland – a bar that was identified and examined by the President of the Family Division in *X and Y (A Child)*[57] – has been removed. That means that a local authority in this jurisdiction can now place a child in secure accommodation in Scotland, just so long as that establishment is one approved by the relevant Scottish authorities[58].

CLAIMS UNDER THE HRA 1998: UNLAWFUL DEPRIVATION OF LIBERTY

9.63 Practitioners are increasingly familiar with the proliferation in claims for declarations and damages under the HRA 1998 and accompanying claims for tortious breaches flowing from the misuse of the CA 1989, s 20. They are dealt with in detail at paras 1.32–1.52. Whilst such claims have in family law focused on the CA 1989, s 20, there is, we suggest, every reason to believe that there exist, and facts will continue to give rise to, a significant number of latent claims under the HRA 1998 against local authorities for the unlawful deprivation of a child's liberty in breach of the ECHR, Art 5.

9.64 For the moment, there is no reported case in the family law arena on this topic. But, we suggest, it remains a space to watch. For when such claims are issued, practitioners should keep to hand and rely on the guidance given by the High Court in issuing claims based on the misuse of the CA 1989, s 20, as set out paras 1.32–1.52.

55 *Re X (A Child) (Jurisdiction: Secure Accommodation), In Re Y (A Child) (Jurisdiction: Secure Accommodation)* [2016] EWHC 2271 (Fam) at [48]–[49].

56 [2018] EWHC 138 (Fam) at [47]–[56].

57 [2016] EWHC 2271 (Fam).

58 Child (Secure Accommodation) Regulations, reg 3(1), as amended by the Children and Social Work Act 2017. The placement must have been approved by the Scottish Ministers under the Public Services Reform (Scotland) Act 2010.

CONCLUSION

9.65 In statutory terms, the area is narrow. The practitioner will need:

(a) the CA 1989, ss 25 and 100;

(b) the Children (Secure Accommodation) Regulations 1991 – and make sure these are up-to-date, to include the amendments made by the Children and Social Work Act 2017.

As for key case law, the two most helpful cases at the time of writing are, we suggest:

— if dealing with a secure accommodation order: *Re W (A Child)*[59]; and

— if involved in an application made under the inherent jurisdiction: *Re D (A Child)*[60].

The decision in *Re A-F (Children)*[61] is also most useful: in particular, regard should be had to the detailed procedural guide at paras [47]–[56].

9.66 Key points and arguments to consider, whatever your position on the application, are:

(a) is this a secure accommodation-type case or an inherent jurisdiction-type case? ie consider the 'gateway criteria';

(b) look at the CA 1989, s 25(1) criteria: which is being relied upon?

(c) if it is an 'absconding criteria' case, is the (new) definition of 'absconding' really met?

(d) irrespective of the wording of the CA 1989, s 25(4) ('*shall*'), is an order necessary and proportionate?

(e) for how long has the child been deprived of her liberty? Should advice be given on a potential claim against the local authority for declarations and damages for breach of ECHR, Art 5?

59 [2016] EWCA Civ 804.

60 [2017] EWCA Civ 1695.

61 [2018] EWHC 138 (Fam).

Chapter 10

SPECIAL GUARDIANSHIP ORDERS

INTRODUCTION

10.1 The starting point of the modern law is the Prime Minister's Review of Adoption in July 2000, which identified the existence of a significant group of children for whom it was not wished to make the absolute legal break with the birth family that characterises adoption. It highlighted that long-term foster care often lacked security and a sense of family. The need for an intermediate status – a placement between fostering and adoption – was explained. The focus was on the requirement for legal security without absolute legal severance.

10.2 Following the Review of Adoption, the UK Government's White Paper, *Adoption: A New Approach*[1], committed the government to the creation of a new private law order – a special guardianship order – that would satisfy the need for legal permanence short of adoption. A few years later, in 2004, through the Adoption and Children Act 2002 (ACA 2002), special guardianship orders were introduced into the Children Act 1989 (CA 1989), with accompanying regulations made.

10.3 A special guardianship order is, of course, one that bestows on the special guardian parental responsibility for a child. That parental responsibility can be exercised to the exclusion of all others, apart from another special guardian (although an exception to that is where the law provides that the consent of more than one holder of parental responsibility is required, for example for the sterilisation of a child). The December 2010 White Paper set out what it described as an 'illustrative case study' of the use of special guardianship orders,

> 'J (13) and S (9) have been in the care of the same foster carers for some time. They came into care as the result of J disclosing sexual abuse, and are unable to return home. The foster carers and the children would like to remain together but J does not want to be adopted. She wants to keep her birth name, have contact with some members of her birth family but live

---

1 December 2000.

with her foster carers. "Special guardianship" would provide her and her sister with a permanent home within their foster family'[2].

10.4 In the decade that followed the introduction of special guardianship orders, there was a year-on-year increase in their use. At the same time, two other trends took hold: the first was a perceived heightening of the threshold required to be met for adoption following the judgments of the Supreme Court in *Re B (A Child)*[3] and Court of Appeal in *Re B-S (Children)*[4] and an accompanying sharp decrease in the number of placement orders made[5]; the second, a growing uneasiness about the pace at which, in any given case, a special guardianship order would be adopted as the preferred outcome by a local authority and approved by a court.

10.5 The latest figures show that, in the year ending 31 March 2017, 3,690 children ceased to be looked after through the making of a special guardianship order. That figure excludes, of course, those children in relation to whom a special guardianship order is made without them first having become looked after (for example where such orders are made in private law proceedings).

10.6 The concern about the fragility of many special guardianship orders remains. In part, the problem is structural, with the statutory scheme not providing for the introduction, matching or settling-in period that is key to adoptive placements, no doubt in reflection of the original expectation that a child and special guardian would be well known to one another. In addition, special guardians often face heightened challenges: in particular, in relation to contact between the child and her birth family (with children subject to these orders frequently having a high level of contact with a range of relatives) and split loyalties that a special guardian, say a grandparent, will feel toward the subject child and her parent(s).

10.7 This chapter is a short one. It addresses the following points:

(a) special guardianship orders: where are we now?

(b) statute, guidance and regulations;

(c) financial provision and support, including judicial review.

For discussion of placing children abroad under special guardianship orders, see Chapter 3 on international public law orders.

2 Derived from an unpublished paper by Selwyn and Sturgess, *Achieving permanency: proposals for UK policy* (2000), and cited by Wall LJ in *Re S (A Child)* [2007] EWCA Civ 54 at [12].
3 [2013] UKSC 33.
4 [2013] EWCA Civ 1146.
5 From 1 September 2013 to 30 June 2014, there was a 54 per cent drop.

SPECIAL GUARDIANSHIP ORDERS: WHERE ARE WE NOW?

10.8 In December 2015, the Minister for Children and Families, Edward Timpson MP, published his report into special guardianship orders. That review reached two central conclusions. The first was that the majority of these orders are made to carers who have an existing relationship with the child and who, with appropriate support, intend to and will be able to care for her until she turns 18.

10.9 Second, and of more concern, the report found that in a significant minority of cases, the required protective factors are not in place. In particular, that absence flows from three factors: rushed or poor-quality assessments – often caused by family members coming forward late in proceedings, court deadlines or challenges to assessments requiring re-assessment; the approval of risky placements – notably, almost half of the cases considered by the review came with a supervision order attached; and inadequate support for special guardians – both for proposed special guardians in terms of information and post-order when difficulties emerge. Underpinning each of these is the need for a good-quality special guardianship assessment.

10.10 Edward Timpson MP's concern echoed the view of Cafcasss and the ADCS who, in October 2015, issued a joint policy statement, 'out of concern about a number of cases where we believe children have been placed at risk through a Special Guardianship Order being made without sufficient consideration of the placement's long-term viability'. It was the Cafcass-ADCS view that special guardianship assessments were being squeezed, not least by the 26-week deadline introduced by the Children and Families Act 2014[6]. To this, one can add, anecdotally at least, the all-too-common tension between the need for DBS checks prior to the making of a special guardianship order and the significant delay in many parts of the country in obtaining these checks.

10.11 The review also noted that we had moved away from the original purpose of special guardianship orders. At the time of their introduction in 2005, it was considered – although not explicitly or implicitly contained in the statute – that this new order would focus on certain groups of children:

— older children who had become separated from their birth family;

— children already settled with a relative or foster carer;

— minority ethnic groups in relation to whom a cultural tension with adoption may exist; and

— unaccompanied asylum-seeking children who require permanence without severance of the strong attachment with family abroad.

6 'The Assessment of Special Guardians as the Preferred Permanence Option for Children in Care Proceedings Applications' (ADCS/Cafcass).

The review found that whilst it was, 'implicit ... that SGOs were originally intended to create a more permanent situation for older children in a placement for whom adoption was not suitable', there had, since 2005, been a steady increase in the making of these orders in relation to younger children and in favour of carers with whom the child is not resident[7].

10.12 The worries about the fragility of special guardianship placements broke into the public consciousness in graphic form in May 2016, following the conviction for murder of the special guardian of an 18-month-old baby, Keegan Downer, killed in distressing circumstances only eight months after she had been placed with the special guardian. The case was picked up on and widely reported by the national press and spurred a number of national organisations into action.

10.13 Following Edward Timpson MP's report, the Special Guardianship (Amendment) Regulations 2016[8] were enacted by the Secretary of State for Education, in a bid to patch up a number of the deficits in the quality and focus of special guardianship assessments. In particular, two points were made explicit:

(a) when considering a child, consideration was required of any harm suffered and any risk of future harm including by the child's parents, as well as of the child's likely future needs; and

(b) when evaluating the relationship between the proposed special guardian and the child, regard must be had to the current and past relationship between them, as well as the proposed special guardian's parenting capacity in terms of understanding of and ability to meet needs, understanding of and ability to protect the children from harm (in particular relating to contact) and ability and suitability to bring up the child until she turns 18.

10.14 Whilst, in legal terms at least, a richer evidential tapestry is now mandated, it remains the case that a squeeze – between family members putting themselves forward late and the 26-week deadline for care proceedings – continues to put pressure on the quality of the assessments that are placed before the court. Equally, the emphasis on the relationship between a child and the proposed special guardians, including the elevation of this into a requirement, in some courts, that they must first reside together, is only now being worked through in the case law, with a settled legal position yet to emerge.

10.15 Nevertheless, and despite the well-founded concerns, it is, even in novel contexts, possible to see the continued and successful application of the founding principle of special guardianship orders: namely, the need for an intermediate status between fostering and adoption and the need for permanence without complete legal severance. In the 2013 case of *Al-Hilli*[9], following the tragic and widely reported fatal shooting in the French Alps of two girls' parents and maternal

---

7 *Special guardianship review: report on findings. Government consultation response* (December 2015) p 23.

8 SI 2016/111.

9 [2013] EWHC 3404 (Fam).

grandmother, Baker J hit on precisely that point in explaining his use of special guardianship orders. His Lordship held:

> 'Such orders are particularly suitable for children who require a greater degree of permanence and stability than is provided by an ordinary residence order, but for whom adoption is not suitable'[10].

10.16 Equally, the importance of special guardianship in a non-familial context – as first flagged up in the December 2010 White Paper – has been reiterated by the Court of Appeal. In the 2012 case of *Re I (A Child)*[11], a case that focused on the legal structure that would govern the placement of a little girl (aged three at the first-instance final hearing) with her foster carers, McFarlane LJ granted permission to appeal on the basis that the first-instance judge had failed properly to consider special guardianship alongside adoption as a suitable welfare outcome.

STATUTE, GUIDANCE AND REGULATIONS

10.17 By way of the ACA 2002, ss 14A–14G were inserted into the CA 1989. These sections make provision for special guardianship orders.

10.18 The Department for Education's statutory guidance in relation to special guardianship orders was produced in January 2017[12] ('Special guardianship guidance'). It is due to be reviewed later in 2018. It supplements and provides further explanation of the Special Guardianship Regulations 2005 and the Special Guardianship (Amendment) Regulations 2016. It is statutory guidance with which local authorities should comply unless exceptional circumstances justify departure (in accordance with the Local Authority Services Act 1970, s 7 and *B v London Borough of Lewisham*[13]).

10.19 Importantly, a special guardianship order may not be made unless the court has received a CA 1989, s 14A(11) report. That report must address a range of matters including, most importantly:

(a) the suitability of the proposed special guardian[14];

(b) the long list of matters set out in the Special Guardianship Regulations 2005, Schedule[15];

(c) the amendments introduced by the Special Guardianship (Amendment) Regulations 2016, as set out at para 10.13, above.

10 *Surrey County Council v Al-Hilli* [2013] EWHC 3404 (Fam) at [6].
11 *Re (A Child)* [2012] EWCA Civ 1217.
12 'Special guardianship guidance' (January 2017), available at assets.publishing.service.gov.uk/government/uploads/system/uploads/attachment_data/file/656593/Special_guardianship_statutory_guidance.pdf.
13 [2008] EWHC 738 (Admin) at [20].
14 CA 1989, s 14A(8).
15 Special Guardianship Regulations 2005, reg 21.

10.20 A full, and very helpful, examination of the key principles of the statutory framework in relation to special guardianship orders was set out by the Court of Appeal in *Re S (A Child)*[16].

10.21 The Court of Appeal in 2015 re-emphasised the provisions at CA 1989, s 14A(3)–(6), which set out: (i) those who can as of right apply for a special guardianship order; (ii) those for whom permission is required; and (iii) the court's jurisdiction to make an order of its own motion[17]. It should not be forgotten that:

(a) those who are entitled to apply as of right for a special guardianship order are: a guardian, a person with whom the child lives under a child arrangements order, a relative or local authority foster parent with whom the child has lived for at least one year, any person with whom the child has lived for a (non-continuous) period of at least three years and those with the consent of parental responsibility (etc) holders[18];

(b) for all other applicants, the leave of the court is required, with the court to have regard to the same considerations to which it would have regard in an application for an order under the CA 1989, s 8[19];

(c) the court retains jurisdiction to make a special guardianship order even though no application has been made[20] but that should 'not be the default position' because of the risk of procedural irregularity of such an order being considered without notice. Indeed, in the view of Ryder LJ, 'It is only where parties agree that an application for a SGO should be dispensed with that the s 14A(6)(b) of the CA 1989 power can be exercised without good reason. In any other case, the use of this power must be reasoned. The parties in this case did not agree and the use of the power was assumed not reasoned'[21].

FINANCIAL PROVISION AND SUPPORT, INCLUDING JUDICIAL REVIEW

10.22 Financial provision is, in many cases, second only to the welfare and contact decisions in terms of the importance that it comes to hold, and the heat of the dispute that it provokes. The relevant provisions are set out in the CA 1989, s 14F and, most importantly, in the Special Guardianship Regulations 2005, Part II.

10.23 The simple point to remember is that, whilst a special guardian may have a right to be assessed, the payment and extent of financial provision is a decision for a local authority to reach. It is, however, amenable in principle to

16 [2007] EWCA Civ 54 at [40]–[77].
17 *Re H (A Child) (Analysis of Realistic Options and SGO)* [2015] EWCA Civ 406 at [26].
18 CA 1989, ss 14A(3) and 10(5)(b)–(c) and (10).
19 CA 1989, ss 14A(3), (4) and (12) and 10(8)–(9).
20 See CA 1989, s14A(6)(b).
21 *Re H (A Child) (Analysis of Realistic Options and SGO)* [2015] EWCA Civ 406 at [26].

judicial review. The key points from the Special Guardianship Regulations 2005, as amplified by the statutory guidance, are:

(a) non-means tested assistance may be given in cash for a particular occurrence. That assistance is a service as opposed to financial support. The examples given in the statutory guidance are the funding of a babysitter to permit the special guardian a break for an evening and money for petrol to get to contact[22];

(b) the assessment and provision of (non-financial, save for cash, as referred to above) support services falls to the local authority in which the special guardian lives, with responsibility passing to a new local authority on any move, save in cases in which a child was looked after prior to the making of the special guardianship order, where, for the first three years of the order, the responsibility remains with the local authority that last looked after the child[23];

(c) in addition, if agreed to before the making of the order, the provision of ongoing financial support (ie that which is paid regularly) remains, under the currency of the order, the responsibility of the local authority who agreed to it, as long as the special guardian continues to qualify[24];

(d) financial support should be payable in accordance with the Special Guardianship Regulations 2005 to help secure a suitable special guardianship arrangement where there is otherwise a financial obstacle to the making of that arrangement. Chapter II of the Special Guardianship Regulations 2005 deals with this in full. Of particular importance are the provisions for financial support where: it is necessary so as to ensure that the special guardian can look after the child; where the child's needs demand special care; where there are past or likely future legal fees; and where it is required for furniture, domestic equipment, adaptations of the home, transport, clothing, toys, etc[25];

(e) in determining the amount of ongoing financial support, the local authority should have regard to the amount of fostering allowance which would have been payable if the child were fostered[26]. Paragraph 65 of the Special guardianship guidance, which merits setting out in full, reads,

> 'In determining the amount of any ongoing financial support, the local authority should have regard to the amount of fostering allowance which would have been payable if the child were fostered. The local authority's core allowance plus any enhancement that would be payable in respect of the particular child, will make up the maximum payment the local authority could consider paying the family. Any

22 Special Guardianship Regulations 2005, reg 3(2); Special guardianship guidance, para [27].
23 Special Guardianship Regulations 2005, reg 5; Special guardianship guidance, paras [31]–[34].
24 Special Guardianship Regulations 2005, reg 5(2); Special guardianship guidance, para [35].
25 Special Guardianship Regulations 2005, reg 6; Special guardianship guidance, paras [37]–[41].
26 Special guardianship guidance, para [65].

means test carried out as appropriate to the circumstances would use this maximum payment as a basis';

(f) remuneration is not paid, save for in the case of a former foster parent, in which case it may be, for an initial (and extendable) term of two years[27];

(g) financial support ceases on the occurrence of trigger events, including the child commencing employment and her turning 18 unless she continues in full-time education or training[28].

10.24 The principles in relation to the calculation of the *amount* of ongoing financial support have been emphasised by the courts in applications for judicial review. In particular:

(a) a local authority may either draw up a general policy on the level of core allowance to be paid to special guardians (considering, in doing so, the circumstances of the typical, hypothetical case) or set allowances on a case-by-case basis[29];

(b) a local authority's fostering allowance should function as a 'ranging shot' for a local authority's consideration of the appropriate special guardianship allowance[30];

(c) a rigid link between special guardianship financial provision and adoption allowances is inappropriate. Instead, para 65 of the statutory guidance gives central importance to the link between fostering allowances and special guardianship financial provision[31];

(d) a general policy that calculates a special guardianship allowance at two-thirds of a fostering allowance is unlawful in that, whilst some (downward) adjustment to a fostering allowance is both acceptable and unavoidably arbitrary in its calculation, the removal in its entirety of the 50 per cent of the fostering allowance that is said to be caused by the additional financial burden of caring for a foster child (as opposed to a 'typical, natural child') ignores para 65 of the statutory guidance[32].

10.25 In addition to financial provision, a local authority is required to make arrangements for the provision of other special guardianship support services, to include counselling, advice and information. Equally, a child who is subject to such an order may qualify for advice and assistance under the Children (Leaving Care) Act 2002 if first looked after by a local authority. Further, the Adoption Support Fund – launched by the government in May 2015 in a bid to provide therapeutic services to adoptive children – was in April 2016 extended to cover therapeutic

---

27 Special Guardianship Regulations 2005, reg 7; Special guardianship guidance, paras [42]–[43].

28 Special Guardianship Regulations 2005, reg 9; Special guardianship guidance, para [45].

29 *R (on the application of TT) v London Borough of Merton* [2012] EWHC 2055 (Admin) at [53].

30 *B v London Borough of Lewisham* [2008] EWHC 738 (Admin) at [47]. Whilst Black J refers to an earlier version of the statutory guidance, the wording is copied over into the Special guardianship guidance.

31 *B v London Borough of Lewisham* [2008] EWHC 738 (Admin) at, for example, [54].

32 *R (on the application of TT) v London Borough of Merton* [2012] EWHC 2055 (Admin).

support for children who live in England, are subject to a special guardianship order and were previously in care.

CONCLUSION

10.26 As can be seen, whilst special guardianship orders continue to play a central role in the family justice systems, a concern about their fragility and ubiquity remains. In addition, the tension between a considered and thorough special guardianship assessment and a 26-week deadline, within which family members may often put themselves forward late, presents difficulties.

10.27 When advising on any case relating to financial provision on the making of a special guardianship order, practitioners should pay close regard to the Special guardianship guidance and the Special Guardianship Regulations 2005, as amended in 2016.

Chapter 11

POST-ADOPTION CONTACT

INTRODUCTION

11.1 Pursuant to the Adoption and Children Act 2002 (ACA 2002), s 1(4)(f), whenever the court or an adoption agency is considering a decision relating to the adoption of a child, it must consider the relationship which the child has with relatives, and with any other person in relation to whom the court or agency considers the relationship to be relevant, including:

(a) the likelihood of any such relationship continuing and the value to the child of its doing so;

(b) the ability and willingness of any of the child's relatives, or of any such person, to provide the child with a secure environment in which the child can develop, and otherwise to meet the child's needs; and

(c) the wishes and feelings of any of the child's relatives, or of any such person, regarding the child.

11.2 The aforementioned provision appears to recognise and place significant weight on the relationship that a subject child might have with his birth family and indeed, the ACA 2002, ss 51A and 51B provide the court with a specific power to direct post-adoption contact, both before and after an adoption order is made. However, as will be explored throughout this chapter, both the statutory provisions and the existing case law make it incredibly difficult for birth relatives to obtain post-adoption contact orders, notwithstanding the social shift towards open adoptions.

ACADEMIC RESEARCH

11.3 Historically, the concept of post-adoption contact with the birth family was considered inconsistent with the purpose of adoption, namely the legal severance of the child from the birth family and her total incorporation into the adoptive family. Yet, this 'clean break' approach to adoption has somewhat shifted over the years. Most children who are placed for adoption in England and Wales have some contact with their birth parents, usually in the form of indirect 'letterbox contact' (the exchange of letters, photographs, cards and/or small gifts, which is usually mediated by the adoption agency)[1]. Face-to-face contact is, unsurprisingly, less common[2].

11.4 This shift towards post-adoption contact has arisen because of concerns surrounding the consequences of closed adoptions, and in particular, the adopted child's feelings of loss, separation, and lack of identity[3]. Even where a child is adopted as a baby – and therefore has no memory of her birth family – research shows that she might experience stress from the loss of genealogical continuity, the loss of biological connection to the adoptive parents, and being different from her peers[4]. Whilst the focus of the family courts is on the welfare of the child, it is also worth noting that closed adoption may be considered unhelpful to birth family members, who must come to terms with the loss of the child and may be further affected by the lack of knowledge of what has happened to the child post-adoption[5].

11.5 According to academic research, the adopted child's experience of post-adoption contact with a birth relative is variable: contact can be positive, negative, or neutral[6]. However, qualitative research indicates that those children who do have post-adoption contact with their birth relatives are generally pleased with their contact and would wish it to continue[7]. Some of the benefits that the children associate with post-adoption contact include:

— continuing a relationship with a relative to whom the child is emotionally attached;

— providing reassurance that the birth relative is safe;

— enabling the child to understand why she was adopted and her birth parents' difficulties, thereby reducing self-blame; and

— assisting with issues of identity[8].

However, adopted children will not necessarily want contact with all members of their birth family, particularly where their birth relatives have been hostile or abusive[9].

11.6 Whilst most adopted children regard contact as a positive experience, this is not true for all children. There are some instances where contact may

---

1 E Neil, 'Post-Adoption Contact and Openness in Adoptive Parents' Minds: Consequences for Children's Development' (2009) 39 *British Journal of Social Work* 5, 6.
2 E Neil, 'Contact after Adoption: A longitudinal study of post adoption contact' (Centre for Family Research, 27 January 2015).
3 E Neil, 'The benefits and challenges of direct post-adoption contact: perspectives from adoptive parents and birth relatives' (2010) 27 *Aloma* 89, 90.
4 Ibid, 90.
5 Ibid.
6 Ibid.
7 Ibid, 91.
8 Ibid, 91–92.
9 Ibid, 91.

unsettle the child, especially where there is poor interaction between the child and the birth relative during contact or a history of maltreatment of the child[10]. Yet, research suggests that in most cases, post-adoption contact with the birth family does not disturb adoptive family relationships or affect the adopted child's adjustment in the adoptive family[11]. It is also worthwhile noting that the academic research challenges the idea that letter contact is 'easier' than face-to-face contact, and suggests that it is less enduring than face-to-face contact[12]. Typically it is the reliability of the arrangements for contact that affects the child's satisfaction with it, rather than the type of contact[13].

RELEVANT STATUTES

11.7 As will be explored in the final section of this chapter, the courts may make orders for contact when making placement orders, pursuant to the ACA 2002, s 26. However, once the court makes an adoption order, any provision for contact under the ACA 2002, s 26 is discharged, as it only has effect while 'the adoption agency is authorised to place the child for adoption or the child is placed for adoption'[14]. In other words, once a child is 'placed' for adoption, which is by definition with 'prospective adopters'[15], or the adoption order is made, the adoption agency ceases to have parental responsibility for the child[16] and the placement order (and concomitant contact order) ceases to exist.

11.8 However, the court must give thought to the issue of post-adoption contact before an adoption order is made. Pursuant to the ACA 2002, s 46(6):

> 'Before making an adoption order, the court must consider whether there should be arrangements for allowing any person contact with the child; and for that purpose the court must consider any existing or proposed arrangements and obtain any views of the parties to the proceedings'.

11.9 Prior to the introduction of the Children and Families Act 2014 (CFA 2014), where the court considered post-adoption contact to be in the child's best interests, it could only order contact by making a 'contact order' under the Children Act 1989 (CA 1989), s 8[17]. However, the CFA 2014, s 9 inserted new ss 51A and 51B into the ACA 2002. The new provisions provide a regulatory framework on how post-adoption contact is to be effected or, in the alternative, curtailed.

---

10 Ibid, 95.

11 E Neil, M Beek and E Ward, 'Contact after Adoption: A follow Up in Late Adolescence (Centre for Research on Children and Families, December 2013) 275.

12 Neil, supra note 2.

13 Neil, supra note 2.

14 ACA 2002, s 27(1)(a).

15 ACA 2002, s 18(5).

16 ACA 2002, s 46(2)(a).

17 See *X and Y v A Local Authority (Adoption; Procedure)* [2009] EWHC 47 (Fam).

11.10 Section 51A applies where 'an adoption agency has placed or was authorised to place a child for adoption, and the court is making or has made an adoption order in respect of the child'[18]. Most cases where an adoption agency is involved will fall under s 51A, in that the agency will have placed the child for adoption, whether by moving the child to prospective adopters or by changing the status of the child's existing foster carers to one of prospective adopters[19]. Section 51A will also apply to non-agency adoption applications where there is a placement order and the applicants, such as existing foster carers, were not approved by the agency as prospective adopters but are either to be granted an adoption order by the court or the court has already made such an adoption order[20].

11.11 Pursuant to s 51A(2), when making the adoption order or at any time afterwards, the court may make an order requiring the person in whose favour the adoption order is or has been made (ie the adopted parent or parents) to allow the child to have contact with the person named in the order or prohibiting the person named in the order from having contact with the child:

> **'51A Post-adoption contact**
>
> …
>
> (2) When making the adoption order or at any time afterwards, the court may make an order under this section—
>
> (a) requiring the person in whose favour the adoption order is or has been made to allow the child to visit or stay with the person named in the order under this section, or for the person named in that order and the child otherwise to have contact with each other, or
>
> (b) prohibiting the person named in the order under this section from having contact with the child'.

11.12 Only certain persons fall under the category of 'person named in the order.' These are specified in s 51A(3) and include the following individuals:

(a) any person who (but for the child's adoption) would be related to the child by blood (including half-blood), marriage, or civil partnership;

(b) any former guardian of the child;

(c) any person who had parental responsibility for the child immediately before the making of the adoption order;

(d) any person who was entitled to make an application for an order under s 26 in respect of the child (contact with children placed or to be placed for adoption) by virtue of subsection (3)(c), (d) or (e) of that section; and

(e) any person with whom the child has lived for a period of at least one year.

18 ACA 2002, s 51A(1).

19 *Butterworths Family Law Service* (LexisNexis, looseleaf) para **3A[4291]**.

20 Ibid.

11.13 Whilst the category of persons who may be 'named' in a post-adoption contact order is wide, the right to apply for an order is circumscribed. The adopted parent(s) and the child have an automatic right to make an application under s 51A(4)(a) and (b). All other persons who are identified as having the ability to be 'named' in the order under s 51A(3) must seek the leave of the court to make the application[21].

11.14 When deciding whether to grant leave to those persons under s 51A(3), the court must consider the following:

(a) any risk there might be of the proposed application disrupting the child's life to such an extent that he or she would be harmed by it (within the meaning of the CA 1989);

(b) the applicant's connection with the child; and

(c) any representations made to the court by: (i) the child; or (ii) a person who has applied for the adoption order or in whose favour the adoption order is or has been made[22].

11.15 Section 51B goes on to set out how s 51A should work in practice. Pursuant to s 51B(1)(a) and (b), an order under s 51A may contain directions about how it is to be carried into effect, and can be subject to any conditions that the court thinks appropriate. It remains in place until the child's 18th birthday, unless revoked[23], and an application for the variation or revocation of the order may be made, without leave, by the child, the adopter, or the person named in the order[24]. The court is required in all cases, including the adoption application itself, to draw up a timetable with a view to determining without delay whether to make, vary, or discharge a s 51A order and to ensure that said timetable is adhered to[25].

11.16 Legal practitioners should be aware that the court could make a prohibition on post-adoption contact under s 51A(2)(b) of its own initiative; however, it cannot do so for an order for post-adoption contact[26]. Further, it is important to note that s 51A (and s 51B) only apply where a court is making, or has made, an adoption order following placement for adoption by an adoption agency. In all other cases (ie a non-agency placement), provision for post-adoption contact will be made under the CA 1989, s 8 and is governed by the welfare checklist in s 1(3).

11.17 When making a decision about post-adoption contact – both in respect of granting leave to make the application and the application itself – the court must determine whether it is in the child's best interests, with reference to both the factors in s 51A(3) and the welfare checklist under the ACA 2002, s 1(4).

21 ACA 2002, s 51A(4)(c).
22 ACA 2002, s 51A(5).
23 ACA 2002, s 51B(1)(d).
24 ACA 2002, s 51B(1)(c).
25 ACA 2002, s 51B(3).
26 ACA 2002, s 5A(6).

As stated in the ACA 2003, s 1(2), the paramount consideration of the court (or adoption agency) must be the child's welfare, *throughout his life* (emphasis added). Legal practitioners arguing in favour of post-adoption contact should therefore seek to address why post-adoption contact would be beneficial to the child both now and in the future.

THE EFFECT OF SS 51A AND 51B

11.18 Replacing the procedure for post-adoption contact under the CA 1989, the ACA 2002, ss 51A and 51B provide the court with a specific power to make orders concerning post-adoption contact, both before and after the adoption is finalised. These orders may be 'positive', compelling the adoptive parents to make the child available to spend time with a named person, or 'negative', preventing the child from having contact with a named person[27]. The new focus on the welfare checklist in the ACA 2002, rather than the welfare checklist in the CA 1989, embodies the recognition that post-adoption contact, like adoption itself, has life-long implications for the subject child[28].

11.19 However, reflecting the general 'pro-adoption' stance of the ruling government, ss 51A and 51B arguably make it even more difficult to obtain post-adoption contact than prior to the enactment of the CFA 2014. Two provisions in particular may be regarded as 'setbacks' to acquiring post-adoption contact:

(i) the need for certain persons to apply for permission to make an application for post-adoption contact, including birth parents and birth siblings; and

(ii) the ability of the court to make a prohibition on contact order of its own volition.

11.20 Prior to the introduction of the CFA 2014, birth parents/siblings did not need to obtain leave from the court to apply for a post-adoption contact order pursuant to the CA 1989, s 8. As such, ss 51A and 51B introduce an additional hurdle to the already Herculean task of acquiring a post-adoption contact order. Likewise, the ability of the court of its own volition to make an order prohibiting contact (albeit not a contact order facilitating contact) exemplifies the dominant aim of the legislation, namely to reduce the allegedly destabilising effect of post-adoption contact on adoptive placements.

11.21 Legal practitioners must be live to the challenges brought about by the insertion of ss 51A and 51B into the ACA 2002 and advise their clients accordingly[29].

27 B Sloan, 'Post-Adoption Contact Reform: Compounding the State-Ordered Termination of Parenthood' (July 2014) 73(02) *CamLaw* 378, 391.

28 Ibid, 393.

29 For a comprehensive discussion of the effects of ss 51A and 51B on post-adoption contact, including the human rights implications, see Sloan, supra note 27.

COMMON ISSUES IN RESPECT OF POST-ADOPTION CONTACT

11.22 Notwithstanding that the CFA 2014 introduced fundamental changes to the law regarding post-adoption contact, the pre-2014 case law is still relevant and raises a number of issues that family law practitioners must be aware of when considering the finalisation of care, placement, and adoption proceedings. Each of these will be discussed below.

Willing adopters

11.23 Although adoptive parents might be open to contact between the adopted child and the birth family, the court has taken the view that where adopters are willing to agree contact, it is unnecessary to make an order binding them to their agreement. For example, in *Re T (Adoption: Contact)*[30], the Court of Appeal granted the adoptive parents' appeal against a post-adoption contact order made by the first instance judge, holding that no order would allow the adopters more flexibility (at 256). Further, the court indicated that it would be an unjust burden on the adoptive family if they had to return to court to stop contact (at 256).

11.24 In some cases, a recital has been included in the order setting out the intention of the adopters to agree contact[31]. Legal practitioners who act for adoptive parents should keep in mind that if the adoptive parents indicate that they are willing for contact to take place but later change their minds without giving adequate reasons, the birth parents might be granted leave to seek a contact order under the ACA 2002, s 51A[32].

Unwilling adopters

11.25 Equally, the case law indicates that the court is unlikely to impose an order for post-adoption contact on unwilling adopters. It is generally held that the issue of contact should be left to the 'good sense' of the adopters and that they can 'be trusted to do what they believe to be in the best interests of *their* [child]'[33]. This quote from Butler-Sloss LJ intimates the recognition by the court that once an adoption order is made, the adoptive parents are the legal parents of the child and the birth parents no longer have any legal status – or Art 8 rights – in respect of her. As such, to make an order requiring the (adoptive) parents to allow contact that they are not in agreement with is a circumscription of their rights as legal parents.

30 [1995] 2 FLR 251.

31 *Re T (Adoption: Contact)* [1995] 258.

32 See *Re R (Adoption: Contact)* [2006] 1 FLR 373.

33 *Re T (Adoption: Contact)* [1995] 2 FLR 251, 255; emphasis added.

11.26 The extent of the court's reticence to making a post-adoption contact order on unwilling adopters may be seen in the case of *Oxfordshire County Council v X, Y and J*[34]. In *Oxfordshire County Council v X, Y and J*, the child, J, was the subject of an adoption order. When making said order, the first instance judge refused the application by the birth parents for the adoptive parents to provide them with an annual photograph of J; the adoptive parents, the local authority, and the guardian agreed that photographs should be made available to the birth parents to view at the local authority offices. The adoptive parents were concerned that the birth parents would use any photographs provided to trace J on the internet.

11.27 The birth parents appealed; however, their appeal was denied. The court reiterated the comments of Wall LJ in *Re R (Adoption: Contact)*[35] that 'under the jurisprudence which has developed, contact orders in adoption proceedings are of themselves unusual'[36] and 'the imposition on prospective adopters of orders for contact with which they are not in agreement is extremely, and remains extremely, unusual'[37].

11.28 A rare example of a case where the court did order a post-adoption contact order is *MF v London Borough of Brent*[38]. In *MF v London Borough of Brent*, a foster carer sought an adoption order for a child in her care. The maternal grandmother who cared for the child's half-siblings supported the order but sought monthly unsupervised contact with the child at her home. The foster carer opposed the making of a contact order on the basis of child protection issues, including that one of the child's half-siblings had mental health problems and had been caught shoplifting whilst with the maternal grandmother[39].

11.29 The court made the adoption order and a limited contact order in respect of the maternal grandmother, as both orders were held to be necessary and in the child's best interests. The court stated that on the facts of the case, the adoption and contact orders were 'inextricably linked' and the 'success' of the adoption order was in part dependent on a minimum level of contact between the child and the birth family, particularly the child's half-siblings and the maternal grandmother[40]. As *MF v London Borough of Brent* makes clear, each case is fact-specific and it is ultimately the court's decision on whether to order post-adoption contact.

11.30 Family law practitioners should keep in mind that when seeking leave to apply for contact pursuant to s 51A, birth family members will need to prove

34 [2011] 1 FLR 272.

35 [2005] EWCA Civ 1128, [2006] 1 FLR 373.

36 [2005] EWCA Civ 1128, [2006] 1 FLR 373 at [47].

37 At [49]. In his article 'Swimming Against the Tide: Challenging Contact Arrangements in the Public Law,' Andrew Bainham queries whether the views of adoptive parents concerning contact should be given the considerable weight that they appear to have been afforded by the courts and whether this gives effect to the best interests of the child (November 2015) *Fam Law* 1356 at 1362.

38 [2013] EWHC 1838 (Fam).

39 At [10].

40 At [34].

to the court that the decision of the adopters to oppose contact is sufficiently contrary to the child's welfare, or sufficiently unreasonable, to justify the court overriding the adopters' discretion about contact[41].

Resistant birth parents

11.31 It is perhaps otiose to add that where birth parents or family members are fundamentally resistant to the adoption of the child, the court is even less likely to order contact. This may be seen in the case of *Prospective Adopters v FB*[42], where the birth mother opposed the adoption order and sought for the child to be returned to her care or, in the alternative, for there to be a 'shared care' arrangement between her and the prospective adopters.

11.32 The court made the adoption order and rejected the birth mother's contact proposals. It held that whilst there were cases where an open adoption would be appropriate, this was not one of them since the mother did not accept the adoptive placement[43]. According to the judge, anything other than identity contact (ie letter-box contact) would therefore run the risk of jeopardising the stability of the adoptive placement[44].

Sibling contact

11.33 It is not unusual to have cases involving multiple siblings (and half-siblings) with different care plans for each child, especially where there is a range in their ages. For example, an older child might be subject to a final care order with a care plan of long-term fostering or a family placement, whilst care and placement orders – with a view to adoption – are made in respect of a younger sibling. The difficulties that this may raise in practice are immediately obvious if one considers that a child in long-term foster care or in a family placement is more likely to have contact with the birth parents/family. As such, contact between the child in foster care or a family placement and the adopted child could result in a breach of the confidentiality of the adoptive placement, and/or the birth parents/family could attempt to undermine or disrupt the adoptive placement.

11.34 As per the ACA 2002, s 51A(9), any sibling or half-sibling who wishes to have contact with their adopted sibling must seek the leave of the court to make an application for a post-adoption contact order; they do not fall into the category of persons who have an automatic right to apply. In other words, there is no special status for siblings or half-siblings. As indicated above, the adoption of a child changes the legal status of her birth parents and eradicates their pre-existing Art 8 rights. The same is true of siblings/half-siblings; they are no longer the legal siblings of the adopted child.

41 *Re T (Adoption: Contact)* [2011] 1 FLR 1805, CA.
42 [2015] EWHC 297 (Fam).
43 At [107].
44 Ibid.

11.35 It is therefore unsurprising that the court's unwillingness to impose contact orders on adoptive parents extends to the adopted child's contact with her siblings or half-siblings. The court's attitude towards post-adoption sibling contact may be seen in *Re TJ (Relinquished for Adoption: Sibling Contact)*[45], though it should be noted that this case is slightly unusual in that the half-siblings were not aware of each other's existence and no party was actively seeking for there to be contact between them.

11.36 *Re TJ (Relinquished for Adoption: Sibling Contact)* concerned the possibility of contact between two maternal half-siblings, one of who was placed with prospective adopters (TJ) and the other who was living with his biological father and stepmother (PL). The local authority, supported by the child's guardian, sought a declaration that they did not need to disclose the existence of TJ to members of his birth family, including PL, as the mother had relinquished TJ at birth, with a view to him being adopted, and was clear that she did not wish her family members to be made aware of his birth.

11.37 The court readily agreed to the wider maternal family not being told of TJ's existence, as neither the maternal grandmother nor maternal great-grandparents had been actively considered as potential carers for PL. There was therefore little benefit to informing them about TJ's birth. However, the question of whether to inform PL of TJ's existence and the potential for sibling contact was less straightforward. Both the prospective adopters and the birth mother were opposed to contact between the siblings and supported the declaration sought by the local authority, although the former did indicate that they would support some indirect contact between TJ and PL if they were required to do so.

11.38 Placing particular weight on the positions of the mother and prospective adopters, Cobb J determined that their concerns outweighed 'limited benefit' to TJ of infrequent indirect contact with PL for identity purposes[46]. Moreover, he confirmed that just as adoption proceedings bring the pre-existing Art 8 rights between a birth parent and an adopted child to an end, the same is true for the Art 8 rights of birth/half siblings[47]. The relationship between TJ and PL therefore did not invoke Art 8, whilst the adopters had clear Art 8 rights in respect of the child. As such, Cobb J made the declaration sought by the local authority and did not make any provisions for contact between the siblings.

Contact application after adoption

11.39 Pursuant to the ACA 2002, s 51A(2), the court may make an order for post-adoption contact even after the adoption order is made. The case law in respect of such applications is scant; however, it suggests that post-adoption applications for contact are rarely successful. As indicated in *Re C (A Minor)*

45 [2017] EWFC 6.
46 At [31].
47 At [27].

(Adopted Child: Contact)[48], adoption orders are intended to be fundamental and final. As such, once an adoption order has been made, the question of contact, including indirect contact, should not be reopened unless there has been a fundamental change in circumstances.

Placement orders

11.40 As the preceding sections suggest, it is incredibly difficult for biological families to obtain an order for contact with an adopted child. In order to increase their chances of success, their advocates should consider whether to advise them to seek a defined contact order whilst the child is in placement. Pursuant to the ACA 2002, s 27(4), before making a placement order, the court must: (a) consider the arrangements that the adoption agency has made, or proposes to make, for allowing any person contact with the child; and (b) invite the parties to the proceedings to comment on those arrangements. Further, under s 26, the court may make an order for contact between the child in placement, either on application by a specified person (which includes the child, guardian, and parents) (s 26(3)) or of its own volition (s 26(4)).

11.41 The provisions for contact whilst the child is subject to a placement order are arguably more flexible than those in respect of post-adoption contact. Indeed, contact at the placement stage has much more in common with contact whilst a child is simply in foster care[49]. According to Andrew Bainham, there are several good reasons for thinking about contact orders at the placement stage:

(a) on a theoretical level, they symbolise the importance that the courts ascribe to on-going contact between the child and her birth family;

(b) if an order for placement contact is in force at the time of the final hearing for the adoption order, it will need to be considered by the court when deciding that application;

(c) if contact does not take place during the course of the placement order, it will be more difficult to argue in favour of post-adoption contact; and

(d) if an order for placement contact is sought, it may place pressure on the local authority to amend its care plan(s) in respect of contact, even where the placement contact order is refused[50].

11.42 Legal practitioners should be aware that there are two arguments that are commonly levelled against making a contact order alongside a placement order:

(a) that the presence of a contact order will put off prospective adopters; and

48 [1993] 2 FLR 431.

49 Sloan, supra note 27 at 386.

50 A Bainham, 'Swimming Against the Tide: Challenging Contact Arrangements in the Public Law' (November 2015) Fam Law 1356, 1360–1361.

(b) that a defined order is unnecessary where the local authority is committed in its care plan to promoting on going contact post-placement[51].

In respect of the first objection, it is unclear what empirical evidence this supposition is based on. As Bainham notes, this argument is unnecessarily 'defeatist,' painting all prospective adopters with 'the same brush' and ignoring the fundamentally 'altruistic' nature of adoption[52].

11.43 Similarly, the second objection does not hold up under scrutiny. By the time the proceedings have been finalised, the care plan(s) might have changed. Moreover, notwithstanding what the care plan(s) says, the local authority, if left to its own devices, might be resistant to post-adoption contact, fearing that it will limit the number of prospective adopters[53]. There is therefore no guarantee that the commitment to contact will survive the making of the placement order without a defined contact order in place as well.

CONCLUSION

11.44 Whilst academic research suggests that there are benefits to post-adoption contact, the changes introduced by the CFA 2014 to the ACA 2002 arguably make it even more difficult for birth families to maintain a relationship with adopted child(ren). Family law practitioners who practise in this area of law must be familiar with both the new statutory provisions and the pre-2014 jurisprudence, which still guides the court's approach to making defined post-adoption contact orders. However, as those who represent birth families in care proceedings are aware, any application for post-adoption contact orders is likely to encounter resistance from the courts.

51 Ibid, 1361.
52 Ibid, 1361.
53 Ibid, 1361.

Chapter 12

ALTERNATIVES TO TRADITIONAL CHILD PROTECTION PROCEEDINGS

INTRODUCTION

12.1 In his '15th View from the President's Chambers', Sir James Munby, President of the Family Division, highlighted that the family court is approaching a 'crisis' for which it is 'ill-prepared' and where there is 'no clear strategy to manage the crisis'[1]. The Lord Chief Justice of the Judiciary of England and Wales, Lord Thomas, echoed this sentiment in his 5th annual report of 2017[2].

12.2 The cause of this 'crisis' is the long and sustained rise in applications for public children law orders since 2016[3]. The Lord Chief Justice highlights in his report that between January and November 2016, the year-on-year increase averaged 20 per cent[4]. Whilst the rate of increase has slowed since the beginning of 2017, the trend is still upwards: there were 5,051 new public law applications in January to March 2017, up 5 per cent on the equivalent quarter in 2016[5].

12.3 In response to this crisis, the President has identified the need for a 'radical rebalancing of the very functions and purpose of the family courts'[6]. Part of

1 Sir James Munby, '15th View from the President's Chambers' (2016) Family Law, 19 September, available at www.familylaw.co.uk/news_and_comment/15th-view-from-the-president-s-chambers-care-cases-the-looming-crisis#.WsoRd0sh1-U.

2 The Lord Chief Justice's Report 2017 (Judicial Office), available at www.judiciary.gov.uk/wp-content/uploads/2017/09/lcj-report-2017-final.pdf, p 22.

3 The reasons for this marked increase in public law applications are not fully known and the exploration of them is beyond the scope of this book. However, in his '15th View from the President's Chambers,' Sir Munby suggests, in principle, three possible causes for the increase: (1) 'that the amount of child abuse is increasing' (which he largely discounts); (2) 'that local authorities are becoming more adept at identifying child abuse/neglect and taking action to deal with it'; and/or (3) 'that local authorities are setting more demanding standards – in other words, lowering the threshold for intervention'.

4 Ibid 22. However, he notes that further research is desperately needed.

5 Ibid 22.

6 '15th View from the President's Chambers', supra note 1.

this includes looking at alternatives to traditional child protection proceedings. This chapter will examine four different pilots, namely the Family Drug and Alcohol Court (FDAC), the London Infant and Family Team (LIFT), settlement conferences, and Pause, which have been introduced to mitigate the increasing numbers of care cases and ensure that the subject child's best interests are served by the family courts.

FDAC

What is FDAC?

12.4 Parental substance misuse is a leading cause of child abuse and neglect, and is associated with a range of child health and developmental difficulties and problems in adult life[7]. In the context of public law proceedings, it is estimated that two-thirds of all care applications involve substance misuse by one or both parents[8].

12.5 Many family law practitioners who undertake public law work will already be familiar with the Family Drug and Alcohol Court, which was first introduced by District Judge Nick Crichton in 2008. Modelled on the Family Drug Treatment Courts in the USA, it offers an alternative 'problem-solving' approach to care proceedings in cases where, as the name suggests, parental substance misuse is a key threshold factor in the decision by the local authority to initiate proceedings[9].

12.6 The problem-solving approach of FDAC is based on the principles of 'therapeutic jurisprudence', which views the court as having an active role in helping to resolve the problems that underlie the problematic behaviour, such as substance misuse[10]. Proponents of a problem-solving approach maintain that its benefit is threefold:

- first, it is a more 'humane' and 'transparent' way of conducting public law proceedings;
- second, it brings about better outcomes for parents and children; and
- finally, it involves financial savings[11].

In respect of FDAC in particular, a five-year study on the implementation of FDAC, which was published in December 2016, found, inter alia, that FDAC mothers were more successful than comparison mothers in stopping their misuse of drugs

7 J Harwin (et al), 'After FDAC: outcomes 5 years later; Final Report' (Lancaster University, December 2016) p 3.

8 Ibid, p 3.

9 Ibid, p 3.

10 Ibid, p 2.

11 Ibid, p 32.

and/or alcohol by the end of the care proceedings, which led to a higher rate of family reunification than in the comparison cases[12].

12.7 The largely positive results of FDAC have resulted in the project being rolled out across the county, with more planned. At present, there are currently ten specialist FDAC Teams, working in 15 courts around the UK and serving families in 23 local authorities in London, Gloucestershire, Milton Keynes and Buckinghamshire, East Sussex, Coventry, South West Peninsula (Devon, Plymouth and Torbay), Kent and Medway, Southampton, Leeds, and Armagh[13]. In April 2015, the FDAC National Unit was set up to support the growth of new FDACs[14].

Relevant statutory instruments and procedure

12.8 Proceedings in FDAC operate under the same statutory framework as ordinary care proceedings, namely the Children Act 1989 (CA 1989). The fundamental difference between them lies in procedure. The FDAC programme is more intensive than ordinary proceedings and involves the parents working with the FDAC multi-disciplinary team, which is separate from the local authority social services team. Indeed, team members are provided by Tavistock and Portman NHS Foundation Trust and the children's charity Coram working in partnership[15].

12.9 The clinical lead of the FDAC team is a child and adolescent psychiatrist, and the team itself is comprised of social workers, substance misuse experts, a domestic violence expert, and parent mentors (parents who have been involved in FDAC proceedings and successfully recovered care of their children)[16]. The team works closely with the court and its role consists of:

— carrying out assessments and directing work with parents;

— devising and co-ordinating an intervention plan;

— enabling and assisting parents to engage and stay engaged with substance misuse, parenting, and other services to address needs identified;

— providing regular reports on parental progress to the court and to all others involved in the case; and

— facilitating additional support for parents through volunteer parent mentors[17].

12.10 In order to understand the benefits of FDAC and its unique approach to care proceedings, it is important to know how FDAC works. In their article,

12 Ibid, p 32.
13 See fdac.org.uk/existing-sites/.
14 S Kershaw, M Shaw and M Ryan, 'FDAC Update' [2017] *Fam Law* 1016.
15 N Crichton, S Kershaw, Dr M Shaw and K Daniels, 'FDAC: the Facts' [2015] *Fam Law* 786 at 787.
16 Ibid, 787.
17 Ibid, 788.

'FDAC: the Facts'[18] the authors very helpfully set out what the process looks like. Whilst it will not be detailed here in full, the salient points are as follows:

(a) Day 1: a participating local authority identifies a case suitable for FDAC. The case is listed on a Monday at 2 pm. The parties attend with their lawyers at 1 pm and meet the FDAC team and learn something of what the programme offers. At 2 pm, they go in front of the judge who will have had an opportunity to have a brief look at the papers. All the judge needs to know is whether or not the family are interested in coming in to FDAC. If they are, the judge will adjourn the matter for two or three weeks;

(b) Day 4: the parents spend all day at the FDAC offices, being assessed by the team;

(c) Day 9: the FDAC social worker and drug treatment worker who assessed the parents meet with the FDAC team manager and consultant child and adolescent psychiatrist to discuss their findings and start to draft the FDAC initial report. When the meeting is completed, the FDAC team hold an 'intervention-planning meeting' with the parents, the children's social worker and guardian and the parent's treatment and support workers, to query with the parents whether there is anything they hope to change in the next six months. The purpose of the meeting is for the parties to agree a 'trial for change', which needs to fulfil three requirements: first, to give the parents the best possible chance of achieving their goals; second, to be achievable with the available resources; and third, to test whether the parents can make sustainable changes in a timescale compatible with the children's timescales and the timescales for the court;

(d) Day 12: the parties' lawyers will have been sent a copy of the 'intervention plan,' which sets out what will be expected of the parents and the professional network in the next six weeks;

(e) Day 15 or 22: the parents return to court with their lawyers, having had a chance to read the assessment and intervention plan. The Judge will want to know whether they are coming into the programme, and if so, they will be asked to sign a simple agreement, agreeing to keep all appointments, to come to court whenever required, and to be open and honest at all times[19].

12.11 Some of the interventions that the FDAC team might prescribe include detoxification, rehabilitation, regular drug/alcohol screening, treatment programmes, CBT, strengthening families courses, domestic violence courses, parenting programmes, and any other appropriate programme for that parent. In respect of assessing the parents' parenting skills and assisting them in understanding the need for attuned interactions with their children, the FDAC team use

18 Nick Crichton (Retired District Judge, Head of FDAC Judicial Training), Sophie Kershaw (Co-Director, National FDAC Unit), Dr Mike Shaw (Child and Adolescent Psychiatrist, Co-Director, National FDAC Unit) and Kieron Daniels (Substance Misuse Expert), supra note 15.

19 'FDAC: the Facts', supra note 15, 787–788.

video-interaction guidance (an intervention whereby the parents are guided to reflect on their taped parent/child interactions).

12.12 After Day 15 or 22, when the parties have officially agreed to partake in the FDAC process, they attend court on a fortnightly basis to meet with the judge, together with the FDAC key worker, the child's social worker, and the child's guardian. The parties' lawyers do not attend court for these discussions. The purpose of this meeting is for the parties to speak with the judge about their progress, what is working well for them, and what is not. In light of the parties' views, the intervention plan may be amended.

12.13 The non-lawyer reviews exist alongside the regular public law hearings, where parties are represented. The practice and procedure within the latter is the same as in non-FDAC care proceedings, save in two important ways. First, there is judicial continuity in FDAC cases: the same judge will conduct the hearings and non-lawyer reviews throughout the proceedings. Second, there is not the same pressure in FDAC cases to conclude proceedings within a 26-week timetable as there is in regular public law proceedings. Recovery from substance misuse is a long and uncertain process, and some studies suggest that it can take at least three years, but often longer[20]. This is obviously at odds with the mandated 26-week length of traditional public law proceedings. However, citing Pauffley J, Munby P made clear in *Re S (A Child)*[21] that 'Justice must never be sacrificed upon the altar of speed' (at [29]). As such, FDAC cases fall into the 'forensic context' of those types of proceedings where an extension of the 26-week time limit in accordance with the CA 1989, s 32(5) might be 'necessary' in order to enable the court to decide the proceedings justly' (at [33]).

12.14 Nevertheless, when considering the timescales of the proceedings, the court will make a 'robust and realistic appraisal', asking the following three questions:

(a) is there some solid, evidence-based reason to believe that the parent is committed to making the necessary changes?

(b) is there some solid, evidence-based reason to believe that the parent will be able to maintain that commitment?

(c) is there some solid, evidence-based reason to believe that the parent will be able to make the necessary changes within the child's timescale?[22]

Where the answers to the aforementioned questions are in the affirmative, the court will more readily direct that the timetable for the proceedings should be extended.

20 Harwin (et al), supra note 7, 3.

21 [2014] EWCC B44 (Fam).

22 *Re S (A Child)* [2014] EWCC B44 (Fam) 38.

LIFT

What is LIFT?

12.15 Introduced in Croydon in 2016, LIFT is a mental health intervention, which operates in the arena of public law proceedings. It is directed at children under the age of 60 months (five years) who have been removed from their parents' care because of concerns around abuse. It focuses on the subject child and his/her attachment relationships. Placing the child at the centre of the intervention, the aim of LIFT is to improve permanency placement decisions for children who have been maltreated and, if possible, rehabilitate them to their birth parent(s).

Relevant statutory instruments and procedure

12.16 LIFT is based on the New Orleans Intervention Model[23] and was developed by the National Society for the Prevention of Cruelty to Children (NSPCC), in collaboration with South London and Maudsley NHS Foundation Trust. A form of it – the Glasgow Infant and Family Team (GIFT) – has been a part of the NSPCC's services in Scotland since 2011, and provided a model for LIFT[24].

12.17 LIFT consists of a twofold approach: first, an assessment of the family by the LIFT team; and second, if the assessment suggests that the parent(s) could potentially look after the child, a bespoke intervention plan to address the problems and strengthen the parent-child relationship. The assessment phase is more intensive than the intervention stage[25], and includes:

- detailed attachment-based assessments of the child and his parents;
- assessment of how well the child is developing;
- an assessment of each parent's health and well-being, including mental health, any addiction issue; and
- the parent's experience of trauma or violence[26].

12.18 The LIFT team, which undertakes the assessment and creates the bespoke intervention package, consists of a child and adolescent psychiatrist, two senior psychologists, two clinical psychologists, three social workers, and one family liaison worker[27]. The team uses structured interviews, observations,

23 The New Orleans Intervention Model was developed by Professor Zeanah at Tulane University, Louisiana in 1998. It is a service approach that focuses on relational assessments and provides intensive assessment and treatment for families of children from birth to five years in foster care, which inform recommendations to the court about adoption or permanent return to birth families.

24 M Baginsky (et al), 'The New Orleans Intervention Model: Early Implementation in a London Borough' (Department for Education, July 2017) 14.

25 Ibid.

26 NSPCC, 'New Orleans Intervention Model: Reducing the risk of abuse and neglect', available at www.nspcc.org.uk/services-and-resources/childrens-services/new-orleans-intervention-model/.

27 Baginsky (et al), supra note 24, 8.

and questionnaires to assess, inter alia, the birth parents' mental health, parental relationship, and the problems and trauma they have faced. The main question for the team, however, is whether the parent can recognise the neglect or abuse, and is capable of reflecting on its causes[28].

12.19 Once the assessment is completed, the LIFT team reports the findings to the local authority social work team and legal representatives. If intervention is seen as appropriate, the LIFT team will create a tailored plan, including therapeutic support, for the family to embark on. This may be delivered with the assistance of partner agencies, depending on the issues that the family must address.

12.20 Specific work that the LIFT team uses as part of its intervention plan include:

(a) circle of security (an evidence-based early intervention based on attachment theory);

(b) parent-infant psychotherapy; and

(c) video-interaction guidance.

12.21 After the intervention has concluded, the LIFT team produce a second report on the work that has been completed. If the parents are able to achieve significant change, the LIFT team will recommend that the children be rehabilitated into their birth families. If no significant change has occurred, the LIFT team will support adoption[29].

12.22 Like FDAC, LIFT operates as an intervention within the public law proceedings. As such the relevant statutory framework remains the same, but the procedure differs. The service works as follows (the weeks are approximations):

(a) Week 1: care proceedings are initiated because of concerns around abuse;

(b) Weeks 1–4: the eligible child is removed from her parents' care under an interim care order;

(c) Week 4: a case management hearing takes place in which the LIFT referral is considered;

(d) Weeks 4–15 (approximately 10 weeks): the LIFT team undertakes the assessment of the family;

(e) Week 16: the LIFT team holds a decision meeting to determine whether the assessment should progress to intervention and the details of said intervention;

(f) Weeks 16–40: the family undertakes the intervention and on completion, the LIFT team produces another report on the results of their work;

(g) Week 40: the court makes a decision regarding permanency[30].

28 Ibid, 12.

29 NSPCC, supra note 26.

30 Baginsky (et al), supra note 24, 27.

12.23 It should be immediately apparent to family practitioners that if intervention is advanced, the proceedings will fall outside of the 26-week timetable. However, as in FDAC, the President of the Family Division gave his permission for LIFT cases to be exempt from the 26-week timetable[31]. Nonetheless, clients need to be advised that the schedule and intensity of LIFT is such that there will not be a lot of flexibility for missed appointments[32]. If the LIFT assessment is negative, the proceedings return to the 26-week timetable.

12.24 As noted above, only children under the age of 60 months (five years) are eligible to take part in LIFT. Where the child has a sibling who is over the age of 60 months, LIFT deals with this on a case-by-case basis. Though the direct work is aimed at children aged younger than 60 months, it is thought that the detailed assessment would be relevant for any older children[33]. Further, GIFT has developed guidelines for social workers working with older siblings as part of the programme, which have been shared with LIFT and continue to be refined for this jurisdiction[34].

12.25 Whilst equally intensive, there is less judicial intervention in proceedings involving LIFT than in FDAC proceedings. The LIFT team, in conjunction with the family, completes the majority of the work, and both the judge and the advocates maintain their regular functions.

SETTLEMENT CONFERENCES

What is a settlement conference?

12.26 Introduced in June 2016, the settlement conference is a court hearing with the 'status' of an Issues Resolution Hearing (IRH), which may be directed during the course of ordinary public (or private) law proceedings, provided that all of the parties consent[35]. However, settlement conferences are in many ways like a form of mediation. During the hearing, a trained family judge takes an 'inquisitorial approach' to the matters at hand, with a view to all of the parties (and their advocates) working collaboratively together to problem-solve and reach an agreement that is in the child's best interests[36].

Relevant statutory instruments and procedure

12.27 As the settlement conference takes place as part of the general public law proceedings, the statutory framework remains the same. However, the Ministry

31 Ibid, 8.
32 Ibid, 31.
33 Ibid, 55.
34 Ibid, 56.
35 *Settlement Conferences Protocol as to Basic Principles with Annexes 1 and 2*, available at www.judiciary.gov.uk/publications/settlement-conferences-pilot/.
36 *Settlement Conferences pilot and evaluation* (Ministry of Justice, July 2017) 1.

of Justice has published 'Settlement Conferences Protocol as to Basic Principles with Annexes 1 and 2' ('the Protocol') and 'Settlement Conferences pilot and evaluation' ('The Pilot'), both of which set out information and guidance on the procedure adopted in this type of hearing.

12.28 Settlement conferences will usually take place after an IRH. At the IRH, parties will be asked if they consent to taking part in a settlement conference and if so, the case will be listed for both a settlement conference and a final hearing (to avoid delays if the case does not settle). The settlement conference will ordinarily be listed quickly and given listing priority to avoid delay[37].

12.29 In contradistinction to the judicial continuity of the FDAC process, the judge who conducts the settlement conference will be a different judge than the one who undertakes case management and the final hearing (if applicable). The two judges will not speak to each other about the settlement conference that took place, and indeed, anything said during the settlement conference – whether by the judge, the parties, or their advocates – is confidential to the settlement process and may not be referred to at any subsequent hearings. The only exception to the expectation of confidentiality is where it becomes evident during the settlement conference that a child is at risk of significant harm. At that point, the judge will immediately conclude the settlement conference and direct whatever steps are needed to safeguard the welfare of the child[38].

12.30 At a settlement conference, a party must be accompanied by his legal representative and is free to speak to her throughout the proceedings. If a party is not represented, the Guardian must be present[39]. Where the parties agree, the judge can see one party without the other parties being present, albeit all of the legal representatives must be in attendance[40]. As the Protocol makes clear, this is only to be entertained where a party's ECHR, Art 6 rights require protection[41].

12.31 The judge may choose to take a more informal approach to the proceedings. She may come down from the bench to position herself closer to the parties and directly engage with the parties themselves in lieu of their advocates. However, family practitioners should be aware that they can raise an objection to a direct dialogue between the judge and their client without the need to give a reason and the judge must respect that decision without question[42]. The conference may involve other family members, potential special guardians, and possibly also the subject children[43].

12.32 As in any hearing, there is no obligation or pressure for parties to agree to anything at a settlement conference. However, unlike traditional public law proceedings, the parties may terminate the settlement conference at any

---

37 *Settlement Conferences Protocol*, supra note 35.
38 Ibid.
39 Ibid.
40 Ibid.
41 Ibid.
42 Ibid.
43 *Settlement Conferences pilot and evaluation* (Ministry of Justice, July 2017) 1.

time. They may also request an adjournment for a period to allow reflection/consideration/further information to be obtained[44]. If a party refuses to partake in a settlement conference or seeks to withdraw from the settlement conference, this will not prejudice their case[45].

12.33 Where the parties are able to agree some or all of the issues, the court will record these in an order, which must be agreed by all of the parties[46]. Where there is no agreement, the order should adjourn the case to the next/final hearing. If the settlement conference results in a determination of the issues on which a judgment is required, the judge shall hand down an extempore judgment, giving reasons[47]. However, this may only be done with the agreement of the parties.

12.34 Advocates should note that since a settlement conference has the status of an IRH, it is regarded as such for legal aid purposes. As such, where parties have legal aid, the settlement conference will be paid as a further IRH when unsuccessful and as a final hearing where successful.

12.35 The settlement conference pilot is still in a trial phase and will be on going until the Ministry of Justice has collected enough quantitative and qualitative evidence to analyse the efficacy of the programme. However, practitioners should be live to the concerns raised in respect of settlement conferences, especially as articulated in the Association of Lawyers for Children's *Guidance to Members on Settlement Conferences*[48], and the judiciary's response to those concerns[49].

PAUSE PROGRAMME

What is Pause?

12.36 Although the Pause programme is not an alternative or adjunct to traditional child protection proceedings, it is an important intervention for family law practitioners to be aware of, especially those who act for mothers who have already lost children to the care system[50]. The statistics regarding repeat removal are staggering: approximately one in four birth mothers appearing as respondents in care proceedings are expected to reappear in a subsequent set of proceedings

44 *Settlement Conferences Protocol.*

45 Ibid.

46 Ibid.

47 Ibid.

48 Association of Lawyers for Children, *Guidance to Members on Settlement Conferences* (7 July 2016), available at www.alc.org.uk/news_and_press/news_items/alcs_guidance_to_members_on_settlement_conferences.

49 Munby, '14th View from the President's Chambers: Care cases: Settlement conferences and the 'tandem' model' (15 August 2016) *Fam Law*, available at www.familylaw.co.uk/news_and_comment/14th-view-from-the-president-s-chambers-care-cases-settlement-conferences-and-the-tandem-model#.WtHJgEsh1R0.

50 This section focuses on the Pause programme in particular. However, there are other Pause-like programmes, including Suffolk County Council's 'Positive Choices'.

within seven years[51]. It is estimated that 60 per cent of repeat proceedings involve at least one child aged less than four weeks, and approximately 70 per cent of women who return to court do so in proceedings that concern an infant who is born subsequent to, or during previous proceedings[52].

12.37 Pause is a voluntary programme that works with women who have experienced, or are at risk of experiencing, repeat removals of children from their care[53]. As family practitioners will be aware, these women have usually experienced neglect, abuse, sexual exploitation, substance misuse, mental illness and/or other challenging issues in their own lives. The Pause programme gives them the chance to 'pause' and focus on their own lives, improving their wellbeing, resilience, and stability in order to reduce the number of children going into care[54].

12.38 During the course of the 18-month programme, participants are provided with an individually tailored intensive package of support, delivered on a one-to-one basis by a dedicated practitioner in collaboration with partner agencies (such as drug misuse, mental health, and domestic violence services)[55]. This includes a bespoke education/career plan and support in accessing stable housing (if applicable). Work may also involve the participant's family, partner, father of her children, and wider friend network.

12.39 Pause does not work with women to recover their children, offer parenting support/parenting classes, or conduct parenting assessments[56]. Instead, it focuses on the woman as an individual, helping her to build healthy boundaries, employ non-adversarial interactions, reflect on responsibility to previous children, address negative issues (when ready), develop aspirations for the future, and reflect on past trauma[57].

12.40 In order to be eligible for the programme, participants must agree to use an effective form of reversible contraceptive for its duration[58]. In general, women who are currently pregnant, have children in their care, have not experienced any child removals for several years, or are not of childbearing age will not qualify for the project[59]. As these conditions on participation suggest, Pause is intended as a preventative, rather than reactive, solution[60].

12.41 The results from the Pause programme have been very promising. The 'Evaluation of Pause: Research Report,' which was published in July 2017 by the

---

51 'Vulnerable birth mothers and recurrent care proceedings – final report' (6 October 2017) *Family Law Week*, available at www.familylawweek.co.uk/site.aspx?i=ed180882.

52 Ibid.

53 K McCracken (et al), *Evaluation of Pause: Research Report* (Department for Education, July 2017) 6.

54 Ibid, 6.

55 Ibid,13.

56 'The Pause Integrated Model – a systematic approach', available at www.pause.org.uk/aboutpause/model.

57 Ibid.

58 McCracken (et al), supra note 53, 14.

59 Ibid, 14.

60 'The Pause Integrated Model – a systematic approach', supra note 56.

Department for Education, found that Pause had a 'positive and significant impact' on the women taking part in the programme, many of whom had 'complex, multiple, and mutually-reinforcing needs'[61]. The research also suggested that the programme reduced the number of pregnancies that would have otherwise occurred during the 18-month intervention[62]. By 2018/2019, Pause aims to have prevented 300 children from entering the care system[63].

CONCLUSION

12.42 As the chapters of this book have shown, public children law is not static; it continues to evolve to meet the changing needs of families and of society as a whole. New approaches have arisen to meet both old and new problems, and it is perhaps one of the most admirable traits of the English family law system that it continues to simultaneously expand, adapt, and refine itself. It is therefore incumbent on family law practitioners to remain up-to-date with the relevant case law, statutory guidance, and guidelines, to ensure that we are not only serving the interests of our clients, but also family justice generally.

12.43 However, it is clear that traditional public law proceedings should not and cannot be the only weapon in our arsenal to fight the on-going crisis in care proceedings. New initiatives, such as those explored above, are vital interventions. They propose unique ways of dealing with families in crisis, whether by focusing on the parents to break cycles of abuse and addiction, or providing the parties the opportunity to 'mediate' with one another under the guidance of a judge. It is only by continuing to challenge our standard practices within family law that we will be able to help children and families and, where appropriate, promote rehabilitation.

61 McCracken (et al), supra note 53, 7.

62 Ibid, 7.

63 E Walsh, 'Pause makes a difference' [2016] *Fam Law* 791.

INDEX